PRAISE FOR
HUMAN CAPITAL MANAGEM

"As the world of work rapidly evolves, so does the focus on people, or the human capital, which underpins every organization. It is exciting to see the development of standards that help define good practices, but also principles of positive people management and corporate governance. This book is the first to pull these all together, providing a strong context and narrative from experienced professionals and academics who have been at the heart of these developments, to create a route map for HR professionals and business leaders, as well as policy makers and regulators."

Peter Cheese, Chief Executive, CIPD

"*Human Capital Management Standards* expounds a compelling and thorough set of principles and guidance material that are applicable across all critical people management processes and functions, and which are relevant to an extremely broad range of industries. It's hard to think of a better book for people and culture/HR practitioners, particularly those bewildered by the modern challenges of business disruption, to use for the restoration and sharpening of their own better work practices and culture for the challenges of the twenty first century."

Peter Wilson, Chairman, Australian HR Institute and CPA Australia, Immediate Past President, World Federation of People Management Associations

"Standards are a vital foundation for maintaining trust and improving effectiveness in all aspects of life, and particularly so in the management of people, the source of intangible and tangible organizational value. Yet to date there has been no commonly agreed set of global standards when it comes to HRM and human capital management and development. Given how rapidly technology is changing the nature of work, this book fills an important gap, with its international, future-focused yet highly practical take on emerging standards. Insightful and thought-provoking, this book is a must-read for any HR practitioner or manager aiming to use standards to unlock human potential and improve organizational effectiveness."

"This is a really important book for those interested in driving improvements in human capital reporting and standards to enhance wellbeing in organizations in the public and private sector. This is a must read for those interested in human capital standards from an outstanding author team."

"This book underlines the global importance of standardization in the field of human capital. Despite its significance to value creation, human capital is not always measured, fully understood or documented. The authors deliver valuable insights in the drivers shaping standards and workforces and how these can affect the future of people management."

"This book gives a comprehensive overview and summary about the first human resources management standards which have been published and the ongoing further activities. This management book should be mandatory in the library for all HR professionals, because it shows how human resource management could create competitive advantage and value for companies and defines the role and responsibilities of Human Resource Management."

"This book gives a comprehensive overview of how to apply quality standards to a range of human capital issues and will be of much interest to managers, organizational leaders and HR professionals. In addition, it takes the reader on a future-focused journey considering governance standards for AI, sensors, robotics, data storage and global sustainability. It is a compelling, thought-provoking read and gives practical tools and insights, which can be used in a range of settings."

"Standards reflect accepted ways of doing things based on a consensus of relevant stakeholders. The international HR standards in this volume offer eminently practical guidance to HR professionals everywhere about how to create value for their organizations by managing their people more effectively."

Wayne F Cascio, Distinguished Professor, University of Colorado, and Robert H Reynolds Chair in Global Leadership; Editor, *Journal of International Business Studies*, The Business School, University of Colorado Denver

"Standards provide a way of codifying and sharing evidence on what works in contemporary organizations. This book is an important step in the movement toward evidence-based practice in management. *Human Capital Management Standards* is a unique collection of guidelines for management-related activities as diverse as recruiting, development, performance management and organizational governance. It is both food for thought and guidance for action."

Denise M Rousseau, H J Heinz II University Professor of Organizational Behavior and Public Policy; Director, Project on Evidence-based Organizational Practices; Heinz College and Tepper School of Business, Carnegie Mellon University; Academic Board President, Center for Evidence-Based Management

"An amazing collection brought to you by global thought leaders discussing the standards developed by the global HR community that will play a significant role in the future of work."

Amy Schabacker Dufrane, CEO, HR Certification Institute

"This book tackles important issues about standards, people and organizations. As Director of a leading business school, and Chair of an international association for universities, reflective practitioners, and learning-oriented organizations, I welcome the way this book enables experts to identify the current value of standards and consider how standards can make sure people management keeps pace with the new data-driven world of business and global competition."

Sharon Mavin, Chair of University Forum for Human Resource Development; Director of Newcastle University Business School and Professor of Leadership and Organization Studies

"Every established profession (medicine, law, accountancy, engineering, etc) is underpinned by standards and evidence-based doctrine. Wilson Wong, Valerie Anderson and Heather Bond have curated a comprehensive collection of people management standards from across the world - an essential resource for all serious HR practitioners. It's a seminal work and proof of how far human resources has come in the last 100 years."

Steve Corkerton, Chief People Officer, National Crime Agency

"This is an insightful and provocative guide to standards in human capital management and development. When our public services are facing ever growing expectations and changing patterns of demand with increasing complexities, the need for excellent standards in leadership and people management have never been so acute. This comprehensive book challenges HR professionals to think more expansively about human capital."

Adrian Smith, Deputy Chief Executive and Corporate Director Place, Nottinghamshire County Council

"It is about time that human capital specialists establish a standard on how to professionally practice HR. This is not a backward-looking standard but a forward-looking one, which is what human resources is all about – continuously adding value to the business through human capital with forward-looking people practices."

Low Peck Kem, Chief HR Officer and Senior Director (Workforce Development), Public Service Division, Prime Minister's Office, Singapore

"This is a valuable, practical and insightful guidebook to the future of the key standards affecting human capital management and development. It is highly recommended. The authors are international authorities on this important topic."

Greg J Bamber, Professor, Monash University, Australia; co-editor, *International and Comparative Employment Relations: National Regulation*, Global Changes

Human Capital Management Standards

A complete guide

Wilson Wong
Valerie Anderson
Heather Bond

KoganPage

First published in Great Britain and the United States in 2019 by Kogan Page Limited

Apart from any fair dealing for the purposes of research or private study, or criticism or review, as permitted under the Copyright, Designs and Patents Act 1988, this publication may only be reproduced, stored or transmitted, in any form or by any means, with the prior permission in writing of the publishers, or in the case of reprographic reproduction in accordance with the terms and licences issued by the CLA. Enquiries concerning reproduction outside these terms should be sent to the publishers at the undermentioned addresses:

2nd Floor, 45 Gee Street
London
EC1V 3RS
United Kingdom
www.koganpage.com

122 W 27th St, 10th Floor
New York, NY 10001
USA

4737/23 Ansari Road
Daryaganj
New Delhi 110002
India

© Wilson Wong, Valerie Anderson and Heather Bond, 2019

The right of Wilson Wong, Valerie Anderson and Heather Bond to be identified as the authors of this work has been asserted by them in accordance with the Copyright, Designs and Patents Act 1988.

Permission to reproduce extracts from BSI and ISO publications is granted by BSI Standards Limited (BSI). No other use of this material is permitted. British Standards can be obtained in PDF or hard-copy formats from the BSI online shop at www.bsigroup.com/shop.

ISBNs
Hardback   978 0 7494 9884 9
Paperback   978 0 7494 8434 7
Ebook   978 0 7494 8435 4

British Library Cataloguing-in-Publication Data

A CIP record for this book is available from the British Library.

Library of Congress Cataloging-in-Publication Data

A CIP record for this book is available from the Library of Congress.

Typeset by Hong Kong FIVE Workshop
Print production managed by Jellyfish
Printed and bound by CPI Group (UK) Ltd, Croydon CR0 4YY

CONTENTS

LIST OF FIGURES AND TABLES

CONTRIBUTORS

Valerie Anderson

is Reader in Human Resource Development at Portsmouth University. She specializes in learning and development in work organizations. She is an expert member of the BSI Committee responsible for standards development in human capital management and development and led the development process for BS PD 76006: *A Guide to Learning and Development*. She is the Convenor of the ISO Working Group to develop ISO 23595: *Learning and Development in Organizations*. In addition to her academic work, she has extensive management and consultancy experience in a range of different public and private sector organizations. She chairs the Research Activities Committee for University Forum for HRD and until 2019 was Co-Editor of *Human Resource Development Quarterly*, which publishes cutting-edge research into all aspects of learning, development and training in work organizations. Valerie is a committed researcher-practitioner, concerned to bring the best of research and practice together to challenge conventional wisdom and generate new ideas and practices. She is author of the CIPD book *Research Methods in HRM*, currently in its third edition.

Heather Bond

joined the CIPD in 2002 and has worked with the CIPD Research team since 2014. As Standards Adviser, she represents the CIPD as an expert on British and International Standards Committees that are developing Standards in human capital and human resource management. A Chartered Fellow of the CIPD, and holder of a judicial appointment as an Employment Tribunal Member, she was previously CIPD's Quality Assurance Manager with responsibility for CIPD qualification development, delivery, assessment and regulatory compliance.

Martin Cottam

is Group Technical Assurance and Quality Director at Lloyd's Register, a global provider of professional services for engineering and technology which improves the safety and increases the performance of critical infrastructures. He is an engineering risk management specialist with risk assessment and safety management experience across several major hazard industries. In the 1990s he led the development of Lloyd's Register's certification of occupational health and safety management systems. He joined the British Standards Committee on OH&S management at that time, contributing to the development and revisions of several British Standards on OH&S management and to the development of OHSAS 18001. He chaired the committee throughout the development of ISO 45001, leading the UK delegation on the ISO 45001 project committee. He now chairs the ISO technical committee for occupational health and safety management (ISO/TC 283), which owns ISO 45001 and is developing additional standards and guidance on OH&S management. Martin was also involved in the development of the ISO 55000 series of standards on Asset Management. He is a member of BSI's Management Systems Expert Group and chair of BSI's Conformity Assessment Policy Committee.

Alaa Garad

is an award-winning executive and academic with extensive expertise in academia, general management, executive education and business development with more than 20 years of experience in designing, leading, implementing and managing projects in various industries and sectors. He has led and managed a client portfolio of 43 organizations and assessed more than 450 firms. He established and chaired two international conferences with overall attendees of 1,300. He is a member of the BSI Human Capital Technical Committee (HCS/1) and has worked and engaged in assignments in 13 countries. A member of seven international and regional professional bodies and a trustee in five charities, Alaa is currently working as Course Leader and Senior Teaching Fellow at the University of Portsmouth. Some of his former roles include CEO, Investors in People, UAE; Director of Emirates Centre for Organizational Learning; and Director of Emirates College of Technology.

Helge Hoel

is Professor Emeritus at the University of Manchester after retiring from his post as Professor in Organizational Behaviour. He is a recognized international expert on discrimination, bullying and harassment in the workplace, having carried out a number of studies related to these issues, including most recently a large-scale study of the workplace experiences of lesbian, gay and bisexual employees. He has written and contributed to many books, articles and reports in the area of bullying and harassment, including commissioned works for the International Labour Organization and the European Parliament. He was commissioned by the Norwegian Labour Inspectorate to develop training courses for investigators of bullying and harassment, which have successfully rolled out within the Nordic countries. As Director of the Fairness at Work Research Centre, now part of the University's Work Equality Institute, he and Professor Anne McBride over-saw the development of the British Standards Institution Management Code of Practice on Diversity and Inclusion (BS 76005). Linked to this develop-ment, he currently represents the UK on the writing panel for a new global standard on diversity and inclusion for the International Organization for Standardization.

Edward Houghton

is the CIPD's Head of Research and Thought Leadership. Since joining the institute in 2013 he has been responsible for leading the organization's people analytics and human capital research, exploring human capital management, measurement and external reporting – with a particular focus on sustainability and transparent reporting. His work has featured in publi-cations by the UK's Financial Reporting Council and Financial Conduct Authority. Recent publications have included *People Analytics: Using people data to drive performance, A duty to care? Evidence of the importance of organisational culture to effective governance and leadership* and *A new approach to line manager mental well-being training in banks*, an independ-ent evaluation of the Bank Workers Charity and Mind partnership to deliver mental health awareness training in the UK financial services sector. In 2018 he was awarded £300,000 of grant funding by the UK Department for Business, Energy and Industrial Strategy as part of the Business Basics Fund for an innovative programme evaluating the impact of people management interventions in small and medium-sized enterprises on firm productivity and performance.

Anne McBride

is a Professor of Employment Relations at the Alliance Manchester Business School, University of Manchester. She chaired the drafting panel for the BSI Code of Practice on Diversity and Inclusion, consisting of members from a range of organizations from the private and public sectors, leading to publication of the standard in 2017. Anne is a member of the Work and Equalities Institute at the University and her work on gender relations at work has been published in *Gender, Work and Organization, Human Resource Management* and *Work, Employment and Society*. She is also a co-director of the Institute for Health Policy and Organization, where she conducts research related to healthcare workforces, such as studying skill mix changes in hospitals and general practice. This research is published in journals such as *Social Science and Medicine, Health Policy* and the *British Journal of General Practice*, in addition to the aforementioned journals.

Sandy J Miles

is the Hutchens Distinguished Professor in the Arthur J Bauernfeind College of Business at Murray State University, Kentucky, and a strategic partner at Organizational Capital Partners. She holds certifications as a Senior Professional of Human Resources and Global Professional of Human Resources through the Human Resource Certification Institute. She also earned the distinction of Academic Fellow through the CIPD in London. Her work has earned the Marquis Who's Who lifetime achievement award for her contributions to the human resource profession. Sandy teaches human resource management courses as well as consulting and researching in strategic human resource management. Her research also earned her an invitation to serve on the Advisory Board for Indiana University's *Business Horizons* and a seat on the Research Council for The Talent Board. She is a board member for the Human Resource Certification Institute, served as the elective Vice Chair for the ISO TC 260 US and was elected as Chair for the US Technical Advisory Group 2017–18. She was nominated by France and elected in 2013 by the ISO TC 260 to lead the work group on recruitment, representing over 20 different countries and publishing one of the first global standards (ISO 30405: Recruitment). She also held a major role in the human governance standards, metrics, and workforce management working groups, and served for five years as one of nine global experts commissioned with advising the ISO TC 260 Chair through the ISO/TC 260 Chairman's Advisory Group (CAG).

Angela Mulvie

is an experienced management consultant and executive coach, having run her own HR consultancy practice for many years following an early career in personnel management and higher education, teaching and researching in HRM. She specializes in performance management and executive development, including executive coaching, and has undertaken assignments in both large corporates and SMEs. She lived and worked overseas from 2001 to 2009 in Asia and the Middle East and continues to work on international assignments for a number of clients. She was for many years an Investors in People Adviser and Assessor with projects undertaken internationally in the USA, the Caribbean, Europe, Africa, the Middle East and Singapore as well as the UK. As a result of some of her research-based work, she has published two books, *The Value of Executive Coaching* (2015) and *Working with External Quality Standards and Awards: The strategic implications for human resource management and quality management* (2018).

Julie Sloan

is the Chief Executive of Workforce Planning Global and a recognized international expert in workforce planning. Earlier in her career, she worked in the Australian Government sector. She has also worked at the United Nations, Centre for Social Development and Humanitarian Affairs and at the International Atomic Energy Agency. A Fellow of the Australian Human Resources Institute, in 2018 she was awarded the Medal of the Order of Australia for services to business, workforce planning and management. In 2017 she received the Standards Australia Meritorious Contribution Award (International) for exceptional achievements in the area of international standardization. Julie is the author of two books on workforce planning, *An Introduction to Workforce Planning* (2008) and *The Workforce Planning Imperative* (2010). She was recognized in the 2008 and 2015 South Australian Government Women's Honour Roll, which pays tribute to women who have made a significant impact on the community, women who are role models and leaders. She has worked in 15 countries and has been an active contributor and member of the ISO TC 260 Human Resource Management (HRM) Committee for 11 years.

Wilson Wong

is Head of Insight and Futures at CIPD. He represents the UK on human capital metrics at ISO/TC260 (HR Standards) and is independent Chair of the Human Capital Standards Committee and Deputy Chair of the

Knowledge Management Standards Committee at the BSI. His career has spanned academia, corporate finance and national ICT policy. Wilson's PhD in Economic Psychology (Behavioural Economics) was on opportunity recognition. He is on the Editorial Board of HRDQ and the *International Journal of HRD Practice, Policy and Research* and is a member of the International Association of Applied Psychology and an Academic Fellow of the CIPD. He is on the Advisory Boards of Nottingham Business School and the Work and Equality Institute, Manchester University. He was called to the Bar in 1990. Research interests include the psychological contract, scenario planning, the future of work, strategic workforce planning, the evolving employment relationship and models of fairness, the future of voice and human capital measurement.

FOREWORD

Throughout the twentieth century the role of consensus standards to support business and industry grew progressively as industry, governments and consumers recognized the value of sharing good practice. This excellent and timely book vividly describes how standards of good practice have evolved as a tool for business transformation beyond product quality and business process and into the softer domains of corporate performance.

The most important resource for companies all over the world is their people and the human capital that they bring through their contribution to the business. Building up the human capital in an organization requires careful thought about the culture and leadership style but may also be affected by a wide range of other factors. Knowing how to be a good employer is a major challenge, especially for small and medium-sized enterprises, start-ups and scale-ups.

Best-practice international and national standards enable businesses of all shapes and sizes to build trust with their employees and external stakeholders and to improve their performance, whatever their ambitions. Companies can rely on the fact that international and national standards are managed through a formal process incorporating full stakeholder engagement, open public consultation and consensus.

International standards organizations such as ISO and their national member bodies such as BSI in the UK and ANSI in the US act as impartial, neutral custodians of the process of reaching consensus, striving all the time to ensure that standards reflect the views of all affected parties.

Many of the great international business standards, some supported by human capital standards on the requisite skills and competencies, had their roots in national standards. This book explores how consensus standards that support better corporate cultures have been developed and adopted identically by organizations everywhere to address subjects as diverse as human resource management and artificial intelligence.

The landscape of standards is constantly evolving. New approaches are being implemented in the leading standards organizations to strengthen diversity and inclusion in standards making and to reflect new, digital technologies that can support communities of experts working together. This book is brimming with insight and information that will support professionals everywhere to realize the true value of human capital standards and to become inspired by the potential they bring to deliver added value as a strategic tool for business performance improvement.

Scott Steedman CBE
Director of Standards, BSI Group, and Vice President (Policy), ISO

Introduction

Valerie Anderson

National or international standards provide a basis for consistent, coherent and effective management of people in organizations. This book is concerned with emerging standards in areas of people management, HR and human capital management and development (HCMD). It is relevant to practising managers who work in organizations of all types and sizes. It should also be of interest to those who are involved with quality assurance and quality improvement processes, and who want to know how external standards of good practice or excellence can contribute to the achievement of organizational excellence.

In an increasingly competitive global environment, organizations face pressure to deploy their resources in the most efficient and effective way. Standards are a prevalent feature of operational management in the contemporary business and social environment, and affect almost all areas of social and organizational life. However, although organizations, especially large companies, operate a range of HR policies and practices, they have developed them without reference to nationally or internationally agreed standards of practice. Standards specifically focused on areas of human capital management (HCM) and HR have only emerged in recent years, and many practitioners are not yet aware of their availability or potential.

This book takes an international focus. Although some parts of the world have more experience of engaging with external standards accreditation, other countries are catching up fast, and are increasingly active in standards development and implementation processes as a feature of their commitment to professionalizing and upskilling the management of people. Therefore, we hope that this book will provide value for professionals overseeing HR and learning and development as well as risk and health and safety. In addition, it has relevance to regulators and workforce strategists wherever in the world they are based.

CHAPTER OBJECTIVES

This chapter sets out to:

- describe the trend towards standardization in work organizations and governance, and the widening purpose of standards as a feature of organizational and management practice;
- discuss the emergence of standardization processes relating to the management and development of people;
- introduce the life-cycle model of HCMD as the organizing frame around which the book is structured.

Key terms

The HR field is replete with acronyms and jargon. In addition, the language used by standards specialists may be somewhat 'off-putting'. In this section, we set out the main terms associated with external and accredited standards and with the HR field. We explain specialized terms associated with the focus of subsequent chapters on a chapter-by-chapter basis. There is also a useful glossary of terms at the end of the book.

Accreditation: This term refers to the process of formal approval and certification, by an awarding body, to recognize the achievement of a standard or level of qualification.

Human capital: The terms 'human capital' and 'human capital resources' are contested expressions. Human capital resources refers to individual, unit or corporate-level capabilities relating to knowledge, skills, abilities and other relevant characteristics (Ployhart *et al*, 2014). Chapter 1 of this book sets out how, at a strategic level, human capital resources are the basis for the achievement of sustainable competitive advantage. The debate about the use of the term revolves around whether the individual contribution that people can make to their workplace is overlooked or undervalued if economic logics associated with terms such as 'capital' and 'investment' dominate decision making in organizations. However, the term human capital as it is used here, and in the book as a whole, connotes our view that people contribute far more than their labour to the organization. People are important sources of value through their individuality, their skills, ideas and networks. These features generate knowledge, ideas and new ways of working that enable organizations to achieve their objectives in a sustainable way. The bottom line is that, regardless of terminological differences, HCM is all about people in the workplace and the combined contribution of skills, attributes, knowledge, talent and expertise that people make in work organizations.

Human resource management (HRM): This term refers to all practices concerned with people in work organizations, taking into account their management as well as their development. This includes systems and practices associated with recruitment and selection, deployment, development and general management of the organization's employees.

Meta-standard: This term refers to management system standards that focus on organization-wide systems and managerial practices that can be audited. Well-known examples of meta-standards are the Quality Management Systems standard, ISO 9001 and the ISO 14001 environmental management systems standard.

National/ international standards: These terms refer to explicitly formulated consensual rules or guidelines published by national or international standardization bodies such as the British Standards Institution (BSI) and the International Organization for Standardization (ISO). They provide an accepted way of doing things relevant to specific products, services or management processes (Anderson, 2017; Mulvie, 2018). Initially, standards served technical design and manufacturing purposes, but over time, accredited standards for organization-wide management systems have been agreed and implemented.

Standardization: This term refers to the process of development, publication and application of guidelines, specifications and rules by a consensus of relevant stakeholders in order to ensure compatibility, interoperability, safety and consistency.

Business excellence, standards and standardization

The influence of standards in organizational and social life has extended profoundly over the last century. Standards now influence market organization and affect benchmarking of products, services and organizational behaviours and practices (Brunsson, Rasche and Seidl, 2012). Early standardization processes were remarkably successful in providing the foundation for design effectiveness, process efficiency and product quality assurance. Without standards, there would be no basis for product reliability and interoperability between components in supply chains. The success of standards in promoting organizational efficiency and inter-organizational effectiveness has led, over time, to interest by national and international standardization organizations, such as ISO, BSI and Standards Australia, to develop and promote a wider range of standards intended for diffusion and adoption by organizations throughout the world. Management system standards, sometimes referred to as meta-standards, have featured as part of standardized practices over the last fifty years. These focus on organization-wide systems as a basis for efficient and consistent operational management practices grounded in common, generically applicable institutional norms (ISO, nd).

Standards are also an important feature of professional life in established and emergent professions, as they provide the basis for 'quality assured', ethical and legitimate professional practice. In the training, learning and development field, the UK Investors in People (IiP) standard, has been available for more than 25 years both in the UK and in other countries (Murphy and Garavan, 2009). Over time the focus of the IiP standard has changed from a focus on learning and development to one directed more at general management and leadership, specifically at practices of continuous improvement achieved through the principles of 'leading', 'supporting', and 'improving' (Mulvie, 2018). Operational practices associated with HRM, such as recruitment and selection, deployment and the management and development of people have, until recently, remained outside the scope of national and international standards (Anderson, 2017).

Standards and standardization for people management and development

In recent years, interest has grown in the potential of standards to contribute to the effectiveness of people management processes in organizations. In an increasingly globally interconnected world, a lack of agreed standards of practice has left HR professionals to acknowledge their vulnerability to the criticism that their field lacks specialized expertise (Monks *et al*, 2013). Corporate scandals of the twenty-first century have also increased interest in the need for standards relating to the way people are managed and treated at work.

In 2016 in the USA, for example, Wells Fargo executives had to admit that they sought to drive growth by putting undue pressure on their employees to hit sales quotas. Such was this pressure that many employees responded by fraudulently opening customer accounts (Conti-Brown, 2017). In Europe, the Volkswagen Emissions Scandal revealed that engineers had been rewarded for developing a gadget that meant that when a car was tested, its performance was different to 'the norm'. Top marks for creative thinking, but bottom of the class for reputable and reliable business practices (Financial Times, 2018).

A further stimulus to interest in standards for the HR domain is that organizations and investors increasingly recognized that people give organizations the 'competitive edge'. People are at the heart of organizations, and every person who works on behalf of an organization contributes in their own way to its success and productivity. In this context a range of employer and employment standards and awards have emerged, such as the Healthy Working Lives Award, the Best Companies Award, the Great Place to Work Scheme and the Top Employers Award. In addition, since 2009, national and international standardization bodies such as ISO and BSI have initiated the development of HR standards.

This book focuses on these national and international accredited standards, and the standardization processes undertaken by ISO and its constituent national standardizing organizations. HR standardization processes were first initiated in the USA in 2009 when ANSI, prompted by SHRM, started work on American national standards in HRM, initiated the development of national HR standards. Two years later, ISO ratified a proposal for the creation of international HR standards, and an ISO Technical Committee, TC260, was established. By 2017, 49 countries were involved as either representatives or observers on this committee (ISO, nd). Alongside the work towards HR standardization in the USA and by ISO at an international level, the UK, through BSI, has also initiated national level standards development. In the UK in 2011, BSI established a committee, HCS/1, and this led to the publication in July 2015 of BS 76000:2015 *Human resource – Valuing people – Management system – Requirements and guidance.*

The argument of this book is that standards can provide a benchmark from which to assert the value-creation role of the HR function (Cascio and Boudreau, 2017). Recognizing the increasing focus in organizations on the management, development, identification and accounting of the intangible value associated with human capital assets in organizations, professions and nation-states, the chapters that comprise this edited collection identify important standards development processes and their potential 'value-add' to the management, measurement and deployment of HR.

The life-cycle model of HCMD

The next chapter of this book points out that two things – money (financial capital) and people (human capital) – are at the heart of all organizations. The grounding premise of this book is that effective standards of practice in the management and development of human capital provides a foundation of trust from which improved and sustained organizational effectiveness can be achieved. Trust between managers and members of the workforce underpins employee commitment and performance. Searle and Skinner (2011) describe HRM as an ongoing cycle of activities necessary to carry out efficient and effective work processes. They characterize this cycle as involving recruitment and selection, learning and development, performance management, and reward. Other processes, such as employment relations and change management, affect all of these parts of the HRM cycle and will affect the ways in which people leave the organization. We argue that in today's context, much of an organization's value is intangible and largely tied to the workforce and the value-creating abilities and potential of those who work on behalf of the organization. Therefore, in our model we refer to the term 'human capital management and development'.

Human assets are as important as, if not more important than, manufacturing and financial assets for sustained organizational performance and flexibility. Adaptability and change are crucial features of the employment relationship in organizations throughout the world. As the basis for this book, we adapt the work of Searle and Skinner (2011) to describe an HCMD model focused on building capability and engaging people (Figure 0.1). The structure of this book reflects this model. The model describes standards of human governance as equivalently important as standards of other forms of corporate governance. Wider organizational processes of change and organizational development form the context and background to a capability building and people engagement cycle that has four elements. These are: entry and pre-entry to the organization, workforce management processes, learning and development, and moving on (or moving out) from the organization.

FIGURE 0.1   HCM model

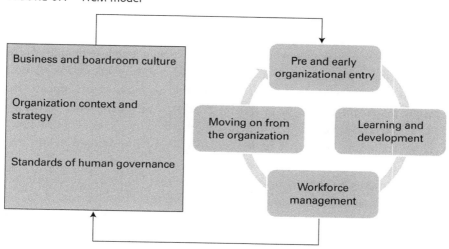

The figure shows the author's model for human capital management, after Searle and Skinner (2011)

Overview of the chapters

Acknowledged experts in a range of HCM domains have contributed chapters to this book. Each chapter highlights the role and purpose of standards and standardization as a feature of HCMD. The process of developing and implementing standards in HR and HCM in organizations of different types and sizes that operate in different regions of the world is not without challenges. Therefore, each chapter author discusses dilemmas associated with developing and adopting national and international standards.

Specific issues that warrant discussion are: what level of detail is appropriate in any HR standard? What time horizon assumptions are appropriate for standardization in the field of HCMD? How should good practice in organization be evaluated to assess achievement in relation to risk, flexibility and innovation?

Chapter 1 introduces different stakeholder perspectives towards the value creation potential of people in organizations. The author, Ed Houghton, discusses the issues of business culture, particularly 'board room culture' and the effect that this has on the human governance processes. They foreground the investor perspective on HCM, stewardship and building and maintaining trust within the organization. In their chapter, they also outline the development of ISO 30414:2018 *Human resource management – Guidelines for internal and external human capital reporting*.

Chapter 2 is contributed by Heather Bond, who is an active participant and expert in many areas of standards development in this field. This chapter addresses wider issues associated with valuing people in organizations. It highlights which standards matter for HCM, and how standards relating to other operational processes recognize the importance of appropriate people management and development processes for operational efficiency and effectiveness. This chapter highlights debates about matters of principle, values and compliance that underpin processes of standards development and revision.

In addition, this chapter discusses the value that HCM standards offer as a basis for mutual understanding, trust and sustained performance.

Chapter 3 is contributed by Julie Sloan, the convenor of the ISO working group to develop standards for workforce planning, ISO 30409:2016 *Human Resource Management – Workforce Planning*. It provides a practical, user-friendly guide to the key elements of strategic and operational workforce planning. In an increasingly global and dynamic business environment, workforce planning is an imperative. Effective workforce planning is required to take account of labour market trends, regulatory or governance requirements and organizational design developments.

This chapter identifies critical success factors associated with workforce planning, and sets out core elements of good practice for the application of quality workforce planning to organizational design processes.

Chapter 4 builds on this trajectory. Dr Sandy Miles, Distinguished Professor at Murray State University and convenor of the ISO workgroup to develop international standards for recruitment and selection (ISO 30405:2016 *Human resource management – Guidelines on recruitment*), argues that attracting and employing talent is critical for organizational success. She indicates the effect of recruitment processes on employee brand and the effectiveness of stakeholder relationships. In a digital and globally interconnected world, recruitment processes are changing fast, and so global standards for recruitment, as a basis from which to manage candidate relationships and subsequent employment relationships, have never been more important.

In addition to the ISO guidance standard on employee recruitment, this chapter also highlights the benefits and development work associated with standards in candidate experience and the delivery of candidate assessment processes and services.

Chapter 5 is written by Valerie Anderson and Alaa Garad. Knowledge and skills are an important feature of organizational and national economic competitiveness, effectiveness and efficiency, and this chapter considers the strategic contribution of learning and development as the basis for productivity and business growth plans. Both employers and individuals play an important part in the continuous processes of 'upskilling' and life-long learning required for a globalized, technologically innovative and volatile context.

In alignment with other chapters, this chapter highlights how organizational competitive capability requires continuous learning at individual, team and organizational levels. An international standard in learning and development is still under development, but the British Standard BS PD 76006:2017 *Guide to learning and development* provides guidance on learning and development in relation to standards for formal and informal learning, training and development. Their chapter also indicates important new practices in relation to the use of technology in learning and development.

Chapter 6 is contributed by Professor Anne McBride and Professor Helge Hoel, who jointly convened the BSI working group to develop a British standard for diversity and inclusion (D&I) (BS 76005:2017 *Valuing People Through Diversity and Inclusion: Code of Practice for Organizations*). In 21st-century organizations, D&I is an issue that distinguishes 'good' employers and sustainable organizational performance. However, individuals around the world are still excluded from a number of opportunities to fully engage with organizations – whether as employees, suppliers or stakeholders.

This chapter focuses on objectives, policies, practices, behaviours and measures that can facilitate greater organizational D&I. It identifies ways in which organizations can minimize the negative consequences of a lack of organizational diversity, and sets out a human capital approach to D&I. It provides examples from BS PD 76005 on how to value people through D&I.

Chapter 7 concerns standards for occupational health and safety (OH&S). Organizations that manage OH&S in an effective way are well placed to reap financial and reputational benefits. In addition, organizations with global supply chains increasingly seek assurance as to the OH&S management of their suppliers. Martin Cottam, the author of this chapter, is Chair of the ISO Technical Committee that owns the first ISO standard addressing OH&S – BS ISO 45001:2018 *Occupational health and safety management systems*. Martin argues that the development of ISO 45001 represents the of ISO management system standards (alongside ISO 9001 and ISO 14001, the equivalent standards for quality management and environmental management). This provides managers with useful standards through which to align and integrate their OH&S management systems and to benefit, if appropriate for the business, from the process of certification.

Chapter 8 focuses on processes and good practice in situations where people move on from the organization. Whatever the 'trigger' to move on, when someone leaves his or her organization the management of the transition process is important for organizational excellence. Sustained performance requires that the right workforce be in the right place at the right time. This chapter, authored by Dr Valerie Anderson, provides a practical and applied approach to areas of good practice that organizations can implement to ensure that they manage the 'moving on' stage in an effective way. This can help managers to minimize negative consequences associated with the moving on process.

Chapter 9 shifts the focus beyond individual organizations, and identifies how standards in HCMD can benefit coordination between organizations in specific sectors, and within organizations that operate across national and regional boundaries. Dr Alaa Garad, a standards expert with global experience, discusses the impact on HCM of new technologies such as artificial intelligence (AI) and smart, autonomous technologies fuelled by data and machine learning (sometimes referred to as Industry 4.0).

This chapter also highlights how integrated management systems across sectors can enable collaboration in important areas for HR, such as occupational safety, employee mental health and wellbeing, and performance management.

The final two chapters of the book address the processes involved in certification and the likely future of standards in the HCM field.

Chapter 10 is written by Angela Mulvie, an experienced executive coach and management consultant with specific expertise in the implementation of standards in all areas of the world. This chapter discusses the principles behind assessment and certification, the steps involved, and how new approaches to accreditation are emerging. It provides an overview of some of the bodies that support the assessment process, and considers how the work of assessment and accreditation organizations is itself quality-assured.

Chapter 11 looks to the future. Dr Wilson Wong, who is Head of Insight and Futures at the Chartered Institute of Personnel and Development (CIPD) and independent chair of the BSI Human Capital Standards committee, looks to the future of standards in the HCM field. In this chapter, he offers a personal analysis of the future of work in a context of technological, digital, social and economic innovation.

This chapter considers the complex interactions of external and internal forces as a mosaic of the landscape of the future of work. The chapter makes the case for practitioners, business leaders, and those involved with developing standards to 'look above the parapet' to get a fresh perspective and take the longer view. This future orientation will be crucial as standardization seeks to influence as well as to respond to emerging patterns, intersections and priorities that affect human capital.

Summary

The development of standards by ISO, BSI, and other national accredited standardization bodies in the broad area of HCMD is relatively recent. This is the first published book in this emerging but important area. The book takes an international focus and the chapter contributors, all experts in their fields, provide unique and authoritative information about the influence of standards on HCMD.

With its integrative perspective, this book provides important new ideas worthy of consideration and implementation by professionals, regulators and strategists concerned with risk, health and safety, learning and development, as well as other HR functions important for sustained organizational performance.

References and further resources

Anderson, V (2017) HRD standards and standardization: where now for human resource development? *Human Resource Development International*, 20 (4), pp 327–45

Brunsson, N, Rasche, A and Seidl, A (2012) The dynamics of standardization: Three perspectives on standards in organization studies, *Organization Studies*, 33 (5–6), pp 613–32

BSI (2015) BS 76000:2015 *Human Resource. Valuing People. Management System. Requirements and Guidance*, https://shop.bsigroup.com/ProductDetail/?pid=000000000030298954 (archived at https://perma.cc/7EGP-BPYW)

BSI (2017) BS 76005:2017 *Valuing People Through Diversity and Inclusion: Code of Practice for Organizations*, https://shop.bsigroup.com/ProductDetail/?pid=000000000030338898 (archived at https://perma.cc/PYG5-P6ZF)

BSI (2017) BS PD 76006:2017 *Guide to learning and development*, https://shop.bsigroup.com/ProductDetail/?pid=000000000030350673 (archived at https://perma.cc/J7Z7-2XU9)

Cascio, W F and Boudreau, J W (2017) Evidence-based management at the bottom of the pyramid, in *The Oxford Handbook of Strategy Implementation*, ed Hitt, M A *et al*, Oxford University Press, Oxford

Conti-Brown, T [accessed 29 March 2019] Why Wells Fargo might not survive its fake accounts scandal, Fortune [Online] http://fortune.com/2017/08/31/wells-fargo-fake-accounts-scandal-2017-tim-sloan/ (archived at https://perma.cc/7HSX-NAJX)

Financial Times (2018) [accessed 29 March 2019] VW faces UK group legal action over emissions scandal, *Financial Times* [Online] https://www.ft.com/content/1e50e9aa-02a7-11e8-9650-9c0ad2d7c5b5 (archived at https://perma.cc/S6MN-YEAU)

Hitt, M A *et al* (eds) (2017) *The Oxford Handbook of Strategy Implementation*, Oxford University Press, Oxford

ISO (2016) ISO 30405:2016 *Human resource management – Guidelines on recruitment*, https://www.iso.org/standard/64149.html (archived at https://perma.cc/BL6L-C7WC)

ISO (2016) ISO 30409:2016 *Human Resource Management – Workforce Planning*, https://www.iso.org/standard/64150.html (archived at https://perma.cc/TDW7-W92A)

ISO (2018) BS ISO 45001:2018 *Occupational health and safety management systems. Requirements with guidance for use*, https://shop.bsigroup.com/ProductDetail?pid=000000000030299985 (archived at https://perma.cc/DP99-H9V7)

ISO (2018) ISO 30414:2018 *Human resource management – Guidelines for internal and external human capital reporting*, https://www.iso.org/standard/69338.html (archived at https://perma.cc/YBL7-5X6U)

ISO [accessed 9 February 2019] Benefits of international standards, *ISO* [Online] http://www.iso.org/iso/home/standards/benefitsofstandards.htm (archived at https://perma.cc/T6EG-XANE)

Monks, K *et al* (2013) Understanding how HR systems work: The role of HR philosophy and HR processes, *Human Resource Management Journal*, 23 (4) pp 379–95

Mulvie, A (2018) *Working with External Quality Standards and Awards: The strategic implications for human resource and quality management*, Routledge, Oxford

Murphy and Garavan (2017) The Adoption and Diffusion of an NHRD Standard: A Conceptual Framework, *Human Resource Development Review*, 8 (1) pp 3–21

Ployhart, R E *et al* (2014) Human capital is dead; long live human capital resources!, *Journal of Management*, 40 (2), pp 371–98

Searle, H and Skinner, D (2011) *Trust and Human Resource Management*, Edward Elgar, Cheltenham

1

Governance, human capital and culture: the role of standards and standardization

Edward Houghton

Introduction

This chapter explores the concepts of culture and the governance of human capital within a business context, and describes the various perspectives that key stakeholders of business have towards the value creation capability of organizations. We also explore the development of industry standards for human capital reporting (ISO 30414:2018 *Human resource management – Guidelines for internal and external human capital reporting*) from an external perspective, reflecting on recent regulatory and investor developments of relevance to the corporate culture and governance debates in organizations today.

This chapter emphasizes the perspective of investors and regulators on human capital and corporate culture, and draws on contemporary research to describe why and how investors are (and aren't) paying attention to the various indicators that describe how organizations create value.

The perspectives of external stakeholders are increasingly important to the leaders of modern organizations who find their businesses subject to various 'megatrends' affecting or likely to affect their business. These trends are numerous and interconnected: from continuing globalization of supply chains and the workforce, via the digitization of work and human relationships, through welcome improvements in global education standards, to the rise of socio-political unrest in western democracies as voters explore alternatives to centrist politics. All these issues lead to uncertainty and instability, and provide little comfort to business leaders and their stakeholders as they attempt to battle against the seductive pull of short-termism and attempt to be more sustainable.

These are just some of the reasons why organizations can benefit from adopting the principles and actions of corporate governance. Corporate governance is designed to ensure that organizations are directed and controlled in a responsible manner, and that management actions are prudent, effective, and in line with the requirements of stakeholders. Key to this is how the organization creates and captures value from the deployment of its people, the cultures and climates within the organization, and the extent to which risks and opportunities are shaping management behaviour. Without a clear understanding of these issues at the leadership level of the business, it is likely the trends highlighted earlier will damage or even destroy the ability of the business to grow and thrive.

In this chapter we consider the role of standards and standardization within the context of corporate governance and the development and deployment of human capital: the knowledge, skills and abilities of the workforce. We look closer at the perspectives of investors to human capital measurement and management, and explore some of the emerging trends in human capital reporting which act as a signal to how boards view the value of the workforce. We explore these ideas with the purpose of enabling boards and senior executives to gain a greater understanding human capital and culture, and to illustrate how the standardization and reporting of these concepts will benefit important internal and external stakeholders.

CHAPTER OBJECTIVES

In this chapter we will explore:

- governance and trust: the role of corporate governance in developing human capital value in organizations;
- culture and standards: why growing interest in business culture, and the culture of boards, highlights a clear need for standards of both behaviour and practice;
- the signals of low levels of trust, and the potential for standards of human capital management (HCM) geared towards building trust;
- human capital reporting, and the role of standardization in providing organization level standards of high quality;
- the investor perspective on HCM and culture.

Key terms

Throughout this chapter we will use the following key terms, and in some cases will provide alternative or more detailed descriptions of their meaning and use.

Corporate governance: This describes the procedures, systems and principles in place to enable effective management of organizations by directors and their stakeholders. Corporate governance standards will differ between jurisdictions. Corporate governance is commonly understood to be concerned with: 'Holding the balance between economic and social goals and between individual and communal goals… the aim is to align as nearly as possible the interests of individuals, corporations and society' (Cadbury, 1992).

Ethical climate: This describes 'correct behaviour, and how ethical decisions should be handled in organizations' (Victor and Cullen, 1987).

Ethical culture: This describes the 'systems, procedures, and practices for guiding and supporting ethical behaviour' in organizations (Kish-Gephart, Harrison and Treviño, 2010).

Human capital: This term describes the value of the workforce: 'the knowledge, skills, abilities and other capabilities which describe individual capacities' (Ployhart *et al*, 2014).

Organizational culture: This describes 'the values, norms and traditions that affect how individuals of a particular group perceive, think, interact, behave and make judgments about their world' (Chamberlain, 2005).

Value and HCM

At their heart, organizations consist of two things: money and people – or, put another way, financial capital and human capital. Understanding how organizations create value through their people is an important step in understanding how organizations work, and to understand this we must appreciate the concept of human capital and why it is of such significance to our understanding of value creation by organizations.

Human capital theory gained prominence in the mid-twentieth century through the work of Schultz (1961), who recognized the value of the knowledge, skills and abilities of the workforce to economic prosperity. For some time, physical capital (eg factories and machinery) had been held up as the main driver of economic growth. However, a number of influential papers called this into question, instead noting that the education of the workforce, and their ability to apply this education, was an important driver (Becker, 1975; Schultz, 1961). For organizations this has obvious ramifications, particularly with regard to understanding skills, people management and training of individuals. Human resource management (HRM) forms the basis for systems to generate value through human capital.

At the organizational level, human capital theory gained prominence when considered as part of various important HRM concepts (Chartered Institute of Personnel and Development (CIPD), nd). It was in management theory where human capital was highlighted as an important concept for understanding how and why management practices deliver value. In this chapter, we highlight how HCM involves three elements – first, the quantification of knowledge and skills as inputs; second, people management and HR as activities; and third, financial value as an output.

There are three human capital perspectives – the education and accumulation perspective, the individual qualities perspective, and the productivity/production orientation. These are outlined below (adapted from Kwon, 2009):

- The education and accumulation perspective: Knowledge and skills developed through compulsory and vocational education (De la Fuente and Ciccone, 2002).

- The individual qualities perspective: Knowledge and skills of an individual (Beach, 2009; Schultz, 1961); Knowledge, competency, attitude and behaviour of an individual (Rastogi, 2002); Knowledge, skills, education and abilities (Garavan *et al*, 2001; Youndt, 2004).

- The productivity/production orientation: Human capital as a fundamental source of economic productivity (Romer, 1990). Human capital as an investment that people make in themselves to increase their productivity (Rosen, 1999). Knowledge, skills competencies and attributes in individuals that facilitate the creation of personal, social and economic wellbeing (Rodriguez and Loomis, 2007).

Human capital is an important strategic concept for boards and HR professionals. It concerns the extent to which the organization can create and capture value. Value arises through the productive activity of employees, the organization's systems of work that support this activity and the encouragement and application of new concepts by innovators and entrepreneurs. It is distributed to individuals in the form of wages and salaries; distributed to shareholders, or invested into the business. Many modern organizations also extract value from other stakeholders; eg through legal tax minimization.

At the heart of an organization's ability to create, capture, distribute and extract value is its relationship with its workforce, and its approach to human capital. In short, human capital is concerned with 'the added value that people provide for organizations' (Baron and Armstrong, 2007) and is a critical intangible asset that organizations must manage.

The integrated perspectives: understanding multi-level human capital

To measure human capital, it is important to consider the different levels at which it exists, and the associated approaches to its measurement. At the macro, societal and economic level, human capital adds to economic productivity and is enhanced through education, healthcare and security. At the organizational and team levels, human capital can be considered a resource or combination of resources important for important outcomes, such as performance and innovation. Finally, at the individual level, human capital represents as the knowledge, skills and abilities of the workforce. These can be measured and utilized to gain advantage from individual differences and complementarities.

These approaches are summarized below.

Societal and economic:

- Economic human capital measurement for purposes of productivity and national performance.
- Human capital development in the form of education, vocational training, healthcare, infrastructure and competitiveness.

Organizational and team:

- Human capital resources, which are the individual and team-level capacities built from the combination of individual knowledge, skills and abilities (KSAs). Enabler of competitive advantage (Coff and Kryscynski, 2011).
- Strategic human capital resources, ie human capital as a basis of competitive advantage, as human capital:

- o influences outputs and quality;
- o is varied between firms, and therefore rare;
- o is hard to imitate (Barney and Wright, 1998; Coff, 1997).

Individual:

- The knowledge, skills, abilities and other capabilities (KSAOs) which describe individual capacities (Ployhart et al, 2014).

This multi-level perspective allows us to understand how human capital interacts and is developed at different organizational levels. Importantly it also provides the basis for human capital measurement. At the societal and economic level, for example, human capital measurement centres on the role of education as a driver of economic prosperity – policy interventions, education systems. Our understanding of the labour market is also influenced by the ways in which education relates to the development of human capital.

At the organizational and team level, organization or system perspectives of the processes, policies and practices that make up HRM form the basis of measurement as they link to the generation of human capital value. At the organization level, human capital is developed through learning, training and development, and there are many more measures available of human capital development, in and beyond learning and development. Measures relating to stress and long-term sickness, performance management, and even innovation capacity are all useful for understanding how human capital is developing and being utilised at the organizational and team level.

At the individual level, human capital is considered more (but not absolutely) tangible, measurable through assessing the knowledge, skills and abilities of individuals in their roles. This information, when codified as skills audits and development plans, provides insight to shape and inform practices existing at the team and organizational levels.

Of course, perfect systems of human capital development and human capital value creation do not exist. There are various interrelated factors which shape the structure, policies and philosophy of firms in their approach to generating value. This intangible level is where the concept of climate and corporate culture has gained much prominence, and as a result is of considerable interest to those interested in generating sustainable value through effective HCM.

Culture, climate and human capital

The term 'organizational culture' is often used to describe the unique social attributes of an organization or team, and in the recent past has come to be recognized as one of the most significant drivers and risk and opportunities in firms (Financial Reporting Council (FRC), 2016). Organizational culture can be described in various ways:

- 'The values, norms and traditions that affect how individuals of a particular group perceive, think, interact, behave and make judgments about their world' (Chamberlain, 2005).
- 'A set of broadly tacitly understood rules and procedures that inform organizational members on what, and how, to do under a variety of undefined situations' (Mavondo and Ferrell, 2003).
- 'Collective programming of the mind which distinguish the member of one organization from another' (Hofstede, 1998).
- 'Patterns of basic assumptions invented, discovered or developed by a given group as it learns to cope with its problem with external adaptation and internal integration' (Schein, 1990).

Organizational culture is widely adopted and has been researched to varying extents – some of the most useful insights highlighting how culture manifests in three specific ways (from Schein, 1990):

- Observable artefacts: signals and objects that individuals observe that describe the culture, such as dress code, formality, annual reports or emotional intensity in employee interactions. Difficult to analyse and often complex given their ambiguity, plus there is a lack of clarity regarding the assumptions associated with analysis.
- Values: these are the norms, ideologies and philosophies of the organization, eg principle-led, commercially driven, customer-centric.
- Basic underlying assumptions: These are often taken for granted or underlying, and act to determine thought processes and behaviours.

Culture change

CIPD research has shown that people professionals play a critical role in supporting culture change as they provide the knowledge, systems, policies, practices and approaches needed to establish behaviours which will enable organizational cultures to develop. Leaders in the business look to HR practitioners to provide a steer on how to define visions of the future, and map current state practices and behaviours against this vision. This is a high value and high impact role for people professionals.

Key questions for senior leaders and HR practitioners in cultural change situations include the following (from CIPD, nd).

HR questions:

- Are we working close enough with the CEO and senior stakeholders to uncover aspects of culture change that are not yet visible?
- Do we have an evidence-based view on the change programme and what is likely to work, and a clearly designed vision against which to set objectives and milestones?
- Are the change team equipped and engaged to partner with senior leaders as they enact culture change?
- Do we have enough engagement from line managers to create and work towards the shared vision of the culture change programme?
- Are the data measurement, management and reporting systems in place to support and steer the roll-out of the culture change initiative?

Learning and development questions:

- Are senior leader and middle manager learning and development needs being developed for the present and future requirements of the organization?
- To what extent is the learning and development team supporting line managers to equip their teams for the culture change programme?
- Are obstacles and challenges in skills and capabilities accurately mapped, and are mitigation processes in place to ensure consistent progression against targets?

Organization design and development questions:

- Does the culture change programme, as designed, fit the development plans for the future of the organization over a set of clear time horizons?
- Is the CEO and senior leadership team equipped with the communication messages, tools and techniques to engage the business in two-way conversations about culture change?
- Is the organization learning from the culture change programme as it develops, and adjusting forecasts, projects and stakeholders in a dynamic way?

- Are the risks and opportunities associated with the culture change programme being accurately captured and managed?

Good governance: protecting and enhancing value

At its heart, governance is about stability. This was best articulated by Sir Adrian Cadbury in his ground-breaking 1992 report: 'Corporate governance is concerned with holding the balance between economic and social goals and between individual and communal goals... the aim is to align as nearly as possible the interests of individuals, corporations and society.'

The Cadbury report, a code of best practice for corporate governance, provides the basis for governance, and has been built on and developed further around the world. In practice, corporate governance describes the rules, processes and practices by which a company is directed and controlled (ICSA, nd). At its bluntest, corporate governance can be described as how a business 'polices' itself, through the management of its own policies and through identifying checks and balances to bring stability.

Governance regimes differ according to regional, national, sectoral and local contexts, and so standards of regulation and principles of governance will differ. However, taken as a whole, understandings and definitions of corporate governance tend to fall into one of two groupings. The first describes the actual behaviour patterns of organizations as signalled by their measures of performance, productivity and growth. The second distinct group of definitions concerns the regulatory or other specific frameworks within which the organization operates. These may include legal, regulatory, labour and financial markets (Claessens, 2007). These two groupings offer a useful way to describe the purpose of corporate governance, and the ways in which it can be understood.

Whichever approach to governance is taken, it involves an interaction between three important economic groups. These are the government (or state), the various sectors or communities within the wider society, and the business or private sector. Governance operates to ensure balance between the perspectives of these groups for political, economic, social and executive decisions. Government Structure and process is critical in enabling good governance, but also important are purpose and vision, effective leadership, collective and individual participation, trust, transparency and accountability. Inherent in all of these is the role of standards and standardization – for governance to work effectively, particularly of human capital, clear and coherent standards must be in place.

Governance is never simple. The interaction between different groups brings tensions for governance to overcome, in particular that which exists between shareholders and other firm stakeholders (CIPD, nd). The Organisation for Economic Co-operation and Development's (OECD's) principles of corporate governance highlight the role of frameworks to protect and facilitate the exercise of shareholders' rights (OECD, 2015). Studies of optimal governance conditions also highlight how shareholder orientation is vital to reduce inefficient management self-interest, and to focus the endeavour of the firm on profit maximization (CIPD, nd). As we will see later, this model of profit maximization is a concept very much up for debate. The issue is, therefore, are the standards of good governance also up for debate?

Governing people: the role of boards in developing human capital

In 2016 the UK FRC conducted an examination of the evidence for the value and importance of culture in the corporate context. Various corporate governance scandals had at the time been linked to a lack of corporate culture at the board level in some major UK businesses, and as a result the regulator (the FRC) responded by looking to address some of the gaps in understanding of culture at board level, and the role boards can play in building effective and healthy organizational cultures.

Much of this has been undertaken with the assumption that measurement and reporting differ considerably worldwide, and even at the national level. While in financial reporting there are clear accountancy standards for reporting financial information, there exists a gap in standards for reporting human capital information, and in particular culture. This is one of several issues that prevents greater understanding and transparent reporting of workforce information.

It is the board level where the values and behaviours of the firm are developed and designed. Here, through their actions and behaviours, leaders craft the set of values and behaviours which the workforce may regard as the standard for the firm. This idea of leading by example is a well-trodden but important concept that describes how and why board behaviour must align with the espoused values and norms of the business. A lack of congruence between espoused and actual behaviours can be a significant issue, as employees no longer see the values in action.

The following issues (from FRC, nd) provide a useful checklist for business leaders to review culture, values and behaviours:

- Recognize the value of culture. A healthy culture should be seen as a valuable asset and key to achieving competitive advantage. To achieve this the board must define the values and purpose of the organization, and align the strategy and business model accordingly with culture in mind.
- Demonstrate leadership. For culture to embed effectively, leaders must embody the desired culture. Boards must deliver when leaders fail to do so.
- Be open and accountable. Openness and accountability are key at every level in the organization, and are evident through the way the business works with its stakeholders and conducts its business.
- Embed and integrate. Company values are key if employees and suppliers are expected to align and deliver against the firm's purpose. Functions such as HR, audit and risk must align for this to work effectively.
- Assess, measure and engage. Indicators and measures must be aligned to outcomes which are of material value. When misaligned, the board must challenge and seek clarity and information. Boards must resource the evaluation and reporting of culture.
- Align value and incentives. Performance management and rewards systems must be aligned to ensure that behaviours are encouraged that are consistent with the company's purpose, values, strategy and business model.
- Exercise stewardship. Effective stewardship by board stakeholders should be encouraged, through better reporting of consistent data. Boards, in their engagement with investors, should articulate their approach on culture and its value.

To summarize, values and behaviours are important concepts. They interact with other firm phenomena to result in forms of corporate culture which are increasingly of interest to regulators, investors, governments and consumers and customers. However, culture in organizations is not static nor generic. Cultures in organizations are dynamic, complex, and exist at different levels within the institution.

For example, a board of directors has a distinct, strategic and leadership-oriented culture. At the same time political and relationship-oriented cultures are evident at executive level within the departments, functions and teams that they manage. The culture at each level, between each team may look very different. It is for this reason that the concept of 'tone from the top' is critical.

Organizations cannot direct or govern the development of cultures. Instead, culture(s) are unique and intangible in nature, and so require 'frames and boundaries', linked to appropriate standards, as points of reference to guide local behaviours and value sets.

It is the role of the executive to develop, maintain, communicate and demonstrate through its leadership the frames and boundaries that guide the various cultures of the organization. Boards of directors both share responsibility with, and oversee, executive or management teams' actions in developing and sustaining the corporate culture.

Points of good practice in relation to organizational culture, values and behaviour that senior leaders should consider include:

- Crisis and reputation management: during periods of significant stress and pressure on the organization, boards must maintain stability and focus on their objectives. Key to doing this is measuring, managing and addressing issues relating to behaviour and culture which may be exacerbating cultural risks, or presenting new risks to the organization. People risk management is a particular approach to managing crises and challenges as and when they occur, and can also enable boards to prepare for potential future issues.

- Challenge and set objectives for the executive team: boards have a central role in setting objectives for the executive and holding them to account in delivering against these. Important in this is the assessment of whether and how objectives align with the organization's strategy and aspirations for its culture. This includes setting stretch targets for culture, and checking on progress against these targets.

- Manage culture through change and transformation: boards have a central role in ensuring change and transformation within the organization is delivered against objectives and in line with the execution plan of the strategy. This is particularly true during times of considerable change, such as during mergers and acquisitions, where compatibility of culture is an important factor for success.

- Manage the development and delivery of corporate strategy: boards, in delivering the corporate strategy, are responsible for ensuring connectedness between strategy and culture. Issues such as competitive differentiation, innovation and long-term planning all rely heavily on the board's awareness of culture throughout the institution.

To summarize, boards of directors and senior leadership teams focus on strategy and execution, and it is clear to see that culture plays an important role. Boards are primarily focused on financial outcomes for their key financial stakeholders: investors and owner-managers. The culture of the firm plays a role in enhancing or reducing the capacity of the business to perform. Boards which are working effectively understand this and focus their attention not only on defining the parameters of the strategy; their purpose, vision and objectives, but also their values.

In short, they ask *how* do we want our business to deliver against its strategy and meet the needs of our stakeholders. Purpose and vision describe the *'why?'* of strategy, culture and the management of operations describe the *how*.

Culture and trust: is measurement possible?

Linked with corporate culture, transparency and trust have become key issues that have risen to the top of the agendas of regulators, investors, consumer and boards. Additionally, environmental, social and governance sustainability (often termed 'impact investing' or 'sustainable investing') have achieved prominence. In terms of corporate reporting, 'integrated reporting' and 'triple-bottom line' reporting have focused attention on measuring and quantifying qualities of sustainability. Key to these, and other, perspectives is the recognition that what makes an effective company is comprised of human, social and relationship resources.

However, these forms of human social and relationship capital are difficult to measure. Nonetheless, investors are interested in quantifying the impact of culture and human capital on firm performance, and on the measurement of the culture of firms as an outcome of responsible investment. This is articulated as part of an investor 'stewardship' agenda, and is an important evolving element of modern investor practice.

A further feature of governance issues relates to culture and trust in organizational partners in supply chain arrangements. As supply chains become increasingly global in scope and impact, investors are keen to see how businesses manage key workplace issues through their product value chains. Many recognize that to innovate, disrupt and remain competitive requires specific behaviours and cultures to be fostered, including within and beyond supply chains and their associated stakeholders.

Trust and culture: the role of corporate governance in building trust

Edelman (nd) argues that the role of corporate governance must go beyond establishing certainty and stability and must also deliver trust as an outcome for all stakeholders in business. However, the prevalence of corporate scandals and governance failures suggests that corporate governance processes are rarely able to deliver the outcome of trust between stakeholders. Indicative of the challenges in this area are:

- Excessive executive pay: in many ways, executive pay has become a key signal of inequality for the key stakeholders of firms, particularly employees. The advent of pay ratios is an important development if they are used to provide a meaningful context to executive pay and are accompanied with a clear narrative around pay decision-making when they are used.

- Inequality and lack of fairness: the issue of inequality is partly an outcome of the differing levels of attention boards have given to different stakeholders in the firm, and partly an outcome of the issue of fairness in reward (eg the executive pay issue, above). A challenge for current boards is how to make decisions that appreciate the impact on their many stakeholders, as well as remaining clearly within the guidelines of the corporate governance code, which is subject to the idea of shareholder primacy.

- Poor people management practices: CIPD research has frequently shown that people management practices across organizations of all sizes is lacking and is most apparent in small and medium sized enterprises, where owner-managers lack the capability and support to be able to establish effective people management practices. These, in combination with a variety of economic factors, have been shown to lead to low levels of trust amongst workers towards institutions, particularly business.

- Low job quality: CIPD research has highlighted that individuals in the UK suffer from mediocre to low levels of job quality, and that positive job quality outcomes are skewed towards the top end of the wage/labour market. There are clear issues for job quality outcomes throughout firm supply chains, and firms are under increasing pressure to demonstrate their actions towards improving job quality in supply chains (Share Action, nd).

- Perception of a lack of power/choice: Globally regulators are starting to trial how boards can improve employee voice at the top table, by introducing recommendations and mechanisms for giving employees a 'seat at the table'. Approaches adopted differ internationally, but there is a growing awareness that the lack of employee voice is an issue that needs to be overcome.

- Perception of fluid and complex economic, social and environmental context: much of the narrative around the world of work today is that multiple forces are in play which act to create complex, dynamic systems, which are difficult for boards to navigate in their decision-making and manage over the long term. This is often an argument put forward to explain the decreasing ability of boards to make decisions over the long-term: that shareholders are increasingly short-term in their thinking, as a result of the perceptions of complex markets, economic systems, and social issues (Dallas, 2011). At the social level boards are under significant pressure to utilize ever-growing amounts of data and information, often objective, but increasingly subjective (eg the views of experts, internal stakeholders, political commentary). Evidence shows that in these situations where data is both objective and subjective in nature boards err towards conformity of views, beliefs and behaviours, resulting in conformity to short-termism (Marginson and McAulay, 2008). This is clearly a difficult risk to overcome.

Building and sustaining trust

Since the financial crisis in 2008, and through subsequent periods of recession and austerity in different areas of the world, measures of trust in corporate institutions have shown a significant and extended decrease (Edelman, nd). In such a context, it is critically important for senior leaders to understand and measure culture as a basis for appropriate remedial or mitigation action to build trust.

These issues are, of course, complex and nuanced. Schein (1990) identifies distinctive issues associated with ethical climate and ethical culture which provide useful ideas in relation to the role of standards in building transparent and ethical practice as the basis for trust:

- Ethical climate: this describes 'correct behaviour, and how ethical decisions should be handled in organizations' (Victor and Cullen, 1987).
- Ethical culture: describes the 'systems, procedures and practices for guiding and supporting ethical behavior' in organizations (Kish-Gephart, Harrison and Treviño, 2010). Ethical culture does not appear overnight

– it is cumulative, developing over time as the organizational ethical perspective is consistently articulated and enacted.

These ideas offer a useful point of departure for understanding the role of human capital, social capital and the various aspects of HRM systems in building trust and achieving transparency in governance. However, culture and trust are difficult issues to measure and report. This is where standards and standardization play a critical role.

Measuring culture: the role of standards

A wide range of consultant-devised tools and systems to capture the 'essence' of culture are available. However, their utility as a basis for benchmarking and comparison is limited, as standardized approaches do not exist. As a result, the outcomes and impact of organizational culture and culture change in dynamic and multi-level contexts are rarely evaluated.

Studies have identified a range of challenges relating to the measurement of culture and human capital. These include the following.
Imperfect indicators:

- A lack of clear measures creates a barrier to trying to measure and understand culture.
- The pursuit of a universal set of indicators prevents firms from establishing contextually relevant and dynamic indicators of culture.

Data blindness:

- When data is available this can create a false sense of security in quality and effectiveness: that the measure adequately describes the construct. This can generate blind spots which are not investigated and managed.

Missing signals:

- Many of the signals of culture are indirect and unobservable, therefore cannot be quantified through measurement.
- Rules or norms which are not observable may often conflict with observable norms. Measuring this relationship is difficult.

Simplistic instruments:

- By their design, cultural indicators need to be flexible to change and accurately report on culture temporally at adequate intervals. Often, indicators will need to operate at different levels and report at different points in time. This can challenge static and simplistic reporting frameworks.

The result of these barriers is that the categorization of cultures is difficult, if not impossible. As management teams are often operating at pace, navigating complexity and executing on strategy, important corporate culture issues may not be recognized. Developing a systematic approach to measuring and reporting on culture is a priority in the HCM field.

Human capital reporting: signalling culture to external stakeholders

A key issue for boards of directors is to 'signal' and communicate their understanding of culture, and the value of their workforce. This mostly occurs through annual reports and engagement processes with investors and other stakeholders. Various data points and narratives are used in this signalling; for example, information about workplace fatalities, gender pay, diversity in the senior leadership team, and investment in learning, training and development.

An outline of the main channels used to signal is illustrated in Figure 1.1.

FIGURE 1.1   Forms of human capital signalling to external stakeholders

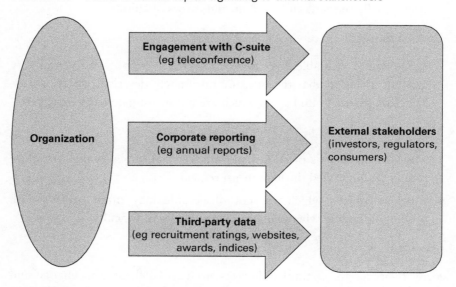

The figure shows the main channels used by directors to signal an understanding of the value of human capital

However, these signals can vary considerably in quality and trustworthiness both within organizations and between them. Standards and standardization, for example ISO 30414, can help to improve how these signals are transmitted, received and understood by investors and other stakeholders.

ISO 30414:2018 HUMAN RESOURCE MANAGEMENT – GUIDELINES FOR INTERNAL AND EXTERNAL HUMAN CAPITAL REPORTING

One important way to improve the quality of the signals about human capital is through standardization, both in terms of measures and methods of reporting (eg annual reports). In 2017, in the US the Human Capital Management Coalition, a group of 26 institutional investors with aggregate assets of more than $3 trillion, petitioned the US Securities and Exchange Commission to require public companies to disclose information about their HCM. The development of ISO 30414 represents an important step towards the development of measures which firms can start to report to stakeholders, both internal and external.

ISO 30414 consists of multiple measures which are divided into nine categories:

1 Ethics: measures which relate to the behaviour of individual employees and compliance against regulation-based business norms.

2 Costs: measures which relate to the total cost of the workforce.

3 Workforce diversity: measures which describe the individual characteristics of the workforce and leadership team.

4 Leadership: measures which demonstrate the extent to which employees trust the leadership capability of organization leaders.

5 Organizational safety, health and wellbeing: indicators which illustrate the extent to which health, safety and wellbeing are managed by the enterprise.

6 Productivity: indicators which highlight the contribution of human capital to organization productivity and performance.

7 Recruitment, mobility and turnover: data which demonstrates the ability of the enterprise to provide adequate human capital through recruitment processes.

8 Skills and capabilities: indicators which demonstrate the quality and content of individual human capital.

9 Workforce availability: measures that highlight the extent to which the enterprise has adequate numbers of individuals to complete work tasks.

In addition to these measures for external reporting, ISO 30414 articulates the importance of disclosing additional categories of human capital information relating to corporate culture and succession planning to internal stakeholders. This information, which is often considered to describe elements of competitive advantage, is important for decision-making at senior leadership level. In addition, it has the potential to offer value to external stakeholders such as institutional investors and regulators.

Risk and opportunity: a new perspective on measuring culture and human capital

The development of standards, as illustrated above, form part of a process to build understanding of HCM issues in organizations and to improve transparency in reporting. This work offers further opportunity to senior leaders in relation to the often overlooked, but crucial, issues of human capital risk assessment.

There are seven dimensions of people risk and opportunity (CIPD, nd):

1 Talent management: issues relating to the attraction and retention of high-quality staff, and to skills shortages, lack of talent and development strategy and poor workforce planning.

2 Health and safety: information regarding health and safety issues that may put employees in danger. This includes issues relating to physical and mental health in the workplace.

3 Employee ethics: issues relating to the risk of inappropriate employee behaviours and ethical breaches of trust, which may lead to regulatory sanctions or litigation.

4 Diversity and equality: a lack of diversity and inclusion in the background of workers in the organization. Risks of having inappropriate or ineffective HCM systems which may lead to bias through systems and processes, resulting in poor diversity outcomes.

5 Employee relations: risks relating to industrial action and poor management practices which may result in a lack of employee voice. This includes risks relating to communications, particularly during mergers and acquisitions or significant organizational change, plus low morale and engagement resulting in reduced or poor productivity.

6 Business continuity: failure to manage the risks that may affect the ability of the workforce to deliver productively, in particular relating to wildcard

events (unexpected in terms of size and magnitude). Exit of key leadership and management talent from the organization with little or no succession planning in place. Changes in the firm's external environment, in particular those relating to the political, social and economic outlook of various important stakeholders to the firm.

7 Reputational risk: major breaches of trust that result in significant corporate or regulatory fines. Poor environmental and social performance which delivers an impact on specific measures of corporate trust, particularly with reference to workforce issues (eg throughout the supply chain).

These human capital risks affect the ability of the organization to deliver on its strategic objectives. Although this information should be of particular interest to external stakeholders, and should inform the content of external reporting by organizations, organizations have made very little progress in this area. Studies have shown that reporting, especially about culture, tends to be formulaic and shallow, lacking any comprehensive and detailed understanding of the issues (CIPD, nd).

Therefore, human capital reporting, making use of international standards, offers an important mechanism for signalling intangible achievements or challenges associated with culture, trust, ethics and transparency. It is this community of powerful stakeholders which may in the very near future be exerting increasing pressure on firms to improve reporting. The question is: are firms ready?

Measuring the immeasurable: the investor view

The corporate CEO mantra of 'employees are our greatest asset' (Mulcahy, nd) is heard frequently by investors. However, workforce-related governance scandals, which are reported on a regular basis, can create scepticism amongst investors. The intangible nature of human capital assets means that people hold *potential value* in the eyes of investor stakeholders. For example, this information is of interest to those who are investing in sectors where value is tied up in intellectual and human capital, such as in the pharmaceutical, high-tech and financial sectors, where R&D and product development processes dominate discussion.

Nonetheless, very little is known about the extent to which investors use human capital/workforce data in their decision-making. This is not surprising given the poor quality and reliability levels of some measures that feature in organizational practices.

However, in recent years environmental, social and governance investors in the investment community have sought information on the workforce and begun to challenge organizations to improve the quality of human capital information. Such interest stems from concern about sustainability and the implications of sustainability for ethical and long-term investments. Emergent ideas about creating shared value highlight that value should be created and distributed between stakeholders, and that those stakeholders should take a deep interest in this process (Moore, nd).

INVESTOR INTEREST

Recognizing that the workforce is one of the key stakeholders of value creation, investors are increasingly motivated to understand how people are being managed and benefiting from value creation and value capture. A CIPD (nd) report highlights the value of human capital reporting from different investor perspectives:

- Investor-director who is using people data: 'HR-related factors end up influencing decisions 100 per cent of the time. Top management is always the big driver. If they are competent, the issues with the rest of the firm are solvable. If there are potential problems with top management... chances are you've got issues further down the line.'

- Investor fund manager using people data to understand skills retention: 'I've been looking at a company that's a high-tech company, and one of my immediate concerns is: how are they attracting staff, and how are they retaining staff in high-skilled roles? Because we know that there are shortages around engineers and around technology roles.'

Human capital reporting and investor decision-making

In spite of evidence of interest from the investment community, no consistent approach has yet been adopted to incorporate human capital data into investor valuation models that might offer 'leading' indicators with relevance to forecasting future returns (Krausert, 2017). Encouraging investors to make better use of human capital data is challenging for many reasons (CIPD, nd):

- Investors seek information which is difficult to measure and report: management quality is a concept which appears in the literature and is described by investors who use the term to describe the experience and/

or reputation of the organization's management team. However, this measure is subject to considerable measurement issues and potential bias within measures, as well as a lack of agreement on what management quality describes.

- Investors tend to seek basic operational data, and not strategic information: for example, the number and change in number of employees; changes in the workforce size, or the size of the workforce over time is also considered to be an important measure. In the eyes of investors, these measures describe stability. However, other information regarding succession planning, recruitment strategy is not sought.

- A lack of good-quality data and poor-quality narrative: the lack of quality has important implications regarding the utility and trustworthiness of data that is reported. It is this barrier in particular which is driving investor interest in standards of reporting, as without good quality data and operationalized reporting frameworks, the data which is being reported is likely to go unused.

At the same time, investors recognize that investment in human capital development (for example skills and training) offers insight on the long-term sustainability of organizations and can shape understanding of likely workforce adaptability or resilience. This type of information, if standardized, could enable comparison between organizations, and provide greater transparency of investment in human capital compared to other forms of capital.

THE WORKFORCE DISCLOSURE INITIATIVE

The Workforce Disclosure Initiative (WDI) was established to enable investors globally to collaborate both within the investment community and with organizations to improve the transparency of reporting on workforce issues. The movement was developed to galvanize action on improving human capital reporting, particularly across supply chains. WDI shines a light on the quality of workforce data, and has a particular focus on improving transparent reporting of supply chain issues – in particular those related to aspects of job quality.

The pilot-year report for the initiative, which is supported by major firms and investors in the UK and the US, found weaknesses in terms of data and reporting quality which prevent information dissemination and discussion of key human capital and culture issues (Share Action, nd). As a result, the WDI continues to push for greater engagement by investors on workforce issues.

Movements such as the WDI, which is a partnership between Share Action, Oxfam and the UK Department for International Development, demonstrate that sentiment amongst investors is growing around the importance of human capital and culture to long-term impact. It provides a welcome example of how interest in human capital reporting is growing amongst the investment and corporate governance community. As this interest continues to grow, there will be more debate on the importance of human capital reporting, and, crucially, more calls for improvements in reporting standards.

Summary

HCM is an important aspect of the human world of work. It recognizes and utilizes the knowledge, skills and abilities of individuals. The importance of people in value creation is recognized by economists and policymakers. However, progress with human capital measurement and dialogue about investment in human capital at the organizational level has been slow and fragmented.

Drawing on research and insights from various fields, this chapter has discussed important issues related to human capital management and measurement. It has considered the role of corporate governance and highlighted emerging trends in the investment community. Standards represent an important opportunity to develop measures and reporting practices to enable HCM and corporate governance to be assessed, evaluated and enhanced. This, we believe, is crucial work if organizations and their stakeholder communities are to fully understand and utilize the value of people for effective and sustainable performance in modern organizations.

References and further resources

Alan, K M A, Altman, Y and Roussel, J (2008) Employee training needs and perceived value of training in the Pearl River Delta of China: a human capital development approach, *Journal of European Industrial Training*, 32 (1) pp 19–31

Barney, J B and Wright, P M (1998) On becoming a strategic partner: The role of human resources in gaining competitive advantage, *Human Resource Management*, 37 (1)

Baron, A and Armstrong, M (2007) *Human Capital Management: Achieving added value through people*, Kogan Page, London.

Beach, M J (2009) A critique of human capital formation in the U.S. and the economic returns to sub-baccalaureate credentials, *Educational Studies: A Journal of the American Educational Studies*, **45** (1) pp 24–38

Becker, G S (1975) *Human Capital: A theoretical and empirical analysis, with special reference to education*, 2nd edn, NBER, Cambridge, MA

Boon, C et al (2018) Integrating strategic human capital and strategic human resource management, *The International Journal of Human Resource Management*, **29** (1)

Cadbury, A (1992) Report of the Committee on the Financial Aspects of Corporate Governance, *European Corporate Governance Institute* www.ecgi.org/codes/documents/cadbury.pdf (archived at https://perma.cc/TA52-NUZ6)

Chamberlain, S P (2005) Recognizing and responding to cultural differences in the education of culturally and linguistically diverse learners, *Intervention in School & Clinic*, **40** (4), pp 195–211

CIPD. Hidden figures: how workforce data is missing from corporate reports, *CIPD* www.cipd.co.uk/knowledge/strategy/governance/hidden-figures-workforce-data (archived at https://perma.cc/687N-BUTQ)

CIPD. The intangible workforce: investor perspectives on workforce data, *CIPD* www.cipd.co.uk/Images/investor-perspectives-on-workforce-data_tcm18-55499.pdf (archived at https://perma.cc/M5KZ-AQ4A)

CIPD. Landing transformational change: closing the gap between theory and practice, *CIPD* www.cipd.co.uk/Images/landing-transformation-change_2015-gap-theory-practice_tcm18-9050.pdf (archived at https://perma.cc/2YED-PX55)

CIPD. Creating and capturing value at work: who benefits?, *CIPD* www.cipd.co.uk/Images/creating-and-capturing-value-at-work_2017-who-benefits-2_tcm18-33097.pdf (archived at https://perma.cc/2BLY-RVGN)

Claessens, S (2007) Global Corporate Governance Forum Focus 1. World Bank, in Stanford, N (ed) (2007) *Guide to organization design: creating high-performing and adaptable enterprises*, The Economist, London

Coff, R W and Kryscynski, D (2011) Drilling for micro-foundations of human capital-based competitive advantages, *Journal of Management*, **37**, pp 1429–43

Coff, R W (1997) Human assets and management dilemmas: coping with hazards on the road to resource-based theory, *Academy of Management Review*, **22**, pp 374–402

Dallas, L L (2011) Short-termism, the financial crisis, and corporate governance, *Journal of Corporation Law*, 37, p 265

De La Fuente, A and Ciccone, A (2002) Le capital humain dans une économie mondiale sur la connaissance, *Commission Européenne*, www.researchgate.net/publication/44830300_Le_Capital_humain_dans_une_economie_mondiale_fondee_sur_la_connaissance_rapport_final (archived at https://perma.cc/BKY6-52HW)

Edelman Trust Barometer: UK Press Release 2018, *Edelman* www.edelman.co.uk/
wp-content/uploads/Website-Edelman-Trust-Barometer-Press-Release-2018.pdf
(archived at https://perma.cc/BD3M-8E3L)

FRC. The UK Corporate Governance Code July 2018, *FRC* www.frc.org.uk/
getattachment/88bd8c45-50ea-4841-95b0-d2f4f48069a2/2018-UK-Corporate-
Governance-Code-FINAL.pdf (archived at https://perma.cc/L5YE-FP96)

FRC. Corporate culture and the role of boards: report of observations, *FRC*
www.frc.org.uk/getattachment/3851b9c5-92d3-4695-aeb2-87c9052dc8c1/
Corporate-Culture-and-the-Role-of-Boards-Report-of-Observations.pdf
(archived at https://perma.cc/5HZ9-8YCW)

Garavan, T N *et al* (2001) Human capital accumulation: the role of human
resource development, *Journal of European Industrial Training*, 25 (2)
pp 48–68

Hofstede, G (1998) Attitudes, values and organizational culture: disentangling the
concepts, *Organization Studies*, 19 (3) pp 477–93

ICSA. What is corporate governance?, *ICSA* www.icsa.org.uk/about-us/policy/
what-is-corporate-governance (archived at https://perma.cc/ZA3R-7MR8)

International Organization for Standardization (ISO) (2018) ISO 30414:2018
*Human resource management – Guidelines for internal and external human
capital reporting*, www.iso.org/standard/69338.html (archived at https://perma.cc/
E4G4-VMVQ)

Kish-Gephart, J, Harrison, D and Treviño, L (2010) Bad apples, bad cases, and bad
barrels: meta-analytic evidence about sources of unethical decisions at work,
Journal of Applied Psychology, 95 (1) pp 1–31

Krausert, A (2017) The HRM-capital market link: effects of securities analysts on
strategic human capital, *Human Resource Management*, 57 (1) pp 1–14

Kwon, D-B (2009). Human capital and its measurement. Paper presented at the
Third OECD World Forum, Busan, Korea, on Statistics, knowledge and policy:
Charting progress, building visions, improving life. https://pdfs.semanticscholar.org/
2f37/bf4af375da23338e42dd85b4227a801fe20d.pdf (archived at
https://perma.cc/L43E-ZQW8)

Marginson, D and McAulay, L (2008) Exploring the debate on short-termism:
a theoretical and empirical analysis, *Strategic Management Journal*, 29 (3),
pp 273–92

Mavondo, F and Farrell, M (2003) Cultural orientation: its relationship with
market orientation, innovation and organizational performance, *Management
Decision*, 41 (3) pp 241–49

Moore, C. Corporate social responsibility and creating shared value: what's the
difference?, *Heifer International* https://cdn.ymaws.com/members.sibf.org/
resource/dynamic/blogs/20140530_112347_15670.pdf (archived at
https://perma.cc/3N8G-88UQ)

Mulcahy, M A. LifeCare, Inc. Conference Features Xerox CEO Anne Mulcahy; Employers Challenged to Motivate and Engage Workforce, *Business Wire* www.businesswire.com/news/home/20030516005369/en/LifeCare-Conference-Features-Xerox-CEO-Anne-Mulcahy (archived at https://perma.cc/8M58-Y5UM)

OECD (2015) *OECD principles of corporate governance*, www.oecd.org/corporate/principles-corporate-governance.htm (archived at https://perma.cc/QW2J-VA6G)

OECD. High-level follow-up meeting of the global deal for decent work and inclusive growth, *OECD* www.oecd.org/about/secretary-general/oecd-sg-decent-work-and-inclusive-growth-new-york-18-september.htm (archived at https://perma.cc/TW75-BN76)

Ployhart, R E *et al* (2014) Human capital is dead; long live human capital resources!, *Journal of Management*, **40** (2), pp 371–98

Rastogi, P N (2002) Knowledge management and intellectual capital as a paradigm of value creation, *Human Systems Management*, **21** (4) pp 229–40

Rodriguez, P J and Loomis, R S (2007) A new view of institutions, human capital, and market standardization, *Education, Knowledge and Economy*, **1** (1) pp 93–105

Romer, P M (1990) Endogenous technological change, *Journal of Political Economy*, **98** (5) pp 71–102

Rosen, H S (1999) *Public finance*, McGraw-Hill, New York

Schein, E (1990) Organizational culture, *American Psychologist*, **45** (2), pp 109–19

Schultz, T W (1961) Investment in human capital, *American Economic Review*, **51**, pp 1–17

Share Action. Workforce Disclosure Initiative – improving the quality of jobs: Pilot year report, *Share Action* https://shareaction.org/wp-content/uploads/2018/04/WDI-Pilot-Year-Report.pdf (archived at https://perma.cc/6YN9-73KP)

Victor, B and Cullen, J B (1987) A Theory and Measure of Ethical Climate in Organizations, *Research in Corporate Social Performance and Policy*, **9**, pp 51–71

Youndt, M A (2004) Intellectual capital profiles: an examination of investments and returns, *Journal of Management Studies*, **41** (2) pp 335–61

2

It's all a matter of standards

Heather Bond

Introduction

This chapter outlines the iterative nature of the standards development process and considers why standards matter. It identifies relevant standards for organizations to review, including arguments for their adoption and consideration of potential benefits, opportunities, challenges and pointers to good organizational practice.

CHAPTER OBJECTIVES

This chapter describes and explains:

- human capital management and development (HCMD) standards that have been published, and those in development;
- the standards development process;
- the different types of standards;
- principles-led or compliance-based approaches;
- why and how standards matter.

Key terms

In this chapter, 'human capital management' (HCM) and 'human resource management' (HRM) are used interchangeably and reflect the focus of the standards being developed nationally and internationally.

Many of the other terms used in this chapter, which are also set out in the glossary at the end of the book (see Appendix 1), will be familiar, but may be defined and understood differently in various national contexts. They are presented in alphabetical order below and as they are defined in the identified standards, notably ISO 30400:2016: *Human resource management. Vocabulary* and BS 76000:2015 *Human Resource. Valuing People. Management System. Requirements and Guidance*, or on the International Organization for Standardization (ISO) Online Browsing Platform (ISO-OBP).

Audit (30400:6.13):	A systematic, independent and documented process for obtaining audit evidence and evaluating it objectively to determine the extent to which the audit criteria have been fulfilled.
Benchmarking (30400:3.17):	Comparing attributes, processes or performance between organizations.
Business continuity planning (30400:3.6):	The process of mutual planning by organizations and other stakeholders.
Business model (30400:3.4):	An organization's approach to operating in its environment.
Compliance (ISO-OBP):	The action of doing what is necessary to meet a specified requirement.
Conformity (ISO-OBP):	The fulfilment of a requirement.
Governance (30400:3.1):	The way in which a whole organization is led, directed, controlled and held accountable.
Human capital (30400:4.1):	The value of the collective knowledge, skills and abilities of an organization's people.
Human governance (30400:7.1):	The system by which an organization is directed and controlled, taking into account the organization's stakeholders as well as human and social factors, at the highest and every level of decision-making.
Materiality (30400:3.15):	A measure of the significance of an element to organizational results.
Organization structure (30400:3.3):	The hierarchical arrangement of authority, responsibility and accountability in an organization.
Organizational culture (30400:3.2):	Values, beliefs and practices that influence the conduct and behaviour of people and organizations.

Organizational values (30400:4.7):	Aspirational or articulated standards, behaviour, principles or concepts that an organization considers important.
People risk (30400:4.10):	Possible negative outcomes that arise as a consequence of the behaviour and activities of people.
Principle (ISO-OBP):	A fundamental, basis for decision-making or behaviour.
Requirement (ISO-OBP):	A need or expectation that is stated, generally implied or obligatory.
Social responsibility (30400:3.9):	The responsibility of an organization for the consequences of its decisions and activities on society and the environment, through transparent and ethical behaviour.
Stakeholder/ interested party (30400:5.1):	A person or organization that can affect, be affected by, or perceive itself to be affected by a decision or activity.
Strategy (30400:3.5):	An organization's approach to achieving its objectives.
Sustainable employability (30400:8.1):	The long-term capability to acquire or create and maintain work. Sustainable employability can be the responsibility of people, organizations or governments.
Strategic planning (30400:3.8):	The formulation, development, implementation and evaluation of factors that are relevant to an organization's long-term or overall interests, and the means of achieving its objectives.
Value (BS 76000:3.26):	The merit and worth of people due to their unique knowledge, skills and abilities (noting that inherent value refers to the principle that people are valued for who they are; not just because they deliver monetary value or money equivalents to their organization).
Values (BS 76000: 3.27):	Principles, ethics or rules applied to make moral judgements, and consequently people's standards of behaviours and attitudes.

Standards that matter to HCMD

There are an increasing number of British and international standards that are firmly grounded in the domain of HCMD. They are premised on the intrinsic value of people and their contribution to organizational performance. These include:

- BS 76000:2015 *Human resource. Valuing people. Management system. Requirements and Guidance*: This standard establishes the principles that underpin a structured and thoughtful approach to people value management in organizations.

- BS 76005:2017 *Valuing people through diversity and inclusion. Code of practice for organizations*: This standard provides a framework of recommendations in support of a principled approach to diversity and inclusion (D&I) in organizations.

- PD 76006:2017 *Guide to learning and development*: This published document helps users navigate the principled use of learning and development to maximize the value of people in an organization.

- ISO 30400:2016 *Human resource management. Vocabulary*: This presents the key terms and definitions used in and across the suite of international HRM standards.

- ISO 30408:2016 *Human resource management – Guidelines on human governance*: This presents guidelines for organizations on the establishment and continuous improvement of processes and practices for effective human governance within organizations.

- ISO/TR 30406:2017 *Human resource management – Sustainable employability management for organizations*: The focus of this technical report is on the principles guiding the development and implementation of sustainable employment policies in organizations.

- ISO 30409:2016 *Human Resource Management – Workforce Planning*: The emphasis here is on the value of workforce planning and the provision of guidance for organizations on responding to the demands of an increasingly dynamic and complex operating environment through effective workforce planning.

- ISO 30414:2018 *Human resource management – Guidelines for internal and external human capital reporting*: The objective of this standard is the principled consideration and transparency of the human capital contribution to the organization.

In addition, in the UK there are also publicly available specifications (PAS) standards that focus on people at work:

- PAS 3000:2015 *Smart working. Code of practice*: The focus is on changes to working environments, practices and technology and a framework of recommendations for organizations to implement smart working.

- PAS 3001:2016 *Travelling for work. Responsibilities of an organization for health, safety and security. Code of practice*: This addresses the responsibilities of an organization for health, safety and security. Attention is given to the various risks that might arise when people are travelling for work on behalf of the organization.

- PAS 3002:2018 *Code of Practice on Improving Health and Wellbeing Within an Organization*: This considers the health and wellbeing of workers, and what is required to ensure health and wellbeing related services are available in organizations.

There are other international standards that have a people value or people risk dimension. These are located under the work programmes of committees of technical experts focusing on governance, security and resilience, sustainability and quality management:

- ISO/AWI 37000 *Guidance for the governance of organizations*: The focus of this new international guidance standard will be on organizational governance. It is scheduled for completion by the end of 2020.

- ISO 37001:2016 *Anti-bribery management systems – Requirements with guidance for use*: The focus and intent of this standard is to guide organizations on establishing and maintaining the measures and controls essential to anti-bribery good practice.

- ISO/NP 37002 *Whistleblowing management systems – Guidelines*: Robust and effective whistleblowing systems for organizations is the scope of this new standard under development.

- ISO 26000:2010 *Guidance on social responsibility*: The principal concern of this standard is the promotion of social responsibility and the contribution of organizations to sustainable development.

- ISO 22330:2018 *Security and resilience – Business continuity management systems – Guidelines for people aspects of business continuity*: These guidelines focus on organizational strategies and plans, policies and procedures relating to managing incidents and the risks to, and adverse effects on, people.

- ISO 27500:2016 *The human centred organization – Rationale and general principles*: This sets out high-level human-centred principles and recommendations for ergonomic related policies and processes, to help organizations optimize performance, minimize risks, maximize wellbeing and enhance relationships with stakeholders.

- ISO/DIS 10015 *Quality management – Guidelines for competence management and people development*: This standard, currently under revision, will present guidelines relating to systems for managing competence and people development in the context of the quality and conformity of an organization's product and services.

- ISO/DIS 10018 *Quality management systems – Guidelines on people engagement*: Another standard under revision, this will shine a light on the importance of engaging and enhancing people's involvement with an organization's quality management system.

The increasing number of standards that are published, or in progress, that focus on people at work is evidence that there is a growing awareness of the importance of the human capital contribution to organizational performance. A full list of the standards developed or in progress under the auspices of the British Standards Institution (BSI) Human Capital Committee HCS1/1 and ISO's Human Resource Management Technical Committee TC260 are provided in Appendix 2.

The remainder of this chapter outlines how different types of standards are developed, and the rationale for their adoption by organizations of all types, size and across different sectors and jurisdictions.

Standards matters – the development process

Standards set out general agreed rules or practices that inform the way products are made, services are delivered, or processes are managed and quality assured. The primary purpose of standardization is consistency, reliability and shared quality outcomes that can benefit both organizations and their stakeholders.

However, what is less well understood is who, and what, is involved in the development of national and international standards that takes place through accredited standardization bodies. This process is outlined in the following section.

Standards bodies, committee structures and the role of experts

British and international standards are developed through the collaboration of technical experts brought together by national standards bodies (NSBs), including the BSI, and the ISO. These standard-setting bodies, and the expert working groups (WGs) they convene, represent government agencies, industry, academia, special interest and user groups, and industry and employer bodies (Chartered Institute of Personnel and Development (CIPD), nd).

British national standards may have been developed in the UK by BSI committees and then gone on to become international standards. For example, the well-known ISO 9001:2015 *Quality management systems – Requirements* was first initiated through a BSI standards development process. Other standards are developed first as international standards, but usually involve considerable UK participation.

THE BSI

BSI is the recognized UK NSB. This is an established position recognized under a Memorandum of Understanding with the UK Government. The Department for Business, Energy and Industrial Strategy (BEIS) has responsibility for standardization policy. BEIS encourages the development of new standards to support economic, innovation, and sustainability goals and provides funding for BSI's activities, including participation in international standards making.

Under its Royal Charter and Byelaws, BSI is identified as a not-for-profit organization. It is required to ensure that its standards making committees represent a wide range of interests and involve key stakeholder groups, for example trade associations, unions, professional bodies, consumer and public interest organizations, academia, and public and private sector employing organizations, which nominate individuals as their expert representatives.

Amongst the numerous BSI standards committees, there are two that focus specifically on the development of human capital standards:

- **Human Capital Committee HCS1/1:** This focuses on UK national standards and draws on the people management and development knowledge and expertise of professionals, academics, consultants and assessment specialists that represent the views of their nominating bodies – for example: the Centre for Assessment, the CIPD, the Chartered Management Institute, the Institute for Employment Studies, the Federation of Small Businesses, Network Rail and the University Forum for Human Resource Development.

- **Human Capital Committee HCS1/2:** This is the UK 'mirror' committee that is solely concerned with the development of international standards in HRM under the auspices of ISO. It has a similar constituency to HCS1/1, and draws on the knowledge of a pool of specialists to ensure the UK has an expert voice on the international standards that the committee votes to support, on behalf of BSI as the UK's NSB as a full and participating member of the relevant ISO committee, TC260.

THE ISO

Founded in 1947, this is an independent, non-governmental international organization with membership constituency made up of NSB representatives. More than 160 countries, represented by their NSB, make up the global ISO membership network.

- Some 120 countries are **Full** members. These are expected to fully participate in the development of ISO strategy, have voting rights on technical and policy matters, and influence the development, promulgation and adoption of international standards nationally.

- Approximately 60 countries are **Correspondent** members. While able to promote the adoption of international standards nationally, they attend technical and policy meetings in the capacity of observers.

- A very small number of countries maintain a watching brief as **Subscriber** members but cannot participate, promote or adopt international standards on a national basis.

Standards-making internationally is governed and managed by ISO's Technical Management Board (TMB). This body is responsible for the ISO Directives that set out the regulations by which standards are developed. The TMB is also responsible for establishing technical committees (TC) and appointing the TC Chairs and Secretariat, and for monitoring the progress of standards as they are developed. Currently there are approximately 300 ISO TCs that bring together the collaborative effort of experts from all over the world.

TC260 Human resource management is the TC responsible for developing standards in the domain of HRM. This TC was established in 2011. Some 28 countries currently participate in the TC through their expert representatives in its 10 different WGs, tasked with developing subject-specific standards and technical specifications. Currently, three of these WGs are led by experts from UK and, in addition, there are UK experts engaged in the development work of another five. There are a further 23 countries that have elected to have observer status.

TC260 also has official liaison relationships with other ISO TCs that have standards in development and where their work intersects on a 'people' dimension, for example TC176 Quality management and quality assurance, which has ISO/DIS 10015 and ISO/DIS 10018 in its wide portfolio of standards.

THE ROLE OF EXPERTS

Standards are developed within this network of committees, and require a significant voluntary contribution and commitment of experts sharing their knowledge and expertise to shape them. These individual experts must become a member of a national committee in order to participate on behalf of their NSB in the work of both national and international standards committees. This requires the support of a nominating organization; for example, a trade association, professional body or academic institution, in order to represent their views. Currently, there are over 11,000 volunteer experts contributing to the work of some 2,000 BSI committees, and in excess of 50,000 experts are active in more than 3,000 ISO committees.

Of these committees, both HCS1/1 & 2 and TC260 focus on developing standards to provide practitioners with a 'toolkit' that encourages and supports good practice in HCMD. These tools can benefit organizations and their key stakeholders such as people who work for or on behalf of the organization, those who access their products and services, and those who are interested in the potential for shareholder value.

The committee structure allows the knowledge of subject experts to be shared, distilled and transferred in the drafting, reviewing and guiding of national and international standards through to publication. The collaborative process involved in standards development is the basis for the credibility and authority of standards and their take-up by organizations and individuals.

The essential components of the standard-making process are:

- **Committees** of experts: These are drawn from a wide geographical and sectoral range working collaboratively to develop the content of the standard.

- **Consensus:** Discussion and decision on the format and content of the standard reached by general agreement by as many committee members as possible, and not by majority vote.

- **Consultation:** Making draft standards widely available for scrutiny and comment to anyone who might be interested or impacted by their content.

The work undertaken in these committees requires in-person or virtual participation by the experts involved, but this is not without its challenges given the dispersed geographical nature of members working across differing time zones. In their 2017 Annual Report (ISO, nd), ISO state that 2,784 technical meetings took place in 56 countries, and that a further number of virtual meetings were organized in that year. On average, 21 technical meetings took place somewhere in the world on each working day of 2017.

THE DEVELOPMENT PROCESS AND TIMEFRAMES

The timeframes and development process protocols are, of course, standardized. The development of national standards in the UK is governed by BS 0 2016: *A standard for standards – Principles of standardization* (BSI, n.d.), and the development of standards internationally, requires adherence to the ISO Directives (Parts 1 & 2) (ISO, nd). But essentially, they have much in common in terms of timelines and procedural stages, as outlined below:

- **Proposal:** For a new item of work that details the rationale, scope and business case to facilitate a committee vote on the approval or non-approval of the type and content of the standard proposed. The development timeframe is confirmed at this stage and can be 18, 24, 36 or 48 months. Once confirmed, this timeframe will be monitored and must be adhered to.

- **Preparation:** A WG of experts is convened to undertake due diligence and further research, and to develop the working draft (WD) standard.

- **Committee:** The WD is shared with the wider committee as a committee draft to allow scrutiny, comment and voting. This stage will be repeated until there is consensus on the technical content and agreement that the committee draft can progress to draft international standard stage.

- **Enquiry:** The draft international standard is submitted for circulation to all ISO members to ensure that everyone has 12 weeks to scrutinize and comment on it in advance of the vote. It is also available for public scrutiny and comment in the same timeframe. To progress further, full consideration of the comments received must be undertaken by the WG, and the draft must have gained approval of two-thirds of the participating committee members, with not more than a quarter of the total votes cast being negative.

- **Approval:** Further consideration of comments and the incorporation of technical content changes take place before progression to final draft stage and circulation to all ISO members for a final eight-week vote. The standard will only be approved for publication if a two-thirds majority of participating members of the TC is in favour, and not more than one-quarter of the total number of votes cast are negative.

- **Publish:** Editorial changes only take place at this stage prior to publication.

Post publication, standards are reviewed at least twice in a five-year period. They are either revised and republished or withdrawn as a result of the review.

TYPES OF STANDARD

In 2017 ISO published more than 1,500 standards, bringing the total published to almost 22,000 standards. Similarly, BSI published approximately 2,500 new or revised standards but at the same withdrew 1,700 standards.

It is important to remember that standards are voluntary, and whilst they have a specific scope and focus, they have the same overarching purpose, share the same structural characteristics and follow similar development protocols. Different types or categories of standard are available:

- **Specification:** These detail a set of objectively verifiable and absolute requirements resulting in non-negotiable criteria for products, services or systems; primarily, the threshold performance criteria.

- **Management systems standard:** These are typically written to reflect the style of a specification. The purpose of this type of standard is to provide a plan–do–check–act (PDCA) model for establishing and maintaining an organization-wide management system. All international management system standards use the Annex SL structure, as set out in the ISO Directives.

- **Code of practice:** These reflect good practice for competent and conscientious professional practice in the form of recommendations and supporting guidance, which can be used to support a claim for compliance depending on the context and content focus.

- **Guide:** These are less prescriptive in approach. A guide provides advice that reflects current theory and practice about a particular subject and contains practical information, guidance and recommendations, but not necessarily to support a claim for compliance.

- **Technical Specification:** These are published for immediate use and to support specific technical aspects of another standard.

- **Technical Report:** These contain information and possibly survey data relating to a specific topic or area of concern.

- **Publicly Available Specification (PAS):** These are published for immediate use and in response to an identified market need. In the UK context, they are always commissioned by external sponsoring organizations that fund the work of a lead technical author or a consortium.

- **Vocabulary:** These support the consistent use of language within a specific field of standards by collating and presenting the terms and definitions used within that field of standards. Terms and definitions from all ISO standards can be accessed via the ISO-OBP.

- **Published documents:** These include standard-type documents that do not have the same status as a standard. Whilst there is no requirement for the same degree of consensus or public consultation, they generally follow the standard development protocols described above and incorporate the essential elements but within a more agile development process.

- **International Workshop Agreement:** These are developed outside the ISO committee system in an open workshop environment to support the engagement and negotiation of stakeholders in key market domains. The resulting published agreement will identify the workshop participants and the negotiated outcomes.

- **Test method:** These provide highly prescriptive procedures that can be repeated and reproduced to support the consistent and valid assessment of a material, product or process.

- **Method of specifying:** These detail the highly prescriptive characteristics of a material, product, process or system to aid customer selection and supplier agreements.

- **Classification:** These provide for the ordering and grading of items for use within a specific field.

Standards are voluntary and are developed nationally and internationally by nominated subject experts working in committees in accordance with the development protocols laid down by the relevant standards body. The category or type of standard reflects its expected functionality and its appropriateness for the subject and target market user.

A specification, the most common type of standard, contains highly prescriptive and absolute requirements, articulated in clauses that adopt '*shall*' to make clear what needs to be done for a claim of compliance to be made and where safety, certainty and assurance are paramount. Codes of practice are developed to provide good practice guidance and flexibility and to support benchmarking and adopt '*should*' to articulate recommendations to follow.

Different subject areas and identified target market users have differing standardization needs or ambitions and HCS1/1 and TC260 have reflected this in the suite of HCMD standards they develop. Generally, these standards are less prescriptive by design, and offer broad, evidence-based guidance on professional standards of practice to enable organizations to improve their approach to HCMD.

Their purpose is to better support optimal individual and organizational outcomes and facilitate measurement, comparability and consistency of HR practices with the ultimate aim of continuous improvement and transparent benchmarking.

Matters of principle or compliance

Seeing standardization as a 'new frontier' for HR, Anderson (2017) puts forward arguments for principles-led approaches in the HCMD domain, but also critiques the requirements-based compliance approach to standardization – deemed to be founded on a unitarist, rather than a pluralist, perspective of different interests and priorities in organizations. This debate is an important issue for those involved in standards. The practical differences that result from these different 'top level' approaches to standards are set out here.

Compliance-based standards

These specify requirements that 'shall' be met by the organizations that adopt them and can be characterized by their focus on:

- detailed rules and requirements to be followed;
- documentary evidence;
- stability;
- shorter-term horizon;
- conformity;

- compliance audits;
- certification.

Such rules and requirements-based standards include management systems and specifications. They adopt a PDCA framework and content clauses that focus on hierarchical 'top management' organizational structures, process efficiency rather than effectiveness, and on an assumption of regular audits to gauge whether the specified threshold requirements have been met and can support a claim of compliance and subsequent certification.

This might be entirely appropriate to the content of some standards, for example ISO 9001. But there is potential for a checklist approach to the prescribed activities to develop, which may give rise to a symbolic adoption of the standard. In addition, changing organizational types, such as hybrid or virtual organizations that increasingly operate transnationally, challenge the effectiveness of a unitary approach.

While there are compliance obligations in standards that may arise from laws or regulations it must be emphasized that standards rarely cite the law within their technical content and organizations still need to meet their legal and regulatory responsibilities.

Principles-led standards

These provide a guiding framework of principles that 'should' be met by the organizations that use them. Standards of this kind can be characterized by their focus on:

- commitment to values, guidance and recommendations for practice;
- integration of content and approach;
- flexibility;
- longer-term horizon;
- self-assessment as a tool for continuous improvement;
- benchmarking;
- options for certification.

Although the arguments for efficiency and optimal interoperability are valid in the context of compliance-based approaches, an overemphasis on rules and procedures can be at the expense of interests of people and their management and development, which requires a strong ethical underpinning.

Standards that focus on people at work need to balance control with flexibility, and if they are to be effective and have impact, provide people with the opportunity to take responsibility and use their initiative in the context of continuous improvement agendas and the volatility of the external environment that organizations and people have to contend with.

Principles and HCM standards

When it comes to principles, the UK showed the way in the realm of standardization with the BS 76000 human capital suite. This framework of standards, developed and published by BSI's HCS1/1 committee, establish and share principles for valuing people, D&I and learning and development in an organizational context:

- 'People working on behalf of the organization have intrinsic value, in addition to their protections under the law or in regulation, which needs to be respected.'
- 'Stakeholders and their interests are integral to the best interests of the organization.'
- 'Every organization is part of wider society and has a responsibility to respect its social contract as a corporate citizen and operate in a manner that is sustainable.'
- 'A commitment to valuing people who work on behalf of the organization and to meeting the requirements of the standard is made and supported at the highest level.'
- 'Each principle is of equal importance.'

These principles were developed independently of the UK CIPD, but are in alignment with the UK professional body's purpose of championing better work and working lives and encouraging principles for the HR profession that clearly articulate principles that matter to it:

- **Work**: Where good work is designed to be purposeful, safe and inclusive, this allows people at work to use their knowledge, skills and abilities and supports the fair recognition of their contribution towards the long-term benefit to people, organizations and society.
- **People**: People should be seen as unique individuals and fundamental to organizations. They should have access and opportunity to share the investment into their wellbeing and development, have a meaningful

voice on work matters, and be treated fairly and in accordance with legally protected rights.

- **Professionalism:** People, specifically those in the people profession, should act with integrity, balancing organizational risks and opportunities when making values and evidence-based decisions and demonstrate an understanding of the implications of their decisions on individuals, organizations and wider society.

Since the publication of the BS 76000 suite, interest in the use of principles as a framework for standards has grown, even in management systems and compliance-based standards. This suggests that there is merit in the principles-led approach, and that future standards may be more inclined towards this route to enable organizations to thoughtfully navigate decision-making and management practice in relation to workplace and workforce futures.

In this part of the chapter, issues of compliance and principles have been reviewed and the practical differences between compliance-based and principles-led standards outlined. The case for a principles-led approach to standards, particularly those that focus on the value of human capital, the workplace and people at work, has been advanced. The foundation principles set out in the BS 76000 family of standards are reflected and mapped against the principles for the people profession articulated by the CIPD.

Furthermore, increasing interest in the principles-led approach to standardization in this domain is cited as a positive signal that the future of work, whilst uncertain, will have a more human focus and that people at work will be appropriately recognized and valued for their inherent merit.

Matters of value and the value of standards to organizations

Who uses standards?

Quite simply, the answer to this question is organizations of all types, size and sector and across geographical boundaries. This includes governments and their departments, multinational companies operating in highly competitive markets, private, public and third sector entities and small businesses operating in niche markets. Organizations determine their approach to, and the scope of, their standardization activities in accordance with their specific circumstances – hence, standards may be adopted for use by an entire organization, or its key component groups or functions, or may be used more narrowly to focus on specific areas. It all depends on their context, operating environment and where they consider it will add value or on what matters most.

What matters

Materiality is a concept familiar to accounting professionals, but is also a key concept for HCMD. In this context it is defined as the 'measure of the significance of an element to organizational results' – specifically, the value of people to an organization, and beyond the notion of costs, and how this is captured and reported.

This reflects a refreshing approach in finance and strategy domains. It deliberately serves to emphasize that 'people matter' and should be central to an integrated approach to organizational strategy, governance, risk, resilience, security and performance – and other material aspects of business such as the UN Sustainable Development Goals (SDGs).

GOVERNANCE AND RISK

Societal expectations of organizational behaviour and performance have changed in the light of recent and high-profile organizational failures of governance. Calls for improved standards of governance have increased. As indicated in Chapter 1, some of the indicators of good governance and the content of international standards intended to support them include:

- a high level of independent and principled oversight that holds organizational leaders to account;
- a focus on overall direction-setting and the management of remuneration and incentives;
- steering the quality and transparency of debate required to drive ethical decision-making;
- attention to the organization's risk, security and resilience controls and mechanisms for whistleblowing and anti-bribery;
- integrated monitoring and reporting of both financial and human capital matters that impact key stakeholders;
- engagement with stakeholders on issues that concern or impact them.

Cognizant of the increasing stakeholder demands for improved governance in ISO TC309 *Governance of organizations*, the development of ISO/AWI

37000 *Guidance for the governance of organizations* has commenced. This work acknowledges that there are existing documents and codes that focus on national perspectives of governance, for example the 'comply or explain' approach.

This work is not intended to replace these, but rather to support them by providing relevant guidance on governance for all types of organizations based on a global consensus of shared knowledge and information. The primary aim is to support organizational effectiveness, sustainability, accountability and fairness and the anticipated benefits of its adoption are cited as:

- clearer accountability, sources and delegation of authority in organizations;
- improved ethical conduct and organizational decision-making;
- creation of space and support for optimal performance and added value;
- greater direction and control to reduce risk and improve organizational stability and viability;
- increased stakeholder trust and confidence;
- better economic, societal, environmental, organizational and individual outcomes.

It is claimed that good governance positions organizations, and society, for success and that perceived abuses of authority, the occurrence of adverse incidents and bribery and corruption are all indicators of a lack of it. Bribery is defined as the offering, promising, giving, accepting or soliciting of an undue advantage of any value, financial or non-financial, and as direct or indirect inducements or rewards that make individuals act in a certain way for the advantage of another – this also includes acting on the organization's behalf or for its benefit.

It is a significantly challenging issue for organizations, particularly those operating globally, and it not only undermines the rule of law but also destroys stakeholder trust and confidence where it goes unchecked.

Efforts to tackle bribery now include ISO 37001:2016 *Anti-bribery management systems – Requirements with guidance for use*, which is intended to help organizations fight bribery and promote an ethical business and organizational culture. It presents a series of measures and controls to prevent, detect and deal with bribery, reflecting good anti-bribery practice. These include leadership commitment to, and responsibility for, tackling bribery wherever it exists in the organization or its supply chain. It also includes the enactment of an effective set of policies and practices to protect the organization and reduce liability where there is evidence of adequate measures having been taken for the prevention of organizational wrongdoing.

These issues also highlight the importance of robust and effective approaches to whistleblowing, which is the intended deliverable of a standard under development – ISO/NP 37002 *Whistleblowing management systems – Guidelines*. The title indicates that this standard will be requirements-based, but it also boasts that three principles will be at its heart: trust, impartiality and protection. In the UK, individuals that raise concerns have protection under the law where they are making a disclosure in the public interest.

The intention of this forthcoming standard is to guide organizations to respond appropriately when concerns of wrongdoing are identified and reported to them, and to assess and address the reported incidence of wrongdoing in order to close the whistleblowing case, bearing in mind the people that are involved and the protections they should be afforded.

ORGANIZATIONAL SECURITY AND RESILIENCE

As indicated in Chapter 9, organizations operate in contexts that are increasingly complex and frequently volatile. Increasing globalization and expectations of workforce mobility present higher levels of exposure to, and the reach of, threats to organizational, societal and individual security and resilience. Organizations face different risks and issues of safety and resilience, and as such challenges grow apace so does the impact on the existence of organizations and the health and wellbeing of people.

Organizations are increasing their global footprint, and often their business models place a greater reliance on a chain of third-party suppliers and on a mobile workforce. But such changes have also ushered in the risks associated with supply chain failures and of remotely located operations, set in the context of rapid technological development and the risks driven by working in a digital economy at high risk of cyber crime.

Rapid organizational change and development can bring opportunities and threats, but can also be disruptive. There are no organizations that are immune to business disruption, so an important consideration is how well they are equipped to minimize the adverse effects of disruption when it occurs.

ISO TC292 *Security and resilience* is responsible for standardization in this domain, and has developed numerous technical requirements standards and guidance and management system standards aimed at enhancing the safety and resilience of society.

Of these, it is ISO/TS 22330:2018 *Security and resilience – Business continuity management systems – Guidelines for people aspects of business continuity* that is relevant to this chapter, because its focus is on organizational preparations and responses to business and supply disruptions and the important human capital aspects of these. The guidelines it provides relate to planning and developing, strategies, policies and procedures essential for an organization's preparation and management of the people risk arising from disruption to business as usual operations over four stages:

- preparation and the use of learning and development to raise levels of awareness;

- responding and coping with the immediate impact and effects of an incident;

- recovery operations and the management of people during the disruption;

- restoration of business as usual and continuing support of the workforce.

The key considerations for organizations are understanding their role in the wider environment and across the supply chain. This enables potential for disruption to be identified and managed. This standard establishes clear expectations in supply chain relationships; ensuring that people in the organization are competent and have clarity about their roles and responsibilities.

It identifies the need for clear and timely communication to underpin impact analysis of potential adverse effects on key stakeholders. This can provide benefits such as a robust approach to business continuity planning, greater understanding of organizational risks, and increased stakeholder trust and confidence in the organization. In addition, employer brand, reputation and market positioning can be enhanced and there is an increased likelihood of benefits arising from increased participation and involvement of the workforce.

SUSTAINABILITY MATTERS

One rationale put forward for the use of standards by organizations is that they help them to operate and perform more productively and competitively. In addition, it is important to consider the extent to which standards can encourage organizations to conduct their activities in a sustainable and socially responsible manner. This is the focus of ISO 26000:2010 *Guidance on social responsibility*. This is not intended to be construed as a management system or used for certification purposes. Rather, its principal concern and stated intention is the promotion of social responsibility and the contribution of organizations to sustainable development. It recognizes that compliance with the law is a fundamental organizational duty, but encourages steps beyond legal compliance to integrate, implement and promote socially responsible behaviour throughout organizations and within their sphere of influence.

The UN SDGs provide a further indicator of the importance of the sustainability agenda. In 2015, UN member states adopted the 2030 Agenda for Sustainable Development and its 17 sustainable development goals:

- Goal 1: No poverty, in all its forms, everywhere.

- Goal 2: Zero hunger, achieve food security and improved nutrition, and promote sustainable agriculture.

- Goal 3: Good health and wellbeing for all at all ages.

- Goal 4: Quality education that is inclusive and equitable and to promote life-long learning opportunities for all.

- Goal 5: Gender equality and empower all women and girls.

- Goal 6: Clean water and sanitation for all.

- Goal 7: Affordable and clean energy for all.

- Goal 8: Decent work and economic growth, full and productive employment for all.

- Goal 9: Promote inclusive and sustainable industry, foster innovation and build resilient infrastructure.

- Goal 10: Reduced inequalities within and among countries.

- Goal 11: Sustainable cities and communities that are inclusive, safe and resilient.

- Goal 12: Responsible production and consumption.

- Goal 13: Urgent action to combat climate change and its impacts.

- Goal 14: Conserve and sustainably use the oceans, seas and marine resources.

- Goal 15: Protect, restore and promote sustainable use of terrestrial ecosystems.

- Goal 16: Promote just, peaceful and inclusive societies; provide access to justice for all and build effective, accountable and inclusive institutions at all levels.

- Goal 17: Revitalize the global partnership between governments, the private sector and civil society to implement the sustainable development agenda.

In their 2017 Annual Report, ISO state that their overarching mission is the provision of global solutions to meet global challenges. This mission, together with their long and active engagement with the UN, results in an increasing ISO focus on the sustainability agenda and a commitment to championing and facilitating through its standardization activities the UN's 17 SDGs. This has resulted in a requirement for all proposals for new standards to demonstrate in their business case their relevance to the SDGs by mapping to specific goals. This will have a material and knock-on effect to the organizations adopting these standards.

Aligned with these strategies, ISO/TR 30406: 2017 *Human resource management – Sustainable employability management for organizations* focuses on the challenging item on the sustainability agenda. Its purpose is to promote organizational capacity and commitment to creating wide stakeholder value. Important stakeholders include the workforce, community, society and economy.

The standard aims to promote practice to ensure organizational capacity and capability to deliver enduring or ongoing employment in the longer term and to support people's ability to gain or maintain good quality work.

PEOPLE MATTER

This book is premised on the view that people are critical to the delivery of an organization's purpose and should be central to an organization's strategy. Organizational systems, processes and HR practice bundles should support the development and sharing of knowledge, skills and abilities and value creation for individuals, organizations and society. In the achievement of this, different assumptions underpin management decision-making and philosophy. The unitarist perspective assumes that people uncritically accept organizational goals and management practices. The pluralist perspective recognizes that there may be disparate and competing interests at work. Management perspectives about this issue, and organizational context, influences how HR is enacted in different organizations and across organizational supply chains. In such circumstances there is a danger that people may not benefit from good HR practice.

The argument of this chapter is that standards are essential to encourage scrutiny of the quality of work and of working lives. Effective business and workforce planning strategies are necessary to support business competitiveness and 'agility'. It is important that individuals are encouraged and supported to learn and develop new knowledge, skills and abilities in a context where matters of equality, equity and inclusivity enable organizations to build good work in an environment that acknowledges both its people risks and opportunities – and to align with the SDGs identified above.

To this end, the BS 76000 suite of standards provide a principled framework to enable organizations to establish managerial accountability and support for flexible, innovative and sustainable HR practices and to ensure they provide good work in an environment where people feel respected and valued for their contribution. These standards matter not only because the framework they present promotes good HR practice, but because they:

- are cognizant of changes in the modern workplace and in the future of work;
- challenge organizations to develop a workplace culture and climate that supports good work and that recognize the intrinsic value of people.

Increasing globalization and reliance on extended supply chains, together with rapid advances of technology and the demands of a knowledge economy and for a mobile workforce, demonstrate the need for standards that support organizations to think about the matters that are material to them and beyond their boundaries. The authority and integrity of organizational governance mechanisms and HR strategies and practices are critical to achieving organizational objectives and social responsibility and sustainability goals. People are central to the achievement of an organization's purpose and they should be given opportunities for good work, and be treated with respect and valued for who they are, in addition to their contribution to organizational outcomes.

Proper consideration should be given to the potential people risks related to business disruption, organizational security and resilience, with an appropriate focus on identifying and addressing individual and organizational wrongdoing.

Summary

Organizations, regardless of their type, size and sector use British and international standards in order to perform their operational responsibilities. Although the use of standards is voluntary in some sectors, or for procurement purposes, certification against a specified standard may be a legal or contractual obligation. Whether or not an organization has a dedicated HR function, reliable guidance related to HCMD provides a consistent and coherent basis for practice, particularly in some smaller organizations and in countries where HRM practices are less well established. This guidance is now available in the standards discussed in this book.

This chapter asserts there is a growing awareness of the importance of the human capital contribution to organizational performance, and cites the increasing number of standards focusing on people at work as evidence of this. It identifies the standards available for organizations to use that provide guidance on good HR practice and protocols to ensure people risk is effectively managed.

It further describes the different types of standards, and how they are developed by committees of subject experts working collaboratively within a process based on consensus and consultation. The debate about the opportunities and challenges associated with compliance-based and principles-led approaches is discussed and the case for a principles-led approach to human capital standards is made. In addition, attention is also drawn to standards that address individual and organizational wrongdoing, and issues of business continuity and disruption that shine a light on the people dimension in these areas.

In conclusion, people, good work, sustainability and standards should all matter to organizations that seek to optimize their performance and differentiate themselves as employers of choice.

References and further resources

Anderson, V (2017) HRD standards and standardization: where now for human resource development? *Human Resource Development International*, 20 (4), pp 327–45

BSI (2015) BS 76000:2015 *Human Resource. Valuing People. Management System. Requirements and Guidance*, https://shop.bsigroup.com/ProductDetail/?pid=000000000030298954 (archived at https://perma.cc/VRE7-WXUM)

BSI (2015) PAS 3000:2015 *Smart Working. Code of Practice*, https://shop.bsigroup.com/ProductDetail/?pid=000000000030324355 (archived at https://perma.cc/8H5S-E3RG)

BSI (2016) PAS 3001:2016 *Travelling for work. Responsibilities of an organization for health, safety and security. Code of practice*, https://shop.bsigroup.com/ProductDetail?pid=000000000030331555 (archived at https://perma.cc/WZ6E-S9A8)

BSI (2017) BS 76005:2017 *Valuing People Through Diversity and Inclusion: Code of Practice for Organizations*, https://shop.bsigroup.com/ProductDetail/?pid=000000000030338898 (archived at https://perma.cc/SR22-7SRY)

BSI (2017) BS PD 76006:2017 *Guide to learning and development*, https://shop.bsigroup.com/ProductDetail/?pid=000000000030350673 (archived at https://perma.cc/TC8X-M777)

BSI (2018) PAS 3002:2018 *Code of Practice on Improving Health and Wellbeing Within an Organization*, https://shop.bsigroup.com/ProductDetail?pid=000000000030384539 (archived at https://perma.cc/6R2D-BHXT)

BSI. BS 0 2016 *A standard for standards – Principles of standardization*, BSI www.bsigroup.com/Documents/30342351.pdf (archived at https://perma.cc/9JCZ-45J9)

BSI website www.bsigroup.com (archived at https://perma.cc/4EKG-5C9L)

CIPD [accessed 2 May 2019] HR and standards factsheet, *CIPD* www.cipd.co.uk/knowledge/strategy/hr/standards-factsheet (archived at https://perma.cc/QZ72-J6HJ)

ISO (2010) ISO 26000:2010 *Guidance on social responsibility*, www.iso.org/standard/42546.html (archived at https://perma.cc/C62D-R2LQ)

ISO (2015) BS ISO 9001:2015 *Quality management systems. Requirements*, https://shop.bsigroup.com/ProductDetail?pid=000000000030273524 (archived at https://perma.cc/QQF4-UDQ8)

ISO (2016) BS ISO 30400:2016 *Human resource management. Vocabulary*, https://shop.bsigroup.com/ProductDetail/?pid=000000000030324720 (archived at https://perma.cc/MV5U-8YQR)

ISO (2016) BS ISO 30408:2016 *Human Resource Management – Guidelines on human governance*, https://shop.bsigroup.com/ProductDetail/?pid=000000000030284701 (archived at https://perma.cc/KR6D-EJMR)

ISO (2016) ISO 27500:2016 *The human-centred organization – Rationale and general principles*, www.iso.org/standard/64239.html (archived at https://perma.cc/SQ9E-Z9P4)

ISO (2016) ISO 30409:2016 *Human Resource Management – Workforce Planning*, www.iso.org/standard/64150.html (archived at https://perma.cc/4ABF-RR6R)

ISO (2016) ISO 37001:2016 *Anti-bribery management systems – Requirements with guidance for use*, www.iso.org/standard/65034.html (archived at https://perma.cc/6S35-4RQM)

ISO (2017) ISO/TR 30406:2017 *Human resource management – Sustainable employability management for organizations*, www.iso.org/standard/72327.html (archived at https://perma.cc/9QP6-AZWB)

ISO (2018) ISO 30414:2018 *Human resource management – Guidelines for internal and external human capital reporting*, www.iso.org/standard/69338.html (archived at https://perma.cc/L7PL-QATA)

ISO (2018) ISO/TS 22330:2018 *Security and resilience – Business continuity management systems – Guidelines for people aspects of business continuity,* www.iso.org/standard/50067.html (archived at https://perma.cc/QV4X-E9KS)

ISO (forthcoming) ISO/AWI 37000 *Guidance for the governance of organizations,* www.iso.org/standard/65036.html (archived at https://perma.cc/2TNG-JHJC)

ISO (forthcoming) ISO/DIS 10015 *Quality management – Guidelines for competence management and people development,* www.iso.org/standard/69459.html (archived at https://perma.cc/4WLG-UQ3F)

ISO (forthcoming) ISO/DIS 10018 *Quality management systems – Guidelines on people engagement,* www.iso.org/standard/69979.html (archived at https://perma.cc/ZY65-6VPB)

ISO (forthcoming) ISO/NP 37002 *Whistleblowing management systems – Guidelines,* www.iso.org/standard/65035.html (archived at https://perma.cc/ZUU6-SKZY)

ISO. Annual Report, *ISO* www.iso.org/annual-reports.html (archived at https://perma.cc/X5PJ-GRBZ)

ISO. Online Browsing Platform (OSB), *ISO* www.iso.org/obp/ui (archived at https://perma.cc/9VDN-TJ3V)

ISO www.iso.org/directives-and-policies.html (archived at https://perma.cc/DHM5-JP4U)

ISO TC260 www.iso.org/committee/628737.html (archived at https://perma.cc/2GK9-YFB5)

Mulvie, A (2018) *Working with External Quality Standards and Awards: The strategic implications for human resource and quality management,* Routledge, Oxford

UN. About the Sustainable Development Goals, UN www.un.org/sustainabledevelopment/sustainable-development-goals/ (archived at https://perma.cc/H4KQ-N3NC)

3

Workforce planning

Julie Sloan

Introduction

This chapter provides a practical, user-friendly guide to the key elements of strategic and operational workforce planning, based on the extensive global experience of the author. It refers to relevant International Organization for Standardization (ISO) human resource management (HRM) standards, and provides information on key workforce planning terminology, a history of workforce planning, and the language and definitions used in workforce planning. Useful advice is provided on why it is important, where it fits in an organization, and the critical success factors associated with workforce planning. Core elements of good practice are identified, together with the application of quality workforce planning to organizational design.

This chapter informs readers about the discipline of workforce planning and its two separate but interrelated components: *strategic* workforce planning (longer term, generally 3–5 years) and *operational* workforce planning (shorter term – generally 12 months).

Workforce planning can enable organizations of all sizes, industries and sectors to respond more effectively to current and projected demands of the labour market. It strengthens the capacity to retain and attract the workforce required now and, in the future, and to manage and mitigate workforce risk using evidence to inform decision-making.

CHAPTER OBJECTIVES

The objectives of this chapter are to:

- describe the important elements of workforce planning to build workforce planning knowledge and capability;
- discuss how standards can provide a guide for effective workforce planning processes;
- identify the challenges and the opportunities of implementing standards for workforce planning;
- propose ways of evaluating the success of workforce management processes.

The information provided is based on ISO 30409:2016 *Human resource management – Workforce planning*, which was developed with input from subject experts in more than 22 countries.

Key terms

As a relatively recent discipline, the language of workforce planning is also somewhat new. Therefore, for monitoring and benchmarking purposes it is important to be consistent with language and to use definitions developed by subject experts, as set out in this list:

capacity management:	The process used to manage the human capital necessary to execute organizational commitments and delivery excellence.
capacity plan:	A view of resource requirements over a defined period that reflects planned numbers of resources by roles and skills. The capacity plan can include consideration of skills development, retraining, redeployment, recruitment, redesign, and use of organizational partners, third-party subcontractors, contingent workforce and volunteer workforce.
career stage:	A distinct phase of a person's career. Can include entry, establishment, advancement, maintenance, transition and maturity.
communications plan:	This informs and engages organization leaders, workforce and other stakeholders in the objectives, methods, deliverables and outcomes of workforce planning.

competence:	The ability to apply knowledge and skills to achieve intended results, particularly those that are essential for an organization's success.
competence framework:	A structure that defines the competence of people within an organization to achieve intended results.
competence model:	The process of analysing and describing knowledge, skills and ability of people.
criticality assessment:	A method applied within the organization to determine level of job role criticality.
current workforce demand:	This is based on current business requirements to deliver business outcomes.
current workforce supply:	Baseline data on the size of the workforce.
divisional workforce plan:	This provides an overview of nominated divisions in relation to the broader organizational plan.
environmental scan:	Gathering and reporting on information on external and internal workforce demand and supply influences.
focus areas:	Those areas identified as important to the organization. May include age, indigenous representation, diversity, areas of undersupply, areas of oversupply, retirement impact, and retirement projections.
future-focused business scenarios:	Identification of plausible alternative future business scenarios. Used to determine workforce shift scenarios.
governance:	The way a whole organization is led, directed, controlled, managed and held accountable.
human capital:	The value of the collective knowledge, skills and abilities of an organization's people.
human capital reporting:	Reporting focused on core elements including human capital costs, structure, skills and capabilities, sustainability, culture and productivity.
human governance:	The way that the people within the organization are led, directed, controlled, managed and held accountable, taking into account human and social factors at the highest and every level of decision-making.
HRM:	The management of people in organizations.
HR management and information systems:	Technology that supports HRM.

insight reports:	Executive summary relating to workforce planning and key elements of core delivery including snapshot reporting on focus areas, workforce shift scenarios and areas for attention, areas to monitor and areas well-placed. These are delivered via automated workforce planning systems.
integrated location plan:	This enables broader scope workforce planning if organization has more than one site/location.
job families:	The segmentation of jobs into similar occupation groups based on related competencies.
key demographic indicators:	These identify organizational demographics by core delivery, core enabling, administrative support and enabling job families.
operational workforce planning:	This typically covers a defined period, generally the ensuing 12 months, and is aligned to the organization's planning cycle. The focus is on gathering, analysing and reporting on workforce risk and risk mitigation.
planning:	The process of thinking about an organization's activity required to achieve a desired outcome.
risk:	The effect of uncertainty – an effect is a deviation from the expected – whether positive or negative. Uncertainty is the state, even partial, of deficiency of information relating to, understanding or knowledge of, an event, its consequence, or likelihood. Risk is often characterized by reference to potential 'events' and 'consequences', or a combination of these. Risk is often expressed in terms of a combination of the consequences of an event, and the associated 'likelihood' of occurrence (ISO Guide 73:2009 3.6.1.1).
risk mitigation strategies:	Approaches designed to reduce workforce risk.
strategic planning:	The formulation, development, implementation and evaluation of factors that are relevant to an organization's long-term or overall interests, and the means of achieving its objectives.

strategic workforce planning:	This usually covers a defined period aligned to organizational strategy – generally 3–5 years or more. The scope of planning can include identifying the workforce, assessments and benchmarking, human resource policy, framework and associated processes related to current and future organizational strategic objectives, structure and design.
strategy:	An organization's approach to achieving its objectives.
succession plan:	A process for identifying and developing current or external employees with the potential to fill key positions in the organization.
workforce:	People who provide a service or labour to contribute to business or organizational outcomes. This may include the contingent, contract, volunteer, and outsourced workforce.
workforce design:	The design of the workforce resulting from workforce planning reports on the efficiency of the current workforce design. It includes design, supply, mobility and utilization.
workforce mix and scenario modelling:	This details investment break-up and the ability to scenario plan workforce needs based on changing demand and business needs.
workforce mobility:	Refers to the intra- and inter- movement of people within an organization.
workforce planning:	The systematic identification, analysis and planning of organizational needs, in terms of people. It is a process used to generate business intelligence to inform an organization of the current and future impact of the external and internal environment on the business, enabling it to be resilient to structural and cultural changes, and thereby to better position itself for the future.
workforce planning process:	An active and continuous process in the organizational planning cycle. Workforce planning is the responsibility of the organization's senior management, and should be aligned and consistent with organizational strategies and governance.

workforce profiling:	Engagement of the workforce in question and answer /surveys identified and or de-identified.
workforce segmentation:	This is used to classify the different types of job families, functions, roles, competencies and/or locations within an organization. It is used to focus workforce planning on the most critical business positions, employee capabilities and locations identified in the strategic and business plan as core to organization performance. There are two basic workforce segmentation approaches: role-based, where jobs are segmented by value or type of work performed and employee-based segmentation by demographic, other observable or inferred characteristics.
workforce supply/ recruitment plan:	This aligns the recruitment plan to affordability and future needs. It includes the stable operating model and the scenario reflecting changing business needs.
work life stage:	Phases of a person's work life, which can include new entry, early, mid, transition and end career. People can move in and out of these work life stages at different ages and life stages.
workplace:	The area(s) in which the worker's activities are carried out.

Standards discussed

The following ISO standards are referred to in this chapter:

- ISO 30409:2016 *Human resource management – Workforce planning*: This standard is the main focus of this chapter. It was developed to meet a worldwide need for workforce planning advice and support to enable industry, organizations and businesses of all sizes to advance their workforce planning capabilities. The processes that are included in this standard enable organizations to respond more effectively to the current and projected demands of the labour market, and to be better prepared for business continuity in a dynamic international business environment characterized by increasing complexity.

- ISO 30400:2016 *Human resource management. Vocabulary*: This document has become a 'go to' resource that helps those involved in any aspect of HRM, whatever their perspective, to understand important vocabulary with relevance to people management and development. It provides a basis from which people whose roles involve HRM or the study of or research into HR issues – standards developers, managers in organizations of all sizes and types, and those who are involved in work through labour unions, work councils or employee representation – to communicate in a consistent and coherent way about important issues.

- ISO 30414:2018 *Human resource management – Guidelines for internal and external human capital reporting*: As outlined already in this chapter, human capital is important for an organization's long-term performance and competitive advantage. This standard sets out guidelines for the measurement and assessment of human capital as a basis for the achievement of sustainable value achieved through people. In common with workforce planning processes, effective human capital reporting relies on the use of standardized and agreed data categories.

Understanding workforce planning

Although processes previously referred to as 'manpower' planning have been important since the early part of the 20th century in many countries and organizations, the discipline of workforce planning is not well known. This section outlines the main features of a robust workforce planning process.

Why is workforce planning regarded as a 'new' discipline?

Workforce planning has been a part of business processes since the 1930s when it was the responsibility of finance managers. Since then it has been evolving from established practices that include manpower planning, manpower forecasting, organization development, organization planning, human resource planning, HRM, strategic staffing, succession planning, strategic planning and organizational development (Sloan, 2008).

Driven by global concern about the impact (numbers, skills and knowledge) of population ageing, it has, since the late 1990s, become an increasingly central component of HRM responsibilities, and has included analysis and reporting on both quantitative and qualitative human resource matters – specifically, the numbers, skills and knowledge within, and risk to, an organization. In the early 2000s, demand for information on the concept, method and process for quality workforce planning increased.

Since 2010 it has been identified as a 'business imperative' (Sloan, 2010) for organizations of all types and sizes, due to the changing, dynamic global business environment and the increasing recognition that people need to be valued as a critical resource in the delivery of business outcomes.

Good quality strategic and operational workforce planning is increasingly recognized for the value it adds to executive evidence-based decision-making on workforce matters, and for its ability to enhance the capacity to retain and compete for the workforce required now and in the future. Demand is at a global all-time high for high level workforce planning capability supported by automated evidence-based data gathering, analysis and reporting within organizations of all sizes. In the present day, progressive organizations have integrated workforce planning into their core business planning processes with outcomes reflected in organizational design and measured by organizational productivity.

The ISO workforce planning standard (ISO 30409:2016) identifies four key phases in the workforce planning process:

1 Getting started: Establishing a workforce planning team and building capability, aligning strategic, business and workforce plans, implementing a communications strategy, segmenting the workforce, reviewing demand and supply data and identifying information gaps, and identifying future-focused business scenarios.

2 Analysis: Analysing the data, undertaking supply and demand gap calculations, and describing workforce supply risk.

3 Risk management: Identifying risk management and risk mitigation strategies.

4 Implementation: Embedding into normal business planning processes and establishing a mechanism for monitoring and measuring workforce planning outcomes.

What is workforce planning?

Workforce planning is defined in ISO 30409 as: 'The systematic identification, analysis and planning of organizational needs in terms of people'.

The standard describes workforce planning as an 'active and continuous process used to generate business intelligence to inform organizations about the current and future impact of the external and internal environment on their business,' and in the process, to become resilient to structural and cultural changes and better positioned for the future.

Two separate but interrelated tasks, requiring different knowledge and skill sets, define workforce planning:

- Strategic workforce planning, which covers a defined period, aligned to organizational strategy, for example, 3–5 years. A strategic workforce plan should include as a minimum:
  - context: a statement about the organization and how it links with the strategic workforce plan;
  - approach: aligned to business strategy and objectives;
  - function: the purpose of the work organization, assignment or evaluation;
  - vision: for the plan;
  - culture: the context of plan to the organization;
  - strategy: what will be achieved by whom and how;
  - measure: how ROI will be measured and monitored.
- Operational workforce planning: which covers a defined period, aligned with the organization's planning cycle, for example 12 months. An operational workforce plan can be tailored depending on available data sets and the specific requirements of an organization:
  - Foundation: could include demographics, classification/remuneration, diversity, gender mix, mobility, or unplanned leave.
  - Intermediate: could include resource cost, segmentation (eg job families), investment mix, workforce projections, attrition, supply projections, or capability.
  - Advanced: could include optimal workforce mix, management layers, workforce design including market standards built in as a comparator, succession and talent time/cost to replace, department impact analysis, supply projections with integrated pipeline and internal mobility pipeline, geo-spatial analysis, or scenario modelling.

Workforce planning is not a mechanism to predict the future, but should be future-focused and based on identifying and exploring a range of alternative future scenarios. It helps organizations to determine:

- the workforce needed to deliver services (demand);
- how the workforce needed for the present and in the future, compares with the current workforce (supply);

- how well these are aligned with the strategic directions and design of the organization.

Workforce planning and workforce development are commonly linked, and these terms are sometimes used interchangeably. They are, however, not the same. Workforce planning enables organizations to identify workforce risk. Workforce development can be one of many risk management and risk mitigation strategies.

Why is workforce planning important?

Workforce planning is important because we live and work in a global knowledge economy that is highly connected and interrelated. Furthermore, the environment within which it operates is uncertain and constantly changing (ISO 30409).

It enables an organization to produce evidence-based workforce insights to strengthen organization design. It can inform discussion on what is happening now, what could happen and what should happen. It can be implemented in phases from foundation, to intermediate, to advanced workforce planning. It can position the organization to prepare for and manage structural, economic, environmental, social and technical change, and be better positioned to compete for the workforce required now, and in the future.

Workforce planning is applicable for organizations of all sizes, as well as for all industries, sectors and regions, and for any organization with a paid or voluntary workforce. Although the objectives and outcomes of each plan are often consistent, the complexity varies with the nature and size of an organization and the level of financial and leadership investment made. It helps all stakeholders, including and especially the workforce, to understand the challenges, opportunities and options for change.

Where does workforce planning fit in an organization?

Workforce planning is intrinsically linked with strategic and business planning, and should be part of the normal business planning process, enabling the organization to identify the workforce implications (current and future workforce) of strategic and business planning. The workforce plan will help the organization identify, and ideally put in place, the human resources needed to deliver the strategic and business plans. It will provide the evidence to justify workforce risk management and risk mitigation strategies.

Workforce planning and human capital reporting are integral to management responsibility and accountability and overlap with other disciplines including HR, finance, policy, communications and information technology. For this reason, an interdisciplinary approach is required for sustainable and quality workforce planning. Indicators of good organizational practice include the following:

- Roles and responsibilities of the agreed custodians of the workforce data gathering, analysis and reporting are clearly defined.
- Communication plans to engage the workforce and key stakeholders in workforce planning are aligned to core communications methods and practices.
- Workforce planning methods and processes are systematic across the organization.
- Human resource metrics are agreed and applied consistently.
- Data are reliable and trusted to inform decision-making across all disciplines.
- Vulnerable data are identified.

What to expect – challenges and opportunities

Workforce planning is a very interesting and rewarding discipline that can bring multiple benefits to the organization, to the current and future workforce, and, most importantly, to the quality of service delivery and organizational productivity. It is, however, a complex task with many critical success factors, some of which represent challenges and others potential opportunities. They include:

- understanding, expectations and level of governance and leadership;
- level of executive engagement and investment in capability building and automated data gathering systems;
- level and quality of management engagement in workforce planning and development;
- level and quality of workforce engagement;
- clarity of expectations about workforce planning deliverables;
- consistency in the approach to design, method, HR analytics and reporting, timeframe and managing stakeholder expectations;

- identification and agreement on future-focused demand scenarios;
- capability (system and people) to produce evidence-based and accurate workforce insight reports;
- respect for workforce planning capability and data quality;
- capability and courage to align workforce planning outcomes to workforce design; and
- capacity to measure and report on the return on investment from workforce planning.

Some of the more complex steps

Workforce planning is best kept as straightforward and as clear as possible. However, depending on the level of investment involved, it can and will become more complex as it evolves. The most complex elements involve a focus on the following:

- governance and leadership – executive, management engagement and accountability;
- communication planning – to achieve workforce engagement;
- workforce segmentation by criticality, aligned with the strategic plan;
- data quality, agreed metrics and definitions to determine the demand and supply gap and consider future-focused business scenarios;
- HR systems capability, analytics and insight reporting;
- sustainable workforce planning capability.

These are discussed in more detail in the next section.

Embedding workforce planning into organizational strategy and direction

Governance and leadership in workforce planning

One of the key elements of successful workforce planning is the level of investment by organization and business entity executives and industry leaders into good quality workforce planning. This requires a recognition by organizational leaders that workforce planning is an intrinsic feature of organizational strategy and planning processes.

Strategic plans are only ever as good as the data that has been analysed to inform them, and so trust in the quality of the data is important. Workforce planner credibility is important if stakeholders are to recognize the relevance and authority of evidence-based outputs and reporting, with the potential to measure the return on investment through human capital savings and/or productivity measures. This is a pre-requisite to effective workforce planning processes.

If workforce planning is to have a meaningful impact on organizational effectiveness, then the processes that are undertaken require collaboration with the leadership team. Senior managers' visible support for workforce data collection and analysis is an important first step. In addition, it is important that senior managers are prepared to review and adjust their business plans as new workforce information becomes available. In this way, an effective workforce planning process will be flexible enough to respond to changing priorities and organizational performance data.

The communications plan

Workforce engagement through accurate information about workforce planning processes and deliverables is equally important to successful workforce planning outcomes. It is important that appropriate messages, using relevant communication channels for different audiences, are utilized. Effective workforce planning communication processes most often involve regular, but not excessive, utilization of online, print and verbal channels of communication. What is communicated, and how this communication is achieved, requires consideration of the audiences that are affected by these processes, such as workers, executives, managers, and other stakeholders.

ISO 30409 recommends that a communications plan is aligned with normal communications avenues such as intra-organization web pages and executive bulletins. The communications plan could include information about methods used, data insights, workforce profiles, workforce risk, and risk management and mitigation strategies. Other relevant workforce information can keep people informed about workforce planning intentions and insights. It is also important to manage any misinformation in the workplace about workforce planning.

Workforce segmentation identified by criticality and aligned with the strategic plan

It is important to create an agreed systematic approach for managers to nominate their critical segments. Criticality involves aligning the workforce segments with the priorities of the organization – that is, identifying the workforce implications (numbers, skills, capability, location, cost) and the timeframe of the strategic direction. The segmentation process is well documented in ISO 30409:2016 *Human Resource Management – Workforce Planning* (6.3.6 – 6.3.10), which outlines two basic workforce segmentation approaches:

1 segmentation by job or role – where jobs are segmented by value or the type of work performed;

2 segmentation by individuals – where employee segmentation is undertaken based on demographic and other observable or inferred characteristics.

Each approach is valid and generally determined by the level of complexity and maturity (workforce planning capability and quality and reliability of data sets) within the organization.

The Workforce Planning Global (2018) three-tiered approach to determining criticality is also a useful model and involves assessment at these three levels:

- *Critical Tier 1:* There is legislative exposure if the role is not filled, the function is not performed and/or the function is performed poorly due to capability challenges. This results in breach of legislation and the likelihood of significant reputational risk – that is, direct legal responsibilities are not fulfilled. This can involve an internal or external focus.

- *Critical Tier 2:* There is regulatory exposure if the role is not filled, the function is not performed and/or the function is performed poorly due to capability. This results in breach of/or failure to fulfil regulatory responsibilities and has the potential for reputational risk and/or lack of public/government confidence to undertake the function – that is, not fulfilling regulatory responsibilities. This can involve an internal or external focus.

- *Critical Tier 3:* There is administrative exposure (that is, limited exposure usually with an internal focus) which would impact productivity/efficiency if the role is not filled, the function is not performed and/or the function is performed poorly due to capability. This may impact reputation or pose a risk, but not of material impact to broader agency/ organizational objectives.

Other assessment of criticality criteria which could be applied includes asking the questions about the job/job family considered to be critical:

- Do they drive a disproportionate share of the key business outcomes?
- Do they influence the value chain significantly?
- Do they require a disproportionate allocation of the organization budget?
- Is there a supply issue – locally, nationally or internationally?
- Are they essential to meeting regulatory or legislative requirements?
- What is the change magnitude requirement for this segment – in other words, what is the future importance of the role? What is the current capability of the people in the role to meet future demand?

Data quality, technology and automation

As previously indicated, data quality is an important issue for effective workforce planning. Agreed metrics and definitions to identify demand and supply gaps and to consider future-focused business scenarios are vital components of workforce planning processes. For this reason it is important to have agreement from management on what data are gathered, why they are being gathered, which definitions are being applied and which metrics are being used. ISO 30414:2018 *Human resource management – Guidelines for internal and external human capital reporting* offers an indicative range of HR metrics and definitions that are extremely useful as a basis for a systematic approach.

Workforce planning can be undertaken manually by following the steps outlined in ISO 30409. However, much workforce planning work involves scenario evaluations designed to enable managers to make decisions based on scenarios that connect workforce planning to strategic initiatives. When these processes are effectively supported by technology, it enables those involved to be proactive rather than reactive.

Where possible, therefore, the use of technology can support the development of an automated approach to generate demand and supply analysis against a range of alternative future-focused business scenarios. It enables organizations to benchmark their workforce data against internal and external points of reference to support managers make better informed HCM decisions.

Automation does not need to be highly expensive – it is possible to establish a data warehouse, eg an Excel spreadsheet, where workforce planning data sets are pulled from various HRM systems and held so they can be accessed for workforce planning purposes to deliver quality workforce planning outcomes. There are a variety of workforce planning systems available in the public domain, but the important thing is to understand the questions that need to be articulated and answered, and to commit to a system supporting those outcomes.

Sustainable workforce planning capability

Although workforce planning is a specialized niche within HRM or HCM, workforce planning capability is a high-demand skill set globally. It is common for people with these skills to be encouraged and attracted to further career opportunities. As a result, as indicated previously, it is important that organizations should ensure workforce planning systems and employee capability are embedded in the normal business planning cycle, with workforce planning management capability and accountability available at all levels.

This can be achieved by establishing annual compulsory workforce planning (strategic and operational) capability building/professional development programmes for middle and executive managers, and by ensuring all managers sign off on their operational workforce plans indicating an understanding of, and agreement with data content, analysis and reporting.

From good practice in workforce planning to workforce design

As will be evident from the earlier sections of this chapter, good practice in workforce planning should reflect a foundation based on a systematic, and preferably automated, method. It requires clearly defined and agreed HR metrics and definitions, and simple and accurate reporting methods for the whole of the organization with comparative analysis reporting capability by division, branch, location and other nominated cohorts:

- Leadership: This must be engaged, and investment made in workforce planning to establish 24/7 credible workforce planning data and insight reporting.

- Segmented critical and priority workforce segments: These should be identified, validated and reviewed in alignment with the strategic and business plans for both the short and longer term.

- Workforce planning capability: Systems and people should be able to:
  - describe what has happened and what is happening now (descriptive);
  - predict what could happen in the future (predictive);
  - prescribe what should happen across the organization or in specified locations, divisions or functions based on a comparative analysis (prescriptive) (ISO 30409:2016, 6.3.22).

- Strategic workforce plans: These should reflect alignment with the organizational strategic plan and include vision, culture, and strategic objectives for meeting organizational people, planning, partnership, skills and knowledge, and innovation goals.

- Operational workforce plans: These should be presented as a graphic snapshot, and in an interesting user-friendly way, such as an 'on-a-page' format. Insight reports should be provided (quarterly or as required) by the whole of the organization, and comparative reporting by division, branch, location or nominated cohort. At a minimum, this should include the following:
  - staffing profile: headcount, full-time equivalent, average staffing, acting, permanent, temporary, classification mix, management span of control, location;
  - demographic profile: gender distribution, age and retirement risk;
  - critical workforce segments: assessment of position risk:
    - on a page – strategic;
    - integrated into normal business planning cycle;
    - succession in workforce planning capability;
    - evolving automation of data gathering and reporting.
  - insight reports: areas for attention; areas to monitor; areas well placed;
  - organizational transformation: achieved through workforce design based on workforce planning outcomes.

- Automating workforce planning: Good workforce planning systems should provide a modern, simple, standardized and effective framework for managing and reporting on the workforce. It should be cost-efficient with future functionality easily integrated. Ideally it should be fit for purpose and sufficiently flexible to enable integration and inter-connection with other human capital reporting systems. The technical architecture should provide as-close-to-real-time-as-possible integration, and enable data warehousing to allow for consolidated reporting and mapping. The user experience should be consistent and straightforward.

Workforce design through evidence-based workforce planning

Workforce design is the end result of quality, evidence-based and credible workforce planning. It involves decisions relating to building capacity in relation to the 'future workforce'. This will incorporate recruitment needs, attention to attraction and retention strategies, strategic frameworks for learning and development and so on. This requires the engagement and participation of senior leaders and is an essential feature of change management processes.

Workforce design is a sensitive process, but is essential for sustainable organizational performance. As indicated in this chapter, workforce design requires several prior stages, each of which require comprehensive scope and effort. Workforce design is particularly appropriate for decisions about issues such as:

- high-level 'greenfield' decisions;
- productivity trends;
- alternative workforce design scenarios/future options;
- worker participation and consultation;
- organizational design and change management.

Evaluating the effectiveness of workforce planning processes

In an increasingly global and dynamic business environment, workforce planning is an imperative. Effective workforce planning is required to take account of labour market trends such as an ageing workforce, as well as geographic distribution of labour. Work that requires advanced technological skills, education, and certification provide challenges to workforce planners, and in many parts of the world regulatory or governance requirements can slow down the recruitment process.

Key questions for organizations that wish to make better use of workforce planning processes include:

- How engaged or involved are senior managers in workforce planning processes?
- What benefits does the organization wish to achieve from investing in a workforce planning process?
- How frequently or regularly are workforce planning processes carried out?
- Are the processes and benefits of workforce planning communicated to managers and other stakeholders in an effective way?
- What forms of stakeholder involvement or participation can be built into the workforce planning process and resulting plans?

Good quality evidence-based workforce planning informs workforce design, structure, investment, capability and risk. It enables the organization to move forward with future-focused change and implement workforce strategy including incorporating employee and representative feedback where appropriate, proposed future workforce structures and designs, transition plans, and appropriate measures and HR processes to employ in order to move towards the Future State models.

Evaluation involves assessment at two levels:

1 the extent to which plans are implemented;
2 assessment of the outcomes of strategic decisions taken on the basis of workforce planning processes.

If outcome assessment is positive, this provides evidence of robust data, analysis and decision-making. If the outcomes are unanticipated then workforce planning data may offer useful evidence to identify the causes of the 'deviation' from the plan.

An important theme of this chapter is that workforce planning is as much about process as outcome. Therefore, evaluation of workforce planning involves assessment of the systems that generate data about emerging trends in workforce supply or demand. In addition, it is important to examine whether workforce planning processes contribute to reducing costs and/or improving efficiency. Evaluation of these issues is complex, as external as well as internal environments are constantly changing. Therefore, evaluation of the responsiveness of workforce planning processes is important as a basis for reviewing the workforce issues associated with strategic 're-thinks' and identifying future workforce opportunities and challenges.

Summary

This chapter has provided a comprehensive, practical and user-friendly guide to the key elements of strategic and operational workforce planning. It reflects the guidelines of ISO 30409:2016 *Human Resource Management – Workforce Planning*, and provides information on key workforce planning terminology, a history of workforce planning, and the language and definitions used in workforce planning. It outlines useful advice on why workforce planning is important, where it fits in an organization, and the critical success factors associated with it. Core elements of good practice are identified, together with the application of quality workforce planning to organizational design.

References and further resources

ISO (2016) BS ISO 30400:2016 *Human resource management. Vocabulary* https://shop.bsigroup.com/ProductDetail/?pid=000000000030324720 (archived at https://perma.cc/4V76-TKCK)

ISO (2016) ISO 30409:2016 *Human Resource Management – Workforce Planning* https://www.iso.org/standard/64150.html (archived at https://perma.cc/AWG3-HLNZ)

ISO (2018) ISO 30414:2018 *Human resource management – Guidelines for internal and external human capital reporting* https://www.iso.org/standard/69338.html (archived at https://perma.cc/8EUL-FQEW)

Sloan, J (2008) *An Introduction to Workforce Planning: Are you ready for crunch time?*, 1st edn, Julie Sloan Management Pty Ltd, Adelaide, Australia

Sloan, J (2010) *The Workforce Planning Imperative*, 1st edn, Julie Sloan Management Pty Ltd, Adelaide, Australia

4

Recruitment

Sandy J Miles

Introduction

Attracting and employing talent is not only a critical cornerstone of human resource management (HRM), but of organizational success. A firm's ability to attract and hire top talent is inextricably linked to strategy execution, operational excellence, and enterprise value. For instance, in complex jobs, high performers are 800 per cent more productive than average performers (Keller and Schaninger, nd). Being able to attract, source, assess and employ (defined as recruitment by ISO 30405:2016 *Human resource management – Guidelines on recruitment*) quality talent is undeniably critical to organizational success.

As organizations strive to attract and employ talent throughout the recruitment process, their brand influences these efforts (positively or negatively) through the way employees carry out the organization's recruitment process and staffing practices (Miles and McCamey, 2018). Effective recruitment serves to build talent pools, as well as enhance or protect other stakeholder relationships held by potential job candidates. As such, the importance of recruitment to an organization is vitally important, given its impact on the employer brand and ultimately the costs associated with an ineffective process or reputation.

This chapter focuses on the body of standards assisting organizations in their recruitment and initial employment of people to positively impact organizational outcomes.

CHAPTER OBJECTIVES

After reading this chapter, you will:

- understand the importance of recruitment;
- know the ISO definition and process of recruiting;
- understand the changing landscape of recruiting;
- understand the benefits of global standards on recruitment;
- be able to link the critical elements of recruiting and how to manage the candidate relationship;
- be able to measure and analyse the success of the recruitment process and talent hired.

Key terms

Assessment:	A systematic method and procedure for ascertaining work-related knowledge, skills, abilities or other characteristics of people or a group of people, or the performance of people or a group of people (ISO 30405).
Critical position:	A job role that has a direct and significant impact on organizational outcomes. Critical positions are identified by organizations as part of their organizational strategy, and will vary by industry, sector and organizational type. They are not always high-level positions.
Employ:	To engage the services of a person, or put a person to work.
Recruitment:	The process of sourcing, attracting, assessing, and employing talent for an existing or new position within the organization (ISO 30405).
Source:	To identify a pool of potential applicants.
Talent pool:	A group of people who possess the knowledge, skills, abilities and other characteristics necessary to carry out a specific job.

Existing standards

This chapter includes references to the following ISO standards and specifications:

- ISO 30405:2016 *Human resource management – Guidelines on recruitment*: This standard provides guidance for organizations on the process and effective practices for recruiting people who are capable of performing the necessary work. The recruitment process is illustrated by the movement of talent through the value chain, and includes all recruitment functions (attract, source, assess, and employ) and practices from the moment a job requisition is opened until it is deemed complete. Patterned after the quality management process of plan–do–check–act, the standard also provides guidance on checking the effectiveness, efficiency, and impact of the recruitment process for continuous improvement.

- ISO/TS 30407:2017 *Human resource management – Cost per Hire*: Cost-per-hire is a standard efficiency metric in recruitment to calculate the economic value attributed to the hiring process. This technical specification includes the globally accepted formula for calculating the costs associated with filling an open position. This standard provides information for internal reporting, as well as comparable reporting enabling comparisons within and outside of the organization.

- ISO/TS 30410:2018 *Human resource management – Impact of hire*: Every organization has at least one position that directly affects organizational performance. Evaluating the recruitment outcomes for these critical positions requires a shift from efficiency and effectiveness to impact measurements. As such, impact measurement assesses the critical positions' contribution to the success of the organization during a defined period. The impact of hire technical specification provides an approach to measuring the impact of a critical position's contribution to maximizing value for the organization. This technical specification defines principles for determining critical positions by using workforce segmentation approaches, as well as measures to determine the impact of critical positions, and the performance of people hired into these positions.

- ISO/TS 30411:2018 *Human resource management – Quality of hire*: The quality of hire metric provides guidance on measuring the quality of talent hired, and their initial effectiveness in doing the job they were hired to do. The more effective people are in performing their jobs, the higher the level of productivity that positively impacts unit and organizational outcomes to impact the firm's outcomes. The formula for this metric is based on the satisfaction of the stakeholders for the performance of the new hire, considering quality as a ratio or comparison of actual against expected parameters. This specification recognizes quality of hire as multi-dimensional, with all dimensions being measurable during a defined period. The specification also includes assistance with interpretations and contextual factors.

- ISO/AWI 30419 (forthcoming) *Guidelines for ensuring a positive candidate experience during the recruitment process*: This standard is under development at time of writing, and focuses on the candidate's experience during the recruitment process. Often organizations only focus on the candidates they are interested in, and often don't communicate with those who are not of interest, resulting in a negative candidate experience. A poor candidate experience damages an employer's brand and can make it more difficult to continue to attract high-quality talent. This standard focuses on guidance for organizations on the practices that should be adopted so that throughout the recruitment process all candidates are treated with courtesy and respect.

- ISO 10667:2011 *Assessment service delivery – procedures and methods to assess people in work and organizational settings (Part 1: Requirements for the client, Part 2: Requirements for service providers)*: A critical part of recruitment is identifying candidates who possess the necessary knowledge, skills, abilities, and other characteristics for a position. Organizations may use assessment tools to identify the best candidates. The assessments as well as the manner in which assessments are conducted not only reflect the employer brand, but when not conducted properly can result in unnecessary legal risk to the organization. ISO 10667:2011 provides guidance on the assessment service delivery process. These guidelines enable organizations to become more effective users of assessments thereby resulting in better hiring practices, and preservation of the employer brand. Clear and concise guidance is provided for providers of assessment services and the clients of assessment service providers, enabling all stakeholders to realize the potential benefits of good assessment practices. This includes defining good practice for assessment procedures and methods; ensuring equity in the application of assessment procedures; and enabling appropriate evaluation of the quality of the assessment service provision.

This body of standards provides a global guide on how to structure the recruitment process as well as providing global terms and definitions. These standards provide the necessary tools for organizations to ensure an effective and efficient recruitment process. The guidance on recruitment metrics for assessing the quality and impact (for critical positions) of talent hired will assist organizations in the recruitment process; a process vital to ensuring the proper talent is hired by the organization.

The nature and importance of recruitment

The extent to which a firm properly sources, attracts, assesses, and employs talent (recruitment) determines the quality of the workforce, and influences performance, retention, attendance, satisfaction, attraction, and engagement of talent to the firm. Effective recruitment helps ensure the firm can meet the demand for labour as well as having the right talent in the right place at the right time. When this happens, talent is considered fit to role, with the firm realizing increases in operational efficiency through higher productivity and lower operational costs, while talent has the capability to innovate at the required level resulting in the creation of enterprise value (Miles and Van Clieaf, 2017). On the other hand, an ineffective recruitment process is quite costly to the firm. For instance, Virgin Media, a British television, telephone, and internet services provider, quantified the costs of a 'poor' job candidate experience during its recruitment process, and determined it cost its brand $6 million in lost revenue annually (Adams, 2016).

Effective recruiting is the lifeblood of any organization. Talent sourced from the correct labour market, with targeted messages to attract talent through communications of its employer brand and employee value proposition, while using reliable and valid assessments to differentiate and match talent to the job and the organization (Fit to Role) and moving the candidate to employment, impacts both current and future firm value.

To assist organizations in the improvement of the recruitment process, the ISO standards not only address the organizational recruitment processes and practices employed by the firm, but also recognize the duality of the decision-making in the choices job candidates make to continue with the process, and ultimately the acceptance of a job offer. As such, the recruitment process (ISO 30405) centres on viewing recruitment from an organizational perspective as talent moves through the pipeline (ISO 30405), as well as providing guidelines for a positive candidate experience (ISO 30419) thereby strengthening the employer brand in the marketplace.

Additionally, specific guidance on the assessment process for candidates (ISO 10667) helps ensure organizations using assessments and assessment services are guided to ensure a positive and value-adding experience. This guidance enables organizations to become more effective users of assessments to make hiring decisions and enhance the potential, wellbeing and employee–organization fit of all their employees, embodied in a fair process to ensure assessment takers are treated fairly (critical to the candidate experience during recruitment).

To complete the process, ISO 30419 recognizes the critical role of the candidate experience on the employer brand and a firm's ability to source and employ high-quality talent both efficiently and effectively. The body of standards under the recruitment umbrella are integrated into the discussion below.

The recruitment process

ISO 30405 recognizes that the recruitment process for an organization is influenced by both environmental and organizational factors. For instance, some countries or industries may rely on specific sourcing outlets, or be constrained by law as to what can or cannot be done. While these factors certainly influence some of the practices used in local situations, the process of attracting, sourcing, assessing and employing remains the same. Figure 4.1 illustrates how the legal/social environment, organizational and HRM policies, organizational needs and workforce planning may impact the recruitment process and activities a firm would have to perform to properly fill an open position.

The extent to which the process is effectively managed impacts talent quality/quantity, recruitment outcomes (metrics), and human resource outcomes. These results feed back into the process as inputs for process improvements. The separation of influencers from the process allows the standard to be effectively adopted by small, medium or large organizations, regardless of the presence of a professional recruiter.

The key elements in the recruitment process are to attract, source, assess, and employ talent in accordance with the recruitment work flow (talent flow), while ensuring the employer brand is experienced throughout the process (ISO 30405). The ability of the firm to perform these functions seamlessly influences the quality and quantity of people available to the organization, as well as influencing other human capital management (HCM) outcomes and firm performance.

JRE 4.1   The recruitment process

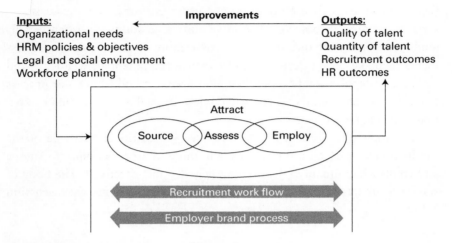

Inputs:
Organizational needs
HRM policies & objectives
Legal and social environment
Workforce planning

← Improvements

Outputs:
Quality of talent
Quantity of talent
Recruitment outcomes
HR outcomes

Attract
Source   Assess   Employ

Recruitment work flow
Employer brand process

The figure shows the inputs and outputs of the recruitment process.

Reprinted with permission from ISO 30405:2016 *Human resource management — Guidelines on recruitment*

Figure 4.2 illustrates the talent supply chain as talent moves through the recruitment process, and the primary focus of the organization in terms of attracting, sourcing, assessing and employing. Mapping out the process in accordance with the talent supply chain helps organizations to balance the candidate experience (ISO 30419) with the activities required to perform the recruitment function effectively and efficiently. As can be seen, the model depicts the talent supply to organize the firm's recruiting activities in recruiting talent through the continuous process of attracting and sequential processes of sourcing, assessing (ISO 10667) and employing (ISO 30405).

The talent supply chain starts with the potential labour pool, and consists of anyone who has or could develop the necessary knowledge, skills, abilities, and other qualities (KSAOs) needed to fill a position. Attention to this group is critical in navigating the modern complexities of recruiting, and the importance of establishing early relationships with candidates and potential candidates (Sahay, 2015). From the potential talent pool, talent then moves through the supply chain to the talent pool, once the talent learns the necessary KSAOs to do the job.

The applicant pool represents the people in the talent pool who decide to apply for a position in the organization. Talent flows through the supply chain through the organization's continual process of attracting and sequential processes of sourcing, assessing, and employing. At each touchpoint in

FIGURE 4.2   Talent flow through the recruitment process

| Potential talent pool | Talent pool | Applicant pool | Candidates for further evaluation | Candidate management | Pre-board | Board |

SOURCE (Confirm/complete inputs/build talent pool)

ATTRACT (Employer brand/recruitment communication)

ASSESS (Screening/selection final decisions)

EMPLOY (Prepare candidate for full employment)

The figure shows the four stages of the talent supply chain

Reprinted with permission from ISO 30405:2016 *Human resource management — Guidelines on recruitment* the supply chain, organizations carry out specific activities to decide which candidates will move to the next phase, while candidates form perceptions and sentiments regarding the organization's processes, practices, information and people to decide whether to continue to engage in the firm's recruitment process.

These exchanges are the foundation from which the candidate experience is determined (ISO 30419) and the candidate's decision to continue in the recruitment process is formed. How the firm manages the progression of talent through the supply chain determines the effectiveness of the recruitment process. Each step is discussed below, from the organizational activities that need to be performed throughout the recruitment process to integration of the candidate experience, and finally measurement of the recruitment process.

The potential talent pool

An important aspect of talent flow is often overlooked during the recruitment process. Prior to the organization seeking talent for open positions, talent commences their search for organizations and positions even before they have the requisite skills. The perceptions formed at this stage can influence future career decisions as well as potential employer preferences. As such, the attraction of candidates through recruitment and employer branding activities even before they have the necessary talent to apply for a position enhances the firm's ability to attract and employ future talent.

From the earliest stages of talent development, a firm starts building an awareness of the organization and the potential for work with that organization just by its operation in the community or positioning in society. Harnessing this opportunity to reach talent at early stages of exploration requires extending recruitment to one step before a job is actually open at the firm, to when talent is first starting to engage in career exploration. Firms able to build a positive image with prospective talent can position themselves as a viable employer as the talent grows and develops. Building and investing in the potential talent pool for critical positions in the company helps to build talent and applicant pools in the years to come.

For instance, consider the organization who knows its long-term strategy depends on the inventions and innovations of its engineers. This is a critical position in the organization, and the need for engineers will carry far out into the future. The more they can influence people who may become engineers in profession and become an employer of choice, the easier it will be to recruit engineers as needs arise. The firm may choose to host science fairs, and/or competitions and allow the engagement of professional engineers employed by the firm to interact with youth and their development through various activities.

In summary, the use of potential talent pools is crucial for critical jobs, or jobs with labour in short supply. At this stage people engage in search behaviours that include investigations into positions and organizations with the goal of identifying a future path for educational development. Organizations may or may not engage at this stage.

For organizations who do choose to engage talent at this stage, they seek to build awareness of their employer brand and an opportunity to attract and supply future talent pools. This is the earliest point at which employers can engage prospective talent and position themselves as a future employer in the minds of critical talent. The prominent focus of the organization is building attraction through building an early foundation for the employment relationship reaching into the future.

The talent pool

The talent pool consists of candidates who have the KSAOs to perform the job. Organizations engage the people in the talent pool through sourcing techniques (eg print, digital or networking) with the goal of motivating talent to apply for a vacancy.

For many jobs, the recruitment process is typically triggered by a job vacancy or requisition notice depicting a certain open position that needs to be filled, and closes when the position is filled and the new hire is employed. This information then indicates the labour market (talent pool) and sourcing practices to be used to move talent from the talent pool to the applicant pool (ie source). To effectively source, the characteristics and requirements of the job and organization are reviewed and verified. A recruitment plan is developed (eg budget, labour market, activities and methods for sourcing, message content, assessments and assessment criteria).

The manner in which the organization interfaces with the candidates in the talent pool through its sourcing techniques contributes to the candidate experience. The information, process or procedure clarity, and opportunity for questions influences the candidate's perception of the organization. For instance, tools used to solicit applications are under scrutiny by the candidates and may influence the candidates' decision not to further engage with the organization. A recent study identified the top five reasons for a negative candidate experience as 'unclear application instructions, extremely long applications, minimal job description, and no link to the application' (Slezak, nd).

It is during this time that candidates look at the information about the job, the process, and the organization and decide if the job is of interest. At any time during this process they may disengage if the process is too onerous. Candidates may also augment their search through social media sites, or third-party sites, for insights into what it would be like to work for the organization. The candidate forms perceptions (either positive or negative) that influence their future behaviour and the manner in which they perceive the organization (Miles and McCamey, 2018). The talent that completes the application process moves forward to the applicant pool, concluding the sourcing process for the organization.

In summary, the organization seeks to engage the talent pool to apply for the open position in the organization. The experience, ease of application, and information regarding employment with the company influences the decision to either apply for the open position, to disregard the opportunity or to drop out of the process. Ensuring there is a clear job description, an applicant-friendly process and a person to contact with questions during the process contributes to a positive experience for the people in the talent pool.

The applicant pool

Talent who have formally applied for a specific employment situation constitute the applicant pool. The candidate's application signals to the organization their interest in employment. For the organization, communication with the candidate is key to ensuring a positive experience through communicating the timeline, process, acknowledgement of application material and status updates as the process unfolds.

As well as engaging candidates in communication to ensure a positive experience, the organization reviews the candidates and determines which ones they are interested in for this specific opportunity. In essence, the organization has two goals: positive candidate experience, and finding the talent to fit the position. As such, the next step is determining if applicants have the necessary job and organization qualifications/competencies required to operate effectively in the position.

The pool of applicants is reviewed and usually divided into three categories: unqualified; qualified and not pursuing; and qualified and pursuing. To continue to identify the person with the best fit, those candidates who are qualified and who the organization wants to pursue are moved into the next stage for further assessment.

Notifying candidates who are not qualified for the position brings closure, a favourable characteristic of the candidate experience (Crispin, nd). It is possible that the candidate is suited for another position, and transitioning them to that applicant pool strengthens the relationship. This is a significant point as it requires the organization to pay attention to how and what it communicates to the candidate to avoid negative effects (Phillips and Gully, 2015). The candidate's experience will determine whether they will apply for another position in the organization (ie reengage), tell a friend, post about their experience on social media and/or continue the stakeholder relationship.

In summary, the employer has two objectives during this stage of recruitment: to continue to provide a positive candidate experience, and to identify a candidate for the position. The key to a positive candidate experience at this point is to ensure that the candidates know the timeline for decision-making, and receive communication from the organization regarding their personal status. After classifying the applicants into unqualified, qualified and not pursuing, and qualified and pursuing, the latter group moves into the next phase for further evaluation.

Candidates for further evaluation

The candidates who are both interested and qualified for a specific employment situation are the candidates for further evaluation. It is important to keep in mind the quality of the candidate experience up to this point, as candidates may lose interest in the position and organization and may opt out of the recruitment process, especially if the process is too long. For the organization, loss of qualified talent during this stage compromises their ability to further assess their capabilities and determine fit for the position and organization.

During the process, the candidate will continue searching for information about the organization. Providing additional information will assist in the candidate's search and continue the relationship with the organization. It should be noted that, just as the organization is looking at all candidates, candidates are looking at other employers as well.

In total, the treatment of the candidate at the various points in the process, as well as the communication process for advancing (or not), contributes to the formation of perceptions about the organization in the mind of the candidate. For instance, a candidate who shows up for an interview and is asked to wait 30 minutes past the scheduled time is likely to feel disrespected. The types of assessments and interviews conducted at this stage are evaluated by the candidate. The perception of fairness and job relevance is key to continuing to deliver a good job candidate experience, as is communicating the timeline for any next steps and decision-making.

Assessments to be used in the recruitment process are selected in accordance with the position, and are designed to measure specific characteristics deemed necessary for effective job performance. Selected candidates may go through a series of assessments that may include cognitive and intellectual tests or work simulations, and may be conducted by dedicated assessment centres or through interviews with key people.

A word of caution about assessments: as important as they are in determining candidate quality, they can also diminish the candidate experience (Handler, nd). Especially notable are pre-hire talent assessments that take too long, are not fun or entertaining, use several technology platforms, or don't appear to be job-related. Balancing the need for quality hires with candidate experience, ISO 10667 focuses on the process of assessment by promoting the provision of standardized, appropriate, and equitable delivery of assessment services to participants. This helps ensure confidence in the assessment process.

The important role of assessments in the recruitment process is critical to the organization's decision on talent selection as well as the candidate's positive perception of the recruitment process. For the organization, assessments provide a scientific process to distinguish between effective and less effective talent, while providing the talent with fair and respectful treatment to provide a positive experience while being assessed. Assessments refer to the method and procedure for ascertaining work related knowledge, skills, abilities or other characteristics of an individual or group of individuals.

ISO 10667 offers guidelines to assist in the process of assessments. Guidelines are provided for both service providers and clients, defining good practice for assessment procedures and methods, ensuring equity in the application of assessments, and enabling appropriate evaluation of the quality of the assessment service provider. ISO 10667 promotes good practice and encourages clear documentation, while ensuring the rights and responsibilities of the assessment participants in relation to the assessments. Attention is given to agreement procedures for all potential parties, pre-assessment procedures, assessment delivery, and post-assessment review. The assessment information is used to determine the level of success at this stage.

It is important to note that, just as the firm seeks more information for candidates, the candidate continues to search for more information about the firm. Providing additional information will assist in the candidate's search behaviour and their decision to continue their relationship with the organization. In total, the treatment of the candidate throughout the process (including assessments) influences the candidate's perception of the organization as an employer, ultimately influencing future attitudes and behaviour towards the firm. The perception of fairness, respect, and relevance is critical to a positive candidate experience. As the market continues to transform from an employer-driven market to a candidate-driven market (Sahay, 2015), focusing on the candidate experience is vital to talent acquisition.

In summary, this stage of the recruitment process commences with organizations identifying the most qualified talent, and engaging them to continue the process. The type of open position will determine the number and types of assessments to be used. Both the candidate and the organization are seeking more complete information about one another before making their respective decisions.

For the organization, the most successful candidates at this stage move into the offer stage. If employment terms are accepted by the candidate, the final stage of recruitment is to complete the requirements to enable the candidate to begin employment. When the candidate shows up for work, the requisition is closed and the candidate becomes an employee.

The offer

The offer stage seeks to complete final decisions regarding interested and qualified candidates, while managing the relationship with the remaining candidates. First is the offer to desirable candidates. Typically, an offer is extended in one of three ways: competitive offer, low-ball offer, and best-shot offer (Henemann, Judge and Kammeyer-Mueller, 2018). The offer itself can affect the candidates' perception of the organization and determine their continued engagement. For instance, receiving a best shot offer, the candidate feels valued and wanted by the organization. Conversely, a low ball offer would have the opposite effect and may even result in the candidate rejecting the offer (especially when other options are available). Understanding the implications of the methodology of the offer is critical to setting the tone of the employment relationship.

Notifying the candidates who did not receive an offer is a critical step in managing the recruitment and candidate experience process. Notification often occurs after the offer has been accepted by the top candidate. The unsuccessful talent may qualify for other employment opportunities in the firm. When this happens, encouraging the talent to redirect their applications to another opportunity in the organization results in not only a positive experience for the candidate, but also enhances the applicant pool for other positions within the firm. The manner in which candidates receive communication signalling closure and/or next steps contributes to a positive or negative candidate experience, and determines the candidate's future interest and continued relationship status with the firm (Miles and McCamey, 2018).

In summary, the intent of the offer process is to solidify an employment opportunity for the top candidate(s). The offer can serve to reinforce a positive perception of the employer or raise concerns. In an employment situation where the candidate has multiple offers, the firm needs to extend the best possible offer to preserve the relationship and transform the recruitment relationship into an employment relationship. Communicating with the candidates who were not selected is a critical step, and inviting them to apply for other opportunities within the organization contributes to a positive employer brand.

Employment

The last stage of recruitment focuses on transitioning candidates who have accepted the job offer to their first day of employment. Retaining a candidate's interest and the completion of critical documentation is the goal of this phase of the recruitment process. Communication continues to play a major role during the employment transition (which may include relocation). When this stage is managed well, candidate engagement and excitement continues to evolve into the workplace. When not managed properly, the candidate experience can be negative, which can become part of the psychological contract impacting employee brand and voice behaviours (Miles and Mangold, 2014).

To ensure this does not happen, the new employee(s) should receive communication to reaffirm their decision, as well as information regarding the job requirements and rewards. This involves carefully planning the new hire's opportunities to forge new relationships within the work unit, ensuring their manager and co-workers are properly introduced and available and providing any necessary assistance in the transitional period.

For success, plans need to include actions directed at the new hire before day one of employment, and careful planning for the first day of employment prior to onboarding activities. Before the new hire's first day the following should be performed:

- Notify the unit of the new hire, and encourage people to reach out and congratulate them on their appointment.
- Plan the first day of work for the new hire with interesting tasks.
- Provide the new hire with their job description and performance expectations, as well as other pertinent information (eg the organizational chart) and the employee handbook.
- Schedule training programmes, if appropriate.
- Provide a benefit packet of information to go over on the first day.
- Schedule a peer to act as a mentor for the first week.
- Schedule key people for the new hire to meet on their first day of work.
- Arrange for any parking pass, building entry pass and work equipment the employee will need for work.
- Arrange for onboarding and an ongoing training plan.

To ensure the new hire gets off to a good start, the following activities are suggested at a minimum:

- Welcome the new hire and discuss the plan for the day.
- Tour the facility and identify where restrooms, break areas and so on are located.
- Introduce the new hire to key people, their mentor and a lunch buddy for their first day (which may be their mentor).
- Provide necessary items (eg a building pass or phone).
- Review documentation (eg their job description, benefits, policies).

Once the new hire shows up and starts working for pay, the recruitment process is technically over (that is, the requisition/vacancy is closed). At this point, the new hire begins onboarding and training, lasting anywhere from days to months depending on the job and the organization. It should be remembered the recruitment process is an opportunity for the organization to build its employer brand and set the stage for employee engagement.

The recruitment body of standards provide a framework for all organizations by providing an overarching process allowing for adaptations for legal and cultural considerations. The process provides guidance on positioning the organization in the minds of prospective talent even before the appropriate KSAOs are developed, through the use of positive messages and interactions with the potential talent pool to build interest in the organization and its job offerings. This allows the candidate to develop the appropriate skill set to apply for jobs when they can be considered part of the talent pool.

For the organization, this contributes to an applicant pool with qualified and interested applicants that are attracted to the organization and its perceived offerings. This level of engagement helps to ensure the candidates the organization is interested in can be successfully pursued, resulting in acceptance of the job offer. Effective management of the recruitment process is a primary factor in building relationships and meeting the organization's talent requirements.

Outcomes, measurement and analysis

Outcomes of the recruitment process result in both internal and external organizational consequences. Internally, the recruitment process determines the quality, quantity, and efficiencies (eg cost and time) of the talent employed. Externally, the recruitment process, practices, and recruiters interface with various stakeholders to affect the firm's reputation as an employer, which can also impact future recruiting efficiencies and effectiveness (Miles and McCamey, 2018). In essence, recruitment outcomes are multifaceted, and the importance of measurement and analysis is critical in measuring both internal and external outcomes.

Traditionally, a common method of measurement for recruitment effectiveness is tracking the movement of candidates along the supply chain (Figure 4.2). This allows for identifying efficiency (eg time and cost), effectiveness (eg number of qualified applicants, number of qualified applicants self-selecting out) and impact (eg recruitment yield and high-quality applicants).

Table 4.1 illustrates measurement of the entire recruitment system.

For instance, assume the 25 vacancies attracted 1,000 applications. We can see the progression to capture the conversion of the talent pool to the applicant pool, and gather the labour statistics for the country and labour market. It may also be prudent to consider unemployment data for the labour market. Other data points can also be added to calculate cost per hire (ISO 30407), quality of hire (ISO/TS 30411), and impact of hire (ISO/TS 30410).

While these measurements assess the overall process in terms of organizational results, data capture on the candidates' experience is not included.

TABLE 4.1 Recruitment system measurement

	Talent pool	Candidate pool	Candidates for further evaluation	Offer	Employ	First day of work	On job six months
Recruitment source							
Company career portal		500	150	25	22	22	19
LinkedIn		500	50	5	3	3	1
Number of people		1,000	200	30	25	25	20
Advance			20%	15%	83%	100%	80%
Time in days		14	21	35	42	44	

The table shows the number of candidates advancing to each stage of the recruitment supply chain

NOTE Recruiting for 25 positions

Adapted from Henemann, Judge and Mueller (2018)

To capture this, an organization can survey and track all applicants and their experience, or enlist the services of a third-party organization. One such organization that conducts comprehensive measurement as well as benchmarking with others in the industry is the Talent Board. The Talent Board also hosts the international event of the CandE Awards, focusing on organizations who deliver the best candidate experience.

Additionally, ISO 30405:2016 *Human resource management – Guidelines on recruitment* provides a measurement framework based on the efficiency, effectiveness and impact outcomes. While the list is not exhaustive, it does provide examples of various metrics used to measure efficiency (cost), effectiveness (quality of talent), and impact of attract, source, assess, and employ. Measurement of the recruitment function based on the four major tasks is further discussed below.

Attract

The ability of a firm to attract high-quality talent with ease is based on its organizational reputation, as well as their reputation as an employer in the marketplace. The reputation of the firm as an employer is referred to as the employer brand. Building a positive employer brand starts well before the formal recruiting process, and first touches the labour market when a firm engages with the potential pool. This early engagement serves to positively position the organization and certain positions within the organization as desirable as one explores future employment opportunities. A firm's ability to capture the interest of potential talent is an important step in succeeding in a candidate-driven market (Sahay, 2015).

Regardless of whether a firm actively works to ensure a positive employer brand, all organizations have a reputation of some kind, whether it be a broad awareness of a firm's activities or consumption of their products or services. Information on the internet (eg on sites such as Glassdoor) also provides insight to potential talent on what life is like working in that organization. As such, measuring and monitoring the 'attraction' is of pivotal importance.

A firm can track and identify its ability to attract talent in many ways. ISO 30405 provides multiple ways to measure the employer brand, including number of job applicants, number of unsolicited applicants, percentage of applicants moving to candidate pools, quality of talent, time to fill positions, job offer to acceptance ratio for each vacancy, number of candidates who show up on the first day, and number of advancements within a short timeframe.

Additionally, ISO 30405 suggests surveying job candidates who have opted out of the process in order to identify whether this was due to organizational practices or personal situations. As mentioned earlier, securing the services of a third-party vendor to survey all applicants through the process also serves to identify those who drop out of the process even during the application phase and never choose to move from the talent pool to the applicant pool.

There is fierce competition to attract and retain talent in a candidate-driven market. Finding talent is critical, before converting them into job candidates and retaining their interest in order to employ and retain them in the long term. It should be noted that the talent's attraction to the firm also impacts on the future satisfaction, engagement, and performance of the new hire (Henemann, Judge and Kammeyer-Mueller, 2018).

Source

The goal of sourcing is to move candidates from the talent pool to the applicant pool. There are multitudes of tools and methods for identifying interested and qualified talent. Talent can reside in the firm, or be sourced externally. External recruitment sources include: applicant-initiated recruitment (eg through a firm career portal), employment websites, employee referrals, social media, professional associations/meeting, and colleges and placement offices.

Given the variety of potential sources, tracking the efficiency, effectiveness and impact of these sources and the talent that is cultivated allows a firm to find quality talent in the most efficient manner. For instance, Table 4.1 illustrates how many applicants were secured from the firm's career portal vs LinkedIn. In this example, the firm's career portal is clearly delivering the best talent. As such, energies and efforts should be directed to managing the portal. Though not included, additional tracking of costs can be calculated as well in accordance with ISO/TS 30407.

Assess

To determine the best match for the position and the organization, assessments are used. Assessments include tests (job knowledge, general knowledge, aptitude, situational judgement or personality tests); work simulations (assessment centre activities, case studies, role play, simulations, work samples or group tasks), other proven instruments (background checks, investigation, interview, medical exams, candidate presentations). Each of these tools measures some aspect of the candidate. Depending on the position and firm requirements one or more of these assessments may be used.

Regardless of the type or quantity of assessments, it is critical to measure the effectiveness of these tools, from the organizational perspective as well as the candidate perspective. For the organization, it is critical to know that the instrument used possesses both reliability and validity. Secondly, the assessment tool used should clearly indicate the most suitable candidates.

While these two dimensions certainly help to ensure a legally sound and scientifically-based system, it is also critical to measure perceptions of the candidates. Assessments can be a source of dissatisfaction among candidates, especially when the assessments do not reflect the job (Miles and McCamey, 2018). ISO 10667 provides extensive guidance on assessments, to include rights and responsibilities both for assessment administrators and assessment takers. The results of the assessment will provide critical information as to which candidates receive the offer. Acceptance of the offer is the last step before moving into Employ. Tracking of this is critical, and is part of the overall recruitment measurement as mentioned above.

Employ

Once a job offer is accepted by a candidate, the employ phase of recruitment begins. This element is critical as it entails all the steps the employer has to take before a person starts work. Depending on the labour market and the needs of the employer, this time will vary. The goal at this stage is to retain interest and desire while ensuring the required documentation is complete and the social/cultural integration begins. The key metrics at this stage is the percentage of the talent who have accepted employment offers who actually show up for the job, and whether those results are within acceptable limits.

Comprehensive measurement of the recruitment process, recording effectiveness, efficiency, and impact for the entire process or specific elements, is critical for optimization of the recruitment process and protection of the employer brand. ISO 30405 further details the collection of data, analysis of results (comparison of existing state to desired state), and the final stage of making an improvement plan where needed.

The changing landscape of recruitment

Talent is the linchpin for any organization. Organizations are currently facing magnitudes of unprecedented changes in scope and speed, with the environment surrounding this unprecedented change commonly referred to as Volatile, Uncertain, Complex and Ambiguous (VUCA). In order to thrive in our VUCA world, organizations have to rethink processes, products, markets, business models, industries and impacts on societies. Take for instance the Toyota leadership, who launched strategic plans to 2050 for zero emissions, supporting the UN Sustainable Development Goals, later reiterated and built on by the Conference of Parties 21 (COP21) in Paris. As Toyota unfolds their plan, they have to be able to map out critical positions (some of which may not be currently in existence), and start the mapping process of how to acquire or develop talent that will see their plan to fruition.

This marks a change in how organizations are starting to view talent needs. As organizations such as Toyota prepare for the future, focus is given not only to the current capabilities of talent, but to the future potential that will be the catalysts in their ability to thrive in a VUCA world (Fernandez-Araoz, 2014).

Clearly, organizational talent needs are changing. As such, organizations will have to look at not only what kind of talent is needed, but the ability to identify and properly assess candidates with high potential, as well as how to employ, develop and retain such talent. With changing needs for talent coupled with the increasing complexity in the recruitment arena spurred by data-driven recruitment and the digitization of recruitment, organizations now more than ever will have to ensure their recruitment process is both capable of identifying, finding, assessing and employing talent that will be able to carry out the firm's long-range goals.

More specifically, data-driven recruitment capitalizes on big data by providing more data points, and hence more information on processes and people to better measure performance and optimize decisions. The guesswork is being taken out of recruitment. For instance, consider Google's capability to project the career trajectory of potential hires (Sullivan, nd). Collecting specific data on candidates allows Google to assess their career progression at top, average and below-average speed in critical areas such as learning, promotion, leadership and innovation. Organizations that can use data in this manner can drastically improve both quality and impact of hire. Sahay (2015) also mentions futurecasting and organizations' ability to interrogate big data generated by the social digital world. Basing hiring strategies and tactics on the insights gleaned will be a game-changer in talent acquisition.

The digitization of recruitment means we have multiple layers of technologies, tools, partners and services embedded in the recruitment process, increasing the complexity and sophistication of recruitment. The complexity of recruitment necessitated the launch of the Association of Talent

Acquisition Professionals (ATAP). This organization is dedicated to assisting talent acquisition professionals (recruiters) in navigating the ever-changing data and digital environment, and the transformation of recruitment from employer-driven to candidate-driven as organizations move from seeking talent with current capabilities to those with potential capabilities.

The candidate-driven recruitment era ushers in the vantage of viewing employer/candidate relationships from a long-term perspective, and requires paying special attention to nurturing relationships in order to ensure an organization is able to secure talent vetted for success for now and the future, as well as being able to secure such talent efficiently and effectively. The ISO standards under the recruitment umbrella were designed in such a way as to view talent from a value chain perspective, highlighting the necessity of managing the candidate relationship to help ensure organizations can continue to navigate the ever-changing world of recruitment.

Summary

Recruitment is an integral component of organizational success. To help organizations improve their recruitment process, experts from around the globe gathered to solve one of HCM's most vexing concerns: how can we provide a process model of recruitment, any organization to be able to follow the general framework, while allowing for the application of local laws and customs, in the ever-changing environment of recruitment. The recruitment standard (ISO 30405) and the family of similar standards were designed and developed to provide minimum guidelines for effectively managing the recruitment process and the candidate experience (ISO 30419).

This chapter explores the process of recruitment as defined in ISO 30405 by illustrating the talent flow, with consideration given to the essential functions of attracting, sourcing, assessing, and employing the necessary talent to meet organizational needs and requirements. Lastly, assistance to provide a common measurement is currently underway, adding more metrics to enable consistent measurement for recruitment for both internal and external comparisons.

References and further resources

Adams, B. (2016) 6 simple steps to revitalizing your candidate experience, *ERE Media* www.ere.net/5-simple-steps-to-revitalizing-your-candidate-experience/ (archived at https://perma.cc/9PZP-PZV9)

Association of Talent Acquisition Professionals https://atapglobal.org/about/ (archived at https://perma.cc/R97D-KZJQ)

Crispin, G. The path to an exceptional candidate experience according to Gerry Crispin, *Jibe* http://info.jibe.com/path-to-an-exceptional-candidate-experience (archived at https://perma.cc/27AB-25JL)

Fernandez-Araoz, C (2014) *It's Not the How Or the What But the Who: Succeed by surrounding yourself with the best*, Harvard Business Review Press, Boston, Massachusetts

Handler, C. Candidate Experience vs. Candidate Quality? Have Your Cake and Eat it Too, *ERE Media* www.ere.net/candidate-experience-vs-candidate-quality-have-yourcake-and-eat-it-too/ (archived at https://perma.cc/6QHH-SLSD)

Henemann, H G, Judge, T A and Mueller, J K (2018) *Staffing Organizations*, 9th edn, McGraw Hill Publishing. New York

ISO (2011) ISO 10667:2011 *Assessment service delivery – procedures and methods to assess people in work and organizational settings (Parts 1 and 2)*, www.iso.org/standard/56441.html (archived at https://perma.cc/3RJV-UE46)

ISO (2016) ISO 30405:2016 *Human resource management – Guidelines on recruitment*, www.iso.org/standard/64149.html (archived at https://perma.cc/DTW6-SUG9)

ISO (2017) ISO/TS 30407:2017 *Human resource management: Cost per Hire*, www.iso.org/standard/62975.html (archived at https://perma.cc/C4D2-E5BW)

ISO (2018) ISO/TS 30410:2018 *Human resource management: Impact of hire*, www.iso.org/standard/68219.html (archived at https://perma.cc/2B9J-SNUT)

ISO (2018) ISO/TS 30411:2018 *Human resource management: Quality of hire*, www.iso.org/standard/68220.html (archived at https://perma.cc/H3DH-R47U)

ISO (forthcoming) ISO/AWI 30419 *Guidelines for ensuring a positive candidate experience during the recruitment process*, www.iso.org/standard/68696.html (archived at https://perma.cc/LEW5-92HN)

Keller, S and Schaninger, B. Focus on the five percent, *McKinsey* www.mckinsey.com/business-functions/organization/our-insights/the-organization-blog/focus-on-the-five-percent (archived at https://perma.cc/DP9A-JQNQ)

Miles, S and Mangold, W (2014) Employee voice: Untapped resource or social media time bomb?, *Business Horizons*, 57 (3), pp 401–11

Miles, S and McCamey, R (2018) The candidate experience: Is it damaging your employer brand?, *Business Horizons*, 61 (5), pp755–64

Miles, S and Van Clieaf, M (2017) Strategic fit: Key to growing enterprise value through organizational capital, *Business Horizons*, **60** (1) pp 55–65

Phillips, J and Gully, S (2015) *Strategic Staffing*, 3rd edn, Pearson Publishing, Hoboken, NJ

Sahay, P (2015) The complexity of recruiting, *Strategic HR Review*, **14** (5), pp 182–87

Slezak, P. Why a poor candidate experience can destroy your business, *Recruit Loop* http://recruitloop.com/blog/why-a-poor-candidate-experience-can-be-bad-for-business/ (archived at https://perma.cc/MGN7-QHBF)

Sullivan, J. Hire like Google – Project the 'Career Trajectory' of your Candidates, *Ere Media* www.ere.net/hire-like-google-project-the-career-trajectory-of-your-candidates/ (archived at https://perma.cc/PFV5-BT7U)

Sustainable Innovation Forum www.cop21paris.org (archived at https://perma.cc/9YJT-E2KA)

Talent Board. CandE Awards, *Talent Board* www.thetalentboard.org/cande-awards/ (archived at https://perma.cc/K6KP-AQXH)

5

Learning and development

Valerie Anderson and Alaa Garad

Introduction

This chapter focuses on the skills and competence base required by organizations and the importance of learning and development for maintaining and improving operations. Knowledge and skills are an important feature of organizational and national economic competitiveness, effectiveness and efficiency. The dynamic nature of the global economy in the 21st century has led organizations to recognize that learning and development is a strategic issue to overcome skills shortages and build organizational resilience to achieve productivity and business growth plans.

Human capital theory (Becker, 2002) highlights that systems of education develop people's initial skills. However, organizational competitive capability requires continuous learning at individual, team and organizational levels. Employers and individuals play an important part in the continuous processes of 'upskilling' and life-long learning required for the globalized, technologically innovative and volatile context in which organizations operate.

This chapter will highlight the importance of standards relating to formal and informal learning, training and development at the level of the individual. It will also focus on processes required to manage and continuously improve a cycle of learning activities within the organization to systematically and consistently promote the development, assurance and maintenance of competent personnel.

Many national and international standards use the terms 'training', 'learning', 'competence' and 'development'. In this chapter, the term 'development' refers to a process that brings out, or enhances, the potential capabilities, knowledge, experience, skills, attitudes, or insights of a person or organization (BS PD 76006:2017 *Guide to learning and development*). The term 'training' is used to refer to instructor or expert-led interventions (whether delivered face-to-face or through technological means) aimed at enabling people to achieve change in knowledge, skills or understanding of work-relevant tasks. The term 'competence' refers to the behaviours and technical qualities members of work organizations must have to enable them to meet required standards of performance. Both training and competence development involve learning.

The term 'learning', as used in this chapter, connotes both an outcome and a process. Learning is the product of growth and fulfilment (knowledge, skills and behaviour), as well as a process of shaping and changing behaviour. Learning can occur in work contexts because of formal or informal processes. Learning is important as it supports adaptation to change, performance improvement, sustainable performance and productivity at individual, team and organizational levels.

CHAPTER OBJECTIVES

This chapter sets out to:

- consider existing standards that have relevance to learning, training and development;
- outline the different contexts for learning and development in work organizations;
- examine the links between individual learning and organizational learning;
- examine the role of technology in learning and development;
- discuss priority areas and opportunities for standards in learning and development.

Key terms

Many of the terms associated with learning and development are well known, but are differently understood in varying organizational contexts. In addition to 'learning', 'training' and 'development', which are defined in the chapter introduction, the following expressions are used in this chapter as follows.

Assessment and evaluation:	In the context of learning and development, th terms refer to formal or informal valuation of the quality, effectiveness and impact of learning, development and competence management systems and processes. Many approaches to assessment and evaluation involve a series of levels to assess the return on investment of learning, training or development interventions, measured through changes in behaviour, competency profiles and levels of productivity, effectiveness and efficiency.
Competency Management System:	This term refers to organizational level systems that take a comprehensive approach to profiling behaviours and qualities needed for organizational performance to a given standard. This involves analysing where skills gaps may be occurring, and planning and managing processes to generate sustainable competency across the organization.
Individual learning:	The process whereby an individual experiences growth and fulfilment (knowledge, skills and behaviours) which result in behaviour change. Individual learning is personal and unless there are opportunities for this learning to be shared, the knowledge, skills and behavioural attributes of individuals are lost from the organization should they leave or decide to withhold what they have learned.
Learning technology:	Although this term is often used as a synonym for e-learning, in this chapter it refers to the broad range of information and communication technologies that can be used to identify learning needs, deliver and assess learning, and provide the basis for organization-wide learning and competency management systems.
Organizational learning (OL):	This term is distinct from the term 'organization-wide learning' below. OL refers to all processes and activities involved in creating, retaining and transferring knowledge both within and beyond organization boundaries. OL is experiential; it requires processes, practices, methods and activities to value 'lessons learned' from within and outside the organization as a feature of systematic performance improvement and adaptability.

Organization-wide learning:	This term refers to the process, rarely achieved in organizations, where all members of the organization are able to access different learning processes, practices, methods and activities (both formally and informally), as individuals and as members of work groups, to systematically and intentionally improve their performance at individual, work group and organizational levels.
Team learning:	Team learning is a social and relational process that occurs when collaborative processes between individuals involve coordination of knowledge and behaviours as a feature of their work processes. Where systemic team learning occurs, it can enhance the performance of the team and can contribute to the improvement of organizational performance.

Learning and development in existing standards

In recent years, standards developers have paid increasing attention to learning and development, competency management systems and valuing people. Six standards are particularly relevant to consideration of learning and development within the organization:

- BS ISO 29993:2017 *Learning services outside formal education – Service requirements*;
- BS ISO 10015:1999 *Quality management – Guidelines for training* (under review);
- ISO 9001:2015 *Quality management systems requirements*;
- ISO 14001:2015 *Environmental management system standards requirements*;
- ISO/IEC/JTC 36 *Information technologies for learning, education and training*;
- PD 76006-2017 *Guide to learning and development*.

They are discussed further here.

BS ISO 29993

This standard focuses on assuring the quality of learning services provided by individuals and organizations externally to the organization and outside of formal educational provision. The standard specifies various elements in the design, delivery, and assessment and evaluation of learning services.

Key features of the standard are the importance of aligning learning activities with business strategy, and having systems in place to evaluate the impact of learning and any quantifiable features of 'return on investment' (see Figure 5.1). At the operational level, this standard applies a systematic approach to learning involving identifying learning needs, design of the learning service, information for learners, sponsors and facilitators, and processes for the assessment of learning and for evaluation of the learning service as well as financial and invoicing practices.

FIGURE 5.1   Key features of ISO 29993

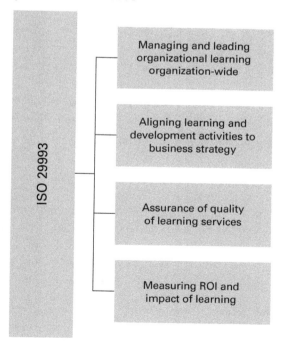

The figure shows the key features of the ISO 29993 standard

This standard has been proved relevant on a global basis. In November 2017, the Ministry of Labour and Skills in India was one of the first government bodies in the world to adopt this standard as part of a project called: 'Come to Learn – Come to Serve'.

BS ISO 10015

The standard is part of the ISO 9000 quality management group of standards. Learning and development form an important part of the achievement of quality management, and the standard has been widely adopted. As of 2018, ISO 10015 is being reviewed prior to relaunch as 'Quality management – Guidelines for competence management and training', with the aim of improving the quality of learning and development programmes in both public and private sectors.

The standard has relevance to training practices in large and small organizations. It encourages a move away from reliance on reactive forms of training towards a proactive and regular assessment of individual skill development priorities, to develop a wider approach to organizational development and upskilling.

Like ISO 29993, this standard focuses attention on the four stages of training: needs assessment, training planning, design and implementation of training and evaluation and assessment of its effectiveness. It further highlights the importance of organizational culture to give workers 'permission' and encouragement to take informed decisions about their learning, so that they can better carry out their duties as a feature of continuous improvement to support organizational performance.

ISO 9001 and ISO 14001

ISO 9001 and ISO 14001 have identical requirements related to generic topics such as people competence. They also align to some extent with knowledge management issues to ensure operational continuity and product and service consistency. In addressing the competence of those who work on behalf of the organization, they require that organizations:

- determine the necessary competence of people undertaking work that affects the performance and effectiveness of the management system;

- ensure that people have the necessary education, training or experience;

- take action, where appropriate, to ensure people acquire the necessary competence;

- evaluate the effectiveness of the actions taken to develop competence.

FIGURE 5.2   Key features of ISO 10015

The figure shows the key features of the ISO 10115 standard

Adapted from Jacobs and Wang (nd)

ISO/IEC/JTC 36

As e-learning becomes more prevalent in organizational approaches to learning and development, standards in this area focus on learning, education and training so that resources can be used and applied in different contexts and so that resources are reusable as appropriate.

PD 76006:2017

This British Standards Institution (BSI) Published Document gives guidance about the contribution that learning and development can make to meet skills shortages. It sets out to provide organizations of all sizes and in all sectors with a useful 'road map' to help them make better use of workplace learning, to support individual and organizational effectiveness.

The document identifies the importance of promoting learning and development amongst a broad range of stakeholders with regard to a) influencing,

b) engaging, c) consulting, and d) aligning learning and development expectations to ensure that the learning and development practices are directed towards the continuous improvement of individual, collective and organizational performance and success.

This document is part of the BS 76000 group of standards. These standards identify that knowledge, skills and abilities of individuals can create value for the organization and its stakeholders. The standards are based on a set of values which are:

- People working on behalf of the organization have intrinsic value.
- Stakeholders and their interests are integral to the best interests of the organization.
- Every organization is part of a wider society and has a responsibility to respect its social contract as a corporate citizen and operate in a sustainable manner.

PD 76006 also sets out the most commonly used methods of learning and development. These are outlined later in the chapter.

Aspects of good practice in relation to learning and development feature in many published national and international standards relating to technical and operational efficiency. This is not surprising as the effectiveness of the skills and competence of people in the organization are fundamental for maintaining and improving operations and service provision. All of these standards emphasize integrating business plans and strategic objectives with processes of monitoring and improving learning and training.

To ensure that learning and development systems are as effective as possible, managers can identify which existing standards might have most relevance to their organizational goals and strategy and ensure the delivery of learning, training and development provision as outlined in these standards.

Learning and development: context and practice

As indicated in the introduction to this chapter, knowledge and skills are important for organizational effectiveness. Learning and development is a strategic issue. Employing organizations and individuals both have an important role to play in 'upskilling' and life-long learning to support continuous development of capability at individual, team and organizational levels.

Different national economies address skills strategies in various ways. In some countries, such as the UK, government, businesses, and individuals share responsibility for skills and capability. The government manages and promotes basic skills formation and development through the education system, and businesses take responsibility for development of the skills required for specific job roles.

In other countries, for example Germany, a pluralist approach is taken where trades unions, employers and the education sector set standards for initial and ongoing learning and development in many sectors. An alternative approach, which is adopted in parts of the Middle East, is for the government to exert strong influence over the nature, form and funding of skills development in education and in the workplace.

Different organizational sectors also require distinctive approaches to initial skills formation and skills development with implications for standards development and standards adoption in different contexts. However, while differences are evident in the approaches and assumptions taken about learning in the workplace, the challenges facing organizations are similar. Organizations require clear management processes to address initial and ongoing training and employability; to identify and meet skills, qualifications and capability shortages or gaps; and to provide access to continuous processes of learning and development for all workers.

Approaches to tackling these issues have changed in recent years. Traditionally, standardized and regulated ways of delivering instructor-led training interventions were common. However, advances in the field of learning and development have led to a more 'person-centred' approach to identifying and meeting learning needs. In this context, coaching, mentoring and e-learning or mobile learning are important and popular learning methods.

Technology is also applied more to manage, deliver and evaluate learning and development in organizations in many sectors of the global economy. This means that organizations can ensure that individuals and teams receive training, and can take forward learning opportunities that enable them to fulfil their potential whilst also contributing positively to the business and the economy as a whole.

A further development in the learning and development field has been the increasing recognition of social learning, where people learn from and with each other. As a result, processes of collaboration, through networking inside and outside the organization, supported where appropriate by social media technologies, supports work-based learning at all levels of the organization in alignment with organizational priorities.

Alongside changes to the learning and development context, changes in the global economic and competitive environment have important implications for the provision of learning and development in work organizations. First, learning and development processes are more likely to occur in large organizations where a learning or training specialist function is available. However, economic competitiveness increasingly relies on smaller, innovative and entrepreneurial organizations and small firms dominate the employment landscape, employing at least 90 per cent of the working age population across the world.

As a result, a high proportion of the working population may not have access to learning and development opportunities beyond their initial education; something that raises concerns as the average age of the working population continues to increase.

Second, employers may be more inclined to invest in learning and development for permanently employed workers. However, the 21st-century employment context relies on increasing levels of 'contingency' employment carried out by people on temporary or flexible (non-standard) contracts. This presents a further challenge for access to work-based learning and development and for consistent levels of skill and service delivery. This context makes skills shortages as well as career obsolescence increasingly likely. Qualities of resilience and adaptiveness are required.

Continuous learning by workers at individual, team and organizational levels is an important way to meet these challenges. The challenge for standards specialists is to ensure that management and sector-wide standards take account of new developments in this field to ensure that learning and development are encouraged and managed at individual, team and organizational levels.

Important questions for organizations to consider, in their specific contexts, include:

- What proportion of people, regardless of their age or contractual status, are operating at acceptable competence levels?

- How quickly do people throughout the organization acquire new skills and abilities to meet change-related opportunities and developments?

- How responsive are all organizational members to new/future business opportunities?

- How successful are knowledge-sharing processes between everyone who works on behalf of the organization (including interns, volunteers, contractors, temporary staff)?

- How effective are levels of cross-functional collaboration?
- How successful is the organization at retaining people who work in priority areas?

Individual learning

Organizations are comprised of individual members. The term 'learning' refers to an outcome (something learned) as well as the process that yields the learning outcome (see Figure 5.3). If individuals do not learn then team learning and organizational learning will also be impossible.

Individuals learn through the accumulation of information, knowledge or skill, resulting in changes to their behaviour, attitudes and competency. Individual level learning is important for operational effectiveness as it can result in the development of new or enhanced skills and competency, increased knowledge, desired behaviours and increased change-readiness.

FIGURE 5.3   The three elements of learning

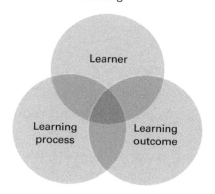

The figure shows the three elements of learning

Traditionally, organizations have focused more on training – the accumulation of specific technical or behavioural skills – rather than on learning and development. Organizations have often relied on classroom-based events as the basis for their training and learning initiatives. However, there is now a growing recognition that the process of learning is experiential – it takes place outside of the classroom at least as much – and probably more – than in formal instructional sessions.

In addition, workplace learning at the individual level occurs through activities required by organizational procedures, policies, and processes.

Because learning is an experiential process, involving activity, reflection, 'sense-making' and the application of new knowledge in applied, work situations, its effectiveness is affected by the quality of relationships between learners and their managers, colleagues, customers, suppliers and other stakeholders.

A further factor that influences the extent to which individual level learning occurs is their position within the organizational structure, the time available to them to participate in learning processes, and the nature and opportunities to learn provided by their job role. In addition, a range of different personal learning preferences, motivations and career aspirations will affect their learning outcomes.

BS PD 76006, which provides a guide to learning and development in organizations, sets out a number of important practices for managers to consider if they are to gain maximum benefit from learning at the individual level:

- Recognize that learning and development is a shared responsibility between the individual and the organization.
- Encourage individuals to learn all the time in accordance with operational objectives that are relevant to the individual as well as to their role and career aspirations.
- Identify 'triggers' for learning, such as:
  o when people are learning to do something for the first time;
  o when they are expanding the breadth and depth of what they have learned;
  o when it is important that they achieve a specific objective;
  o when they encounter problems or things do not work out in the way that was expected;
  o when changes are occurring to the workplace, role or skills that will be required.
- Assist individuals to identify their own preference and approach to learning which might vary from the approach that works best for others. Encourage people to develop their own learning skills and, where possible, organize learning activities that are appropriate for the individual's specific needs.
- Encourage individuals and their managers to regularly determine priority learning needs, taking into account the context of the individual, the organization and their current skills and knowledge.

- Allocate time, resources and support for individuals to learn through their immediate work environment.

- Make sure that learning can be put into practice so that further skills can be developed and shared in the workplace.

- Leverage the enabling features of technology to accelerate learning and development through digital resources that can be accessed at any time to suit individual circumstances and self-directed learning to suit circumstances and individual learning priorities.

INFORMATION TECHNOLOGY AS A FEATURE OF HEALTH AND SAFETY LEARNING AND DEVELOPMENT

Reframe Ltd is a small contracting business providing design and build services for larger infrastructure projects where safety is critical. Health and safety, and wider risk management, is an important priority for the organization. However, most Reframe employees work away from the head office all the time and face a wide range of environments in which different risks are always present. Centralized, classroom-based training was not feasible in such an environment.

As part of their commitment to flexible, but effective risk management and safety training, the company developed an electronic directory so that any employee, wherever they are working, can download advice and guidance relating to new practices as well as up-to-date regulations and guides on all relevant topics. The company actively encourages people to consult the directory before starting a new project so that they are confident in the risk and safety options and can challenge site practices if standards are not appropriate.

Supervisors are also briefed to ensure that potential enhancements to safety provision are discussed at monthly meetings with client organizations, and the company ensures that Reframe staff feel that they have company support from the highest levels to raise concerns and improve practices on any project with which they are involved.

This decentralized and technologically-organized approach to health, safety and risk management learning has resulted in an outstanding safety record for the company, and larger client organizations with which Reframe has worked are now considering how they might achieve similar standards. New clients can also see that Reframe take health and safety seriously, and employees recognize and value the commitment of the company to keep them safe in every working environment.

Team learning

Learning at the group level is often overlooked in work organizations, and yet most people spend much of their work-life in groups and learn from each other (consciously or unconsciously). New employees, for example, learn the 'unwritten rules' and find out about organizational culture and norms from others in their workgroup. Novice workers often learn the job from other workers and most management learning occurs through experience and networking with other managers.

Although unrecognized, team-level learning is an important contributor to organizational effectiveness as it enables team-members to co-create knowledge, share knowledge with others external to the team, and interact effectively as a feature of adaptation to changing situations. Team learning also leads to improved performance within the team, a key feature in organizational performance (Figure 5.4).

Research shows that effective team learning requires opportunities for team members to engage in practices that include knowledge sharing and knowledge 'co-construction' and, where appropriate, to feel permitted to express 'constructive conflict' (Decuyper, Dochy and Van den Bossche, 2010). It enables people to go beyond theoretical or 'brain-based' learning to understand application in practice and to further reflect and understand organizational and team-based priorities.

The quality of team leadership makes a significant difference to the likelihood that team learning will be achieved and team structure and the level of interdependence of team members are also important 'building blocks' of team learning (Decuyper, Dochy and Van den Bossche, 2010). An appropriate organizational culture will encourage team learning, but a culture where mistakes are punished and 'blame' rather than learning is prevalent will inhibit it. Team learning cannot be achieved where team members lack trust and a sense of 'psychological safety'.

As with all learning, time-related factors are important for team learning as it takes time for a group to develop into a team and for team 'dynamics' to be established. Effective teams are characterized by shared responsibilities when failures occur, but also by their commitment to increasing and optimizing their capacity to learn from both successes and failures.

As a collaborative process, team learning requires focus on a common aim. At this level, most learning occurs from experience through dialogue, discussion and 'letting go' of defensive or unconstructive conversations.

FIGURE 5.4   Individual, team and organization-wide learning

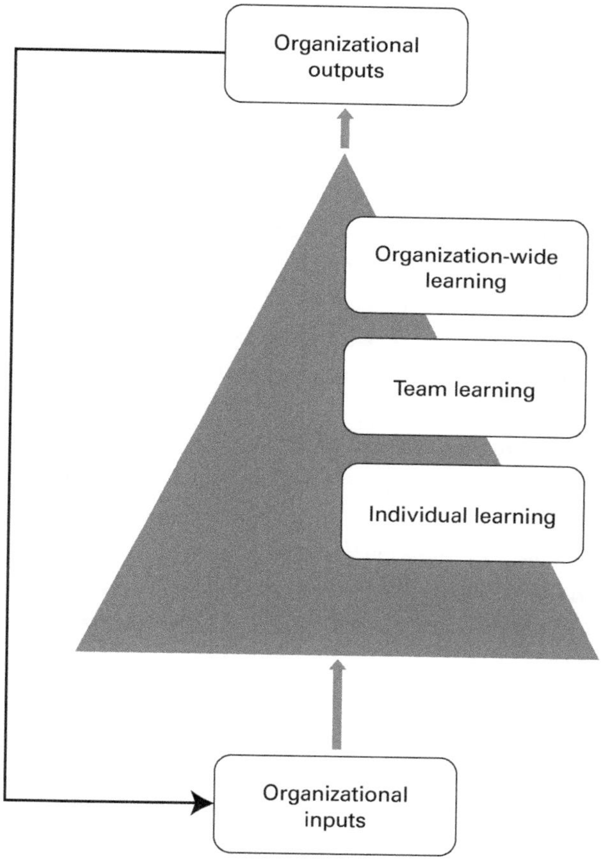

The figure shows how individual, team and organization-wide learning interrelate

Within operational systems, team learning can be facilitated by processes such as 'After Action Reviews', where the aim is to learn lessons for the future through team discussion about 'what happened, why it happened, and how to sustain strengths and improve weakness in performance'. This process involves team members in investigating a situation, and adopting a process to identify strengths and weaknesses in the procedures and activities, propose solutions where problems have occurred, identify areas of good practice to be further developed and adopt a course of action for the future.

Such a process requires appropriate learning behaviours such as reflection, openness, active participation, and critical evaluation, which can provide a basis for a commitment by the team to the application of this learning to future situations.

TEAM LEARNING IN THE HOSPITALITY SECTOR

Chillout Hotel is one of a group of three hotels providing seaside holidays for families that include provision for children's activities, as well as opportunities for adults to participate in wellness and spa treatments. However, although the hotel guests normally enjoyed a relaxed time, it was becoming apparent that staff retention at the hotel was poor (a common feature in the hospitality sector) and that employee (lack of) wellbeing was a cause for concern.

The leadership team came to realize that this situation might be tackled through a commitment to team working that was more positive, creative and entertaining. This required a serious re-think at the top of the organization to ensure that productive team working and learning behaviours would be rewarded and affirmed. To enact this change staff and senior managers were encouraged to engage in formal conversations to share insights about the work and team experience for most employees and how it might be improved.

Following these discussions, the hotel management made it possible for people to work in a range of departments, rather than being confined to one function. One employee recounted: 'I believe teamwork is helping to improve. I myself am involved in four teams and that's normal here. You can see everyone is a member in at least two to four teams at the same time.' Another highlighted: 'I have worked in nearly all the departments now ... I really understand how the place works for visitors.'

Greater flexibility of shift patterns was introduced, and managers, as well as team leaders, made a big effort to get to know people's names and situations so that team members could be confident that they could discuss any problems they faced 'at any time'. To enhance levels of trust within teams, socializing, both inside and outside work, was encouraged, and greater attention was paid to career opportunities for workers, regardless of whether they were employed to work full-time or part-time.

A team review process was introduced to discuss any issues, complaints or problems reported by guests about other visitors and this team learning process became a valued feature of team relationships where communication, idea-sharing and problem-solving behaviours were expected and encouraged.

When Chillout Hotel came to review and evaluate this change to their systems, they identified three important dimensions of team learning. First, to value the position of 'team leader'. Team leaders' informal and casual interaction, whilst centred around work, became less formal, more 'fun', and this encouraged new idea generation and application. Second, prompt sharing of information, at all levels of the organization, through briefings that take place at appropriate times is a vital feature of team learning. Third, when people have contributed ideas or new practices as an outcome of the learning process, it is important that their contribution is acknowledged and affirmed.

Team learning is often unrecognized as a feature of organizational effectiveness. It is a good example of the ways in which learning from experience and from day-to-day work practices can be achieved. The opportunity to co-create knowledge, share knowledge with others both within the team and externally, and interact effectively with colleagues can make a significant contribution to organizational effectiveness.

However, organizational culture and systems that are not conducive to team learning are also prevalent. Areas of good practice that organizations can consider, if they wish to promote more effective team learning include:

- distinguishing between team coherence and 'groupthink', where it becomes difficult for people to think or act in ways that are different from the norm;

- ensuring that responsibility for learning outcomes is shared among team members;

- encouraging team leaders not to dominate, but to welcome conversations in the team where everyone's perspective and ideas are respected and affirmed;

- encouraging team members to have confidence to express their true feelings rather than say what they think others wish to hear;

- ensuring that teams do not carry 'passengers' – those who do not participate in activities but expect to take credit for the achievements of other team members;

- discouraging 'social loafing', where people invest less commitment to the team than if they were to take on a task on their own;

- ensuring that conflict, where it occurs, is constructive and is not allowed to escalate to inhibit team performance and psychological safety.

Organization-wide learning and organizational learning

In this section the distinctive qualities of both organization-wide learning and organizational learning are identified and discussed.

Organization-wide learning

Organization-wide learning is all the activities, processes and practices, both formal and informal, through which people at all levels of the organization are able to learn and apply their learning in their work roles. Everyday learning can make an important contribution to performance at individual, work group and organizational levels. Where organization-wide learning occurs, there is more likelihood of successful problem solving and business development.

Organization-wide learning is distinct from organizational learning (considered next) as it occurs internally, within the boundaries of the organization, and without reference to learning from and with other external stakeholders such as organizational partners, suppliers, customers, clients and local communities. In many organizations, the trigger for organization-wide learning is problem solving, something which involves two elements relating to learning: the development of insights and understanding in relation to the issue under consideration, and the outcomes of that insight-development process as applied to organization structures and processes.

Organization-wide learning involves provision of, and encouragement of, a wide range of different learning methods that will suit different business and individual contexts. Some will involve off-the-job forms of learning, such as e-learning or classroom-based instruction, and others will involve one-to-one interaction, such as coaching or mentoring. Figure 5.5 illustrates some of the methods that are outlined in BS PD 76006:2017 *Guide to learning and development*, which include off-the-job and work-based forms of learning as well as individual and group-based methods.

Effective organization-wide learning does not always require high levels of financial investment, but time and other resources to ensure an effective learning environment and climate are necessary as follows.

The organization must:

- identify where learning and development is most relevant to the effectiveness of the organization and which areas of the business would benefit most from learning and development;

FIGURE 5.5   Methods of learning and development from BS PD 76006

Individual focus

Work-based	Coaching Learning on the job New starter 'buddy' systems Stretch assignments	Mentoring New starter/induction programmes Reflective learning	Off-the-job
	Leader role-modelling Team learning	Formal learning activities Technology-enhanced learning	

Group focus

The figure shows learning methods outlined in BS PD 76006:2017 *Guide to learning and development*

- equip senior managers to support the need for learning to boost performance;

- equip managers to support individuals in their learning, including providing constructive feedback opportunities;

- provide varied learning opportunities that are accessible to all individuals, as appropriate;

- encourage knowledge sharing within the organization;

- identify the most appropriate (and user-friendly) ways of gathering evidence about the strengths and weaknesses of important learning and development activities, adapting and improving them wherever possible.

Line managers must:

- provide role model support for learning activities and development processes for all individuals including identifying their own learning needs and evaluating learning and development they have undertaken;

- discuss with team members their learning needs and the application of their learning and create opportunities for team members to practise newly acquired skills;

- encourage team members to share learning with others and remove as many barriers as possible to learning and its application;

- manage the expectations of team members of how the organization can help/support learning;
- identify the level of change-readiness of individuals and prepare them for their next career move (where appropriate).

Individuals must:

- regularly speak to their manager and others in the organization who can support their learning and development;
- undertake continuous self-assessment for learning priorities achievements and future learning opportunities, reflect on learning and practice, using new or enhanced skills and knowledge;
- be willing to learn during formal and informal learning events and activities and provide constructive feedback to those who organize or facilitate learning;
- share their skills and knowledge with others.

Organizational learning

The term 'organizational learning' refers to all processes and activities involved in creating, retaining and transferring knowledge both within and beyond organization boundaries. Organizational learning is not an incidental process; it requires intentional commitment at the level of individuals, groups and the organization to use learning as a way to achieve sustainable performance through the continuous transformation of the organization.

Advocates of organizational learning suggest that organizations can benefit from this accumulation of experience, as it enables appropriate responses to changes in the internal and external environment of the organization. Garad and Gold (2018) highlight that the process of modifying organizational behaviours through the use of different learning processes, practices, methods and activities results in a 'learning-driven' organization able to systematically improve and sustain performance.

Figure 5.6 illustrates the relationship between individual, team, organization-wide learning, and organizational learning.

Other advocates have acknowledged that organizational learning is more of an aspiration than an outcome. It requires organizational systems to ensure that all people are able to access learning opportunities and are able to share and apply their learning at team and organizational levels. Organizational learning is also a social and relational process. This means

FIGURE 5.6   The relationship between individual, team, organization-wide learning, and organizational learning

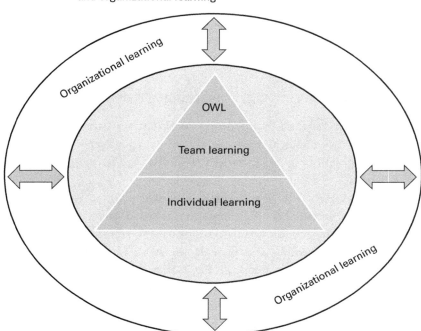

The figure shows the relationship between the different types of learning

that lack of two-way communication, reflection and feedback processes can inhibit it.

Organizational learning also relies on people valuing both formal and informal learning across functional and hierarchical levels. This might set challenges where previous assumptions must be 'unlearned', and new practices and patterns of behaviour taken up, to provide the appropriate environment in which organizational learning can flourish.

Questions that can help organizations examine the extent to which they can benefit from organizational learning include the following:

- To what extent do leaders establish and nurture a learning culture organization-wide?
- In what ways do leaders act as role models for learning?
- How evident is trust across the entire organization?
- How is teamwork encouraged and rewarded?
- How are people recognized for learning and knowledge sharing?

- What channels are in place for the organization to listen to its customers, partners and other stakeholders?.
- How, and to what extent, is feedback from all stakeholders (internal and external) considered and acted upon?

The role of technology in learning and development

Technology is an increasingly important component of work. This section examines how technological tools can contribute to effective learning and development practices in organizations at individual, team and organization-wide levels.

As indicated earlier in this chapter, the term 'learning technology' is understood in different ways, but refers to the broad range of information and communication technologies that can be used to identify learning needs, deliver and assess learning and provide the basis for organization-wide competency management systems. BS PD 76006 indicates that other terms that might be used in relation to learning technology are digital learning, e-learning, online learning, mobile learning, web-based training, televideo-conferencing and audio-conferencing.

Technology can also provide learning opportunities through online interaction via forums, blogs, emails and discussion boards. Learning technologies can be used in an asynchronous way, where different learners engage with the learning technology at different times. Alternatively, it can be organized so that groups of learners engage in the learning process at the same time. Although advocates for learning technology highlight its potential benefits, investment in such systems is only justified when technology presents the opportunity to enhance individual, team or organizational learning processes and practices.

The 'anytime, anywhere' availability of internet-enabled technology provides a convenient and flexible basis through which workers under time pressures, working non-standard hours or at remote locations, can access learning materials. Cost savings are also possible, as resources required for travel or attendance at traditional face-to-face learning events are not required. In addition, learning technologies present opportunities for self-directed and person-centred approaches to learning and development.

A further advantage of technology is the increased range of topics, depth of coverage, and learning media (via computer, mobile phone, tablet device and so on). Additionally, technology is widely used and valued by people in their daily lives for information gathering, communication and collaboration, and so may be a more familiar environment in which they can learn than would be the case with a formal classroom-based event.

Informal learning through technology is often unrecognized and goes unrecorded within the organization, but research has shown that individuals engage extensively with learning, through informal (self-directed) learning achieved using social media platforms such as YouTube, Facebook and TED talks. Other organizationally bespoke systems for learning can underpin formal processes of individual level development. These may involve interaction and facilitation with a tutor or the learner working in a self-managed way to address learning outcomes relevant to the organizational context.

Technologically enabled learning systems include:

- Mobile learning: Learning that is facilitated through the medium of any number of devices such as mobile phones, tablets and so on, which can deliver learning at the point of need.

- Collaborative learning tools: File-sharing software for networked or collaborative working can enable informal and work-based learning opportunities. Specific tools to facilitate interaction between learners to encourage knowledge sharing, reflection and the development of knowledge, understanding and skills are also available.

- Game-based learning: Systems that use elements of software-enabled games to enable learning through experience and immersion in simulations.

These forms of learning are increasingly attractive to large organizations that operate internationally or have high numbers of remote workers. In many cases some form of blended learning may be appropriate, involving the flexible use of more than one learning method. Blended learning enables individual learning to be tailored to suit the cost, time-availability and location of both the learners and the learning providers.

In addition to these forms of learning technology, research studies (Open University, 2018; Chartered Institute of Personnel and Development (CIPD), nd) have suggested that newer trends in relation to the use of technology to facilitate organization-wide learning will include:

- 'Knowledge curation' of open-access resources: Free resources are available online – for example TED Talks, YouTube and Massive Open Online Courses. Some organizations direct workers to these resources for learning which can provide cost and time advantages. Some (but not all) resources incorporate good practices for learning, such as interactivity and reflection. However, these resources are unlikely to be fully relevant to specific organizational contexts.

- Artificial intelligence (AI) tools: These are an emerging learning technology, with opportunities to incorporate both augmented reality and AI into learning and development activities.

- Learning through social networks: Technologically-enabled social networking and messaging tools, either internal or externally managed, are increasingly evident in organizational practices. These have the potential to enable collaborative learning, user-generated content and opportunities for continuous learning and reflection.

In spite of the many advantages of technology for learning, technological-based systems can be ineffective at an organizational level if they are introduced without regard for their purpose and scale. Key issues are:

- Organization-wide learning priorities: Technology as a basis for learning is appropriate to widen access and increase flexibility of provision where they are consistent with existing workflow processes and there are problems relating to hours of work and remote working.

- Organization culture: Technology can provide meaningful opportunities to promote reflection, continuous personal development, knowledge sharing, collaboration and learning from external as well as internal networks. However, where assumptions about control, regulation, governance and compliance dominate organizational culture, these benefits will not be achieved.

- Organizational strategy for learning: As indicated already in this chapter, organizations invest in learning and development with different assumptions and expectations. These also influence the ways in which technological systems can support and enable learning. Where information dissemination is a priority, standardized e-learning 'modules' with a focus on instructor content may be appropriate. However, where deeper learning, understanding and application is required, web-based learning with opportunities for interaction with other learners and feedback processes will be necessary.

In summary, the fast-changing nature of technological development means that organizations committed to integrating learning and technology find that the costs of adoption, implementation and maintenance can be high. Technologies may also be superseded and can be rendered obsolete. However, used appropriately learning technologies can be more cost- and time-effective than traditional classroom-based interventions. Clarity about the purpose of technology for learning is required at organizational level, and the appropriate selection of technological tools to achieve this purpose is a priority.

The following steps can be helpful to organizations in deciding whether to move forward with technology to facilitate learning and planning the implementation process:

1 Determine the level of need and demand – what learning is currently available and what benefits would be gained from using technology? Who supports the proposed change? How would people find out about it? How might end users be involved in the decision-making process?

2 Decide whether technology is appropriate to meet the need you have identified – how large and geographically distributed is your group of intended learners? What barriers might they experience accessing resources via technology? Is it appropriate to have technology only, or some form of blended learning? What is the expected life span of the learning need and the technology you are considering? How frequently will it need to be updated? Does data on learner progress, results and completion rates need to be collected, and who needs this information?

3 Find out what already exists – which resources are already available or in development? Can you share or re-use existing resources?

4 Develop a specification of requirements, and give as much information as possible so that developers or purchasers can have clarity. Specify how often updating will be required.

5 Be clear about the success measures that will be applied to judge the effectiveness of the resource – this may include usage data, learner satisfaction, impact on practice, and/or time/cost savings. Establish a baseline that can be measured against once the learning resource is being used.

Summary

The standards outlined in this chapter identify the importance of alignment between learning and development activities and organizational strategic objectives. However, while the benefits of learning and development are well established, studies show a pattern of skills shortages and a lack of effective learning systems in many organizations (OECD, nd). Many organizations overlook the potential power of effective learning. Where systems are not in place, the evidence suggests that workplace learning opportunities are overlooked. This approach leaves many learning needs unidentified and unmet.

Many organizations do not have the resources for a well-established training function. However, the practices highlighted in this chapter can provide a framework through which managers can develop the approach of their organization to make better use of learning. In addition to individual performance and capability improvements, effective learning systems can lead to increased levels of workforce engagement, organizational resilience and adaptability, talent development and organizational capability.

Future directions for standards in learning and development

Work undertaken over the last five years at ISO and at national standards body levels highlights the importance of developing standards that relate to HRM and human capital management and development. Patterns of 'skills obsolescence' and a requirement to re-structure work patterns to take account of increasing automation and new business directions require investment in learning at individual, team and organization-wide levels to provide for organizational and individual resilience to these factors. Although issues of learning and development are well represented in existing standards, knowledge of these standards is limited.

Recently, ISO have approved a proposal to develop an international standard in learning and development. This work will focus on clarifying the value of learning and development. It will promote organizational practice that is aligned with current evidence and research and which contributes to individual, group and organizational performance.

This standard will also provide the basis for the generation of a common terminology about learning and development to enable effective management and continuous improvement with the potential to aid in benchmarking and measuring effectiveness as a feature of human capital practices.

References and further resources

Becker, G S (2002) The age of human capital, in Lazear, E P (ed.) *Education in the twenty-first century*, Hoover Institution Press, Palo Alto, CA

BSI (2015) BS 76000:2015 *Human Resource. Valuing People. Management System. Requirements and Guidance* https://shop.bsigroup.com/ProductDetail/?pid=000000000030298954 (archived at https://perma.cc/N2JR-LRA9)

BSI (2017) BS PD 76006:2017 *Guide to learning and development* https://shop.bsigroup.com/ProductDetail/?pid=000000000030350673 (archived at https://perma.cc/H5ZF-JYDA)

CIPD. Digital learning factsheet, *CIPD* www.cipd.co.uk/knowledge/fundamentals/people/development/digital-learning-factsheet (archived at https://perma.cc/NL5U-D7WF)

Decuyper, S, Dochy, F, and Van den Bossche, P (2010) Grasping the dynamic complexity of team learning: an integrative model for effective team learning in organizations, *Educational Research Review*, 5 (2) pp 111–33

Garad, A and Gold, J (2018) *The Learning Driven Organization Model: An ecosystem for organizational learning*, independently published

ISO (1999) ISO/IEC/JTC 36 *Information technology for learning, education and training*, www.iso.org/committee/45392.html (archived at https://perma.cc/QU5Q-YEQT)

ISO (1999) ISO 10015:1999 *Quality management – Guidelines for training* www.iso.org/standard/21231.html (archived at https://perma.cc/9VZS-Q5B2)

ISO (2017) ISO 29993:2017 *Learning services outside formal education – Service requirements*, www.iso.org/standard/70357.html (archived at https://perma.cc/GT82-9JWR)

ISO. ISO 14000 family – Environmental management, *ISO* www.iso.org/iso-14001-environmental-management.html (archived at https://perma.cc/DDP4-MEHM)

ISO. ISO 9000 family – Quality management, *ISO* www.iso.org/iso-9001-quality-management.html (archived at https://perma.cc/AXB8-U8XV)

Jacobs, R L and Wang, B [accessed 5 April 2019] A Proposed Interpretation of the ISO 10015 and Implications for HRD Theory and Research, *Ohio State University* https://files.eric.ed.gov/fulltext/ED504782.pdf (archived at https://perma.cc/5C5X-4WR8)

OECD. The Future of Education and Skills: Education 2030, *OECD* www.oecd.org/education/2030/E2030%20Position%20Paper%20 (archived at https://perma.cc/NBD9-VPNF)(05.04.2018).pdf

Open University (2018) *Trends in Learning 2018* www.open.ac.uk/business/apprenticeships/blog/trends-learning-report-2018 (archived at https://perma.cc/96EL-87PN)

6

Diversity and inclusion
Anne McBride and Helge Hoel

Introduction

This chapter will focus on the objectives, policies, practices, behaviours and measures required to facilitate greater organizational diversity and inclusion (D&I). Whether called equal opportunities, managing diversity or the more recent concept of D&I, each of these interventions has been created to encourage greater D&I in organizations. Despite decades of initiatives (and legislation) worldwide, however, individuals are still excluded from a number of opportunities to fully engage with organizations – whether as employees, suppliers or stakeholders (Fairness at Work Research Centre (FairWRC), 2015).

Exclusion from organizational interactions is often associated with belonging to a particular social group (such as women) or several intersecting social groups (such as being both a woman and a member of a minority ethnic group). As studies indicate, exclusion for these reasons is a waste of resources – it ignores talent inside and outside the organization and it creates unnecessary conflict and stress for employees. Such outcomes run counter to the human capital approach to managing organizations (FairWRC, 2015; Deloitte, 2017). Developed as a longer-term, more sustainable means of managing, a human capital approach focuses on valuing people in terms of their actual or potential contribution to the organization.

This chapter identifies the strategic and operational actions for organizations wishing to minimize the negative consequences of a lack of organizational diversity and sets out a human capital approach to D&I. It provides examples from a national standard (BS 76005) to value people through D&I. It is also informed by a broad evidence-based literature review (FairWRC, 2015).

CHAPTER OBJECTIVES

This chapter sets out to:

- describe different forms of exclusion and discrimination that people may experience;
- discuss how national and international standards and regulations can provide guidance for effective management practice in relation to D&I (using examples from BS 76005);
- discuss the opportunities and challenges of adopting this range of objectives, policies, practices, behaviours and measures;
- propose ways of evaluating the success of management processes associated with D&I, and enabling continuous improvement.

Key terms

In this chapter, the following terms (presented in alphabetical order) are used as follows:

Business case: This is a concept that describes how organizations value individual differences as commodities to be attracted and exchanged for value. The business case for recruiting individuals from minority ethnic backgrounds, for example, has been promoted as a means of enabling the mirroring of the demographic make-up of potential consumers, capturing the knowledge of different cultures and contributing to organizational renewal and innovation.

Diversity ISO 30400:2016: *Human resource management – Vocabulary* defines diversity as 'characteristics of differences and similarities between people'. Two supplementary notes are included in this definition:

- 'Diversity includes factors that influence the identities and perspectives that people bring when interacting at work.'

- 'Diversity can foster learning from others who are not the same, about dignity, respect and inclusiveness for everyone, and about creating workplace environments and practices that foster learning from others to gain advantages of diverse perspectives.' (ISO, 2016: 9.1)

Equal opportunities: This term refers to a type of management initiative or legislation that requires all candidates and employees to be treated equally. It is a means of eliminating discrimination against members of particular social groups and is often motivated by a desire for social justice.

Human capital management (HCM): Managing from a 'human capital' approach involves valuing people in terms of their actual (or potential) contribution flowing from their unique skills (Chartered Institute of Personnel and Development (CIPD), 2019). When applied to D&I, this approach entertains the notion that a diversity of human capital can lead to the creation and maintenance of social capital within the organization.

Inclusion: Inclusion is defined in ISO 30400 as the 'practice of including all stakeholders in organizational contexts'. The standard further notes that 'stakeholders from different groups are to be accepted and welcomed (eg offered opportunities on the basis of abilities, talents and skills)' (ISO, 2016: 9.5). This definition is used in BS 76005 (D&I) with two additional notes. The first note identifies a range of factors that can lead to exclusion (such as language/dialect or bodily appearance), and the second indicates that embedding an inclusive culture requires a transparent approach that goes beyond legal compliance.

Intersectionality: This term can refer to the intersection of oppressions (eg racism and sexism) and/or the intersection of social groupings (eg as defined by ethnicity and gender). It is a useful means of identifying the complex and subtle ways in which disadvantage is sometimes manifest in relation to these intersecting characteristics, and has become an important consideration in the discussion of diversity.

Managing diversity:	This term refers to a range of management interventions designed to encourage diversity of individuals, rather than only applying to those in protected groups. This approach has been criticized by concentrating on all the ways in which individuals differ, without referring to issues of equality and fairness, and some argue that it risks diversity becoming 'meaningless' (Tatli, 2011).
Protected groups:	This term refers to those social groupings against whom it is unlawful to discriminate (eg in the UK, this covers age, gender reassignment, marriage and civil partnership status, pregnancy and maternity, disability, race, religion and belief, sex, and sexual orientation).
Social groupings:	This term is defined in BS 76005 as 'groups of people recognized by law, self-identification or self-organization, who share a set of similar characteristics that are defined through demographic attributes for societal exclusion'. The term may include protected groups (noted above) as well as those who might share characteristics but who are not protected by legislation (such as those sharing similar economic backgrounds).
Top management:	Terms like 'management' and 'leadership' are often used interchangeably. Since 2012 ISO has prescribed how ISO management system standards should be written (ISO, nd), and this includes core definitions for words that are frequently used. Top management is one such term, and in this chapter, following this document, the term 'top management' is taken to refer to the person or group of people who direct and control an organization at the highest level. In a non-hierarchical structure, top management implies ultimate decision-makers, who might be business owners.
Under-representation:	This is defined in BS 76005 as the 'disproportionate absence or recognition of people from social groupings', with a note that the 'under-representation of social groupings can be an indication of exclusion and could lead to subsequent disadvantage'. This is a useful way of ensuring that diversity can refer both to individuals and to groups of individuals who might share similarities.

Acknowledgements

The standard BS 76005 for valuing people through D&I was developed by a drafting panel sponsored by the British Standards Institution (BSI) consisting of fifteen members with expertise in the area of D&I. They represented organizations within private industry such as the construction and transport industries, small businesses and management consultancies; the public sector including representatives from Universities; and key industry bodies such as the CIPD, the Advisory, Conciliation and Arbitration Service (ACAS) and the Chartered Institute of Management (CIM).

Existing standards

A number of standards exist that identify the need for organizations to develop holistic approaches to the long-term sustainability of their operations through the provision of fair employment practices and social responsibility to the communities in which they operate. A component part of these standards is their reference to diversity as a key objective. Four notable standards are identified below, including one BSI standard devoted specifically to D&I:

- ISO 26000:2010 *Guidance on social responsibility*: This international standard is intended to provide organizations with a framework that will guide them to contributing to sustainable development. It provides guidance on seven core subjects. A number of these inform the standards in relation to the area of D&I, such as labour practices and human rights.

- ISO 27501:2019 *The human-centred organization – Guidance for managers*: This international standard provides seven principles of human-centredness that enable organizations to reflect on their impact on customers, employees and the wider community. In relation to D&I, the first principle specifically indicates that individual differences should be considered as an organizational strength. Another relevant principle indicates that ensuring health, safety and wellbeing are business priorities.

- BS 76000:2015 *Human Resource. Valuing People. Management System. Requirements and Guidance*: This national standard sets out a number of principles for valuing people in an organization (and is further discussed in Chapters 2 and 3). The standard indicates that 'valuing people' goes beyond the calculation of monetary value and short-term returns on investment. It provides organizations with the means of developing their own objectives, behaviours and measures for embedding strategic, long-term thinking about the value of their people into their management systems. The standard for D&I was developed as a component of the management system, visualized in BS 76000. It indicates that for organizations to realize the full value that people bring to an organization, they need to value people through D&I.

- BS 76005:2017 *Valuing People Through Diversity and Inclusion: Code of Practice for Organizations*: This British standard provides a framework and recommendations for valuing people through D&I. It recommends a holistic approach to valuing D&I to capture individual difference, life experience, social context and historical, economic and cultural exclusion. This standard also encourages dialogue on these issues with a broad range of stakeholders and indicates an approach to take to recognize, value and embed diversity within its operations and relationships with customers/clients, supply chains and communities.

In summary, this chapter identifies the actions that organizations need to take to maximize the full potential of diversity within, and outside, their organizations. International and national standards indicate that organizations need to engage with broader, socially responsible actions that minimize the risk of their organizations being unsustainable in the future. D&I is an essential part of this longer-term thinking.

Taking action in the area of D&I requires organizations to going beyond earlier initiatives that have focused on either the needs of legally protected groups, or the needs of the business. This broader perspective of D&I is indicated in the full definition used in the standard BS 76005.

Employment experiences of exclusion and discrimination

Two-thirds of chief executive officers in Deloitte's 2017 Global Human Capital Trends survey identified diversity as an important issue. The global aspect of many large companies makes 'religious, gender, generational, and other types of diversity a business reality' (Deloitte, 2017: 109). There is also a risk to team cohesion, pay equity and employee engagement if D&I is ignored.

Five examples are provided below of the inequalities that can exist in organizations and wider society. Evidence is also presented of the huge loss of potential when the opportunity is not taken to facilitate the greater diversity of employees (FairWRC, 2015).

1 At a national level, states are starting to identify the economic cost of discrimination. For example, a shortfall of between 3 per cent and 14 per cent of gross domestic product (GDP) is indicated as the 'cost' of discrimination in France (France Stratégie, nd). The under-representation of people from black and minority ethnic backgrounds is estimated to cost the UK economy 1.3 per cent of GDP in lost potential and productivity (whilst they are out of work or working in jobs where they are overqualified and underutilized) (Department for Business, Energy and Industrial Strategy (BEIS), 2017).

2 Whilst many parents may consider it vital to be able to reduce working hours for a period, or take time out, any career break or period with reduced working hours is likely to come at a cost. Many part-time jobs are relatively low paid and even when reduced hours are negotiated within a previously full-time job, the part-time member of staff may be given different tasks to perform and have more limited chances of promotion.

3 54 per cent of Europeans believe that a candidate's age, if over 55 years, would be a disadvantage in seeking employment. Half of the respondents in the same survey were also worried that employers tend to favour people in their 20s.

4 Of particular concern in the UK is that entry into professions has become significantly more difficult for less privileged people during the past 30 years. Research indicates that diversity can be limited when high proportions of interns are on traditional, full-time, degree-based entry pathways and attend one of the top universities.

5 A secular workplace can contain in-built discrimination, such that it might follow Christian practices but cannot easily accommodate, say, Islamic holidays, which might ultimately put potential candidates off applying for some jobs/organizations.

Embedding D&I in organizational practices

Encouraging organizations to increase D&I is nothing new. In a number of countries, from the 1970s onwards, equal opportunities legislation has been used to eliminate discrimination against members of particular social groups. Whilst this was a necessary condition for change, it has never been sufficient. The concept of 'managing diversity' was a subsequent attempt to go beyond the equal opportunities approach, and encourage managers to value difference as a way of gaining competitive advantage. The emphasis on the business case for diversity, however, attracted much criticism for privileging managerial interests. This approach also infers that diversity will not be pursued if there is no material advantage to be gained from it.

As the above statistics indicate, neither approach has led to the elimination of inequality. It has been argued that 'organizations do not know how to translate the diversity discourse into practical interventions that are progressive and inclusive and go beyond legal compliance' (Tatli, 2011).

The remainder of this section illustrates how a standard is an effective mechanism for presenting practical interventions that any organization can take in the area of D&I. It also illustrates the holistic nature of change envisaged within a human capital approach to D&I.

The four components noted below are key to developing effective management practice in the area of D&I (and are included in BS 76005). Each component is described below to enable managers to start addressing four essential questions:

- Who is responsible for leading change?
- Where do we start?
- Which stakeholders should be involved?
- What activities should be included?

Who is responsible for leading change? – top management

Leadership commitment is an integral part of a human capital approach to managing people. A number of studies identify the importance of leadership in achieving meaningful change in the area of D&I (FairWRC, 2015). This has been translated into recommendations within the BS 76005 standard:

1 There needs to be 'a commitment to value people who work on behalf of the organization and to meeting the recommendations of this standard which is made and supported at the highest level' (BS 76005:2017: 1).

2 There is a need for 'leadership commitment in actively supporting a culture that acknowledges the value of diversity and inclusion' (BS 76005:2017: 3).

3 It is possible to recommend objectives, policies, practices and behaviours that embed leadership commitment to D&I (BS 76005:2017, 24).

4 Leaders need to put in place mechanisms to enable organizations to assess the context of their business/organization.

Where do we start? – assessment of context

Tackling D&I in a comprehensive manner can appear daunting and an important first step must be to consider the context of the organization in relation to D&I. In keeping with the human capital approach to valuing people, this requires organizations to identify the opportunities and risks that are related to increasing D&I in relation to (i) people working in and on behalf of their organizations, and (ii) a number of other stakeholders (BS 76005:2017: B1, 25).

Once this assessment has taken place, the organization can then establish objectives for increasing D&I within the organization and start planning the necessary changes, providing the necessary support and identifying how performance can be measured and evaluated (see later in this chapter for further details on evaluation).

The following questions may be useful as a basis for senior management discussion and commitment:

- Who are the key internal and external stakeholders who can affect the effectiveness of an inclusive D&I plan?

- How can key internal stakeholders across the organization be engaged in the D&I agenda, so that D&I goes beyond the remit of human resource management (HRM)?

- How can the value of D&I and its potential impact be clearly communicated to:
  - clients and customers?
  - supply chain partners?
  - local and wider communities within which the organization operates?

- How consistent and coherent are current behaviours, practices and policies that have implications for D&I? To what extent do people at all levels of the organization have confidence to challenge the status quo?

- What new commitments do organizational leaders need to make to a human capital approach to D&I?

Which stakeholders should be involved? – multiple stakeholders

Diversity management should involve multiple stakeholders both outside and inside the organization to ensure a move away from the narrow managerial objectives noted above. Development of BS 76005 shows that it is possible to identify objectives, policies, processes, practices and behaviours that support D&I in relation to:

- the organization that is implementing D&I;
- customers/clients of the organization;
- supply chain partners of the organization;
- communities with which the organization engages.

Each of the above stakeholders is identified in the standard's 'framework for valuing people through diversity and inclusion' (BS 76005:2017: 2). A normative framework for establishing D&I with each stakeholder group external to the organization is also included in the standard. These frameworks are contained in separate annexes, with each beginning with a commentary and rationale for establishing relationships with the stakeholder group.

For example, the framework for establishing relationships with supply chain partners (BS 76005:2017: 30) states:

> By taking an inclusive approach to procurement and commercial relationships, organizations can acquire a leadership position in influencing change in the communities where they operate... By aligning strategic objectives through communication, engagement and contracting, greater outcomes can be delivered. Addressing risks such as skills shortages, changing demographics and divided communities might provide the resilience and sustainability needed to build longevity into both the organization and its supply chain partners.

It is recommended that D&I activities are developed with each stakeholder group. These activities can be organized around a core set relating to the following activities, with examples provided below for each stakeholder group:

- communication;
- consulting;
- exploring further potential;
- commitment to improve.

CUSTOMERS/CLIENTS

Good practice can be vulnerable to change if clients use their financial power to insist on contradictory practices (such as working late) (FairWRC, 2015).

It is therefore important to enter into cycles of 'consulting, responding, aligning and innovating to identify shared opportunities and risks for organizations and their customers' (BS 76005:2017: 28). Also recommended is the informing of customers/clients 'of the intentions of the organization to value people through diversity and inclusion' and the agreeing shared goals in D&I (BS 76005:2017: 28). Suggestions for exploring further potential are provided (such as two-way mentoring and shared event hosting).

The commitment to improve processes includes a recommendation to develop a suite of performance indicators to achieve common goals for D&I.

SUPPLY CHAIN PARTNERS

Any attempt to increase D&I needs to be applicable to sub-contracting employers as well as employees. D&I also needs to be a recommended practice for procurement within supply chains – such that procurers are encouraged to think of the diversity of their suppliers, as well of the work-forces of their suppliers.

Whilst some organizations are limited in the extent to which they can control the activities of sub-contractors, good practice is for organizations to satisfy themselves of the 'competence of commercial partners to under-stand, control and monitor their performance with regards to diversity and inclusion'.

Where an organization believes that a supply chain partner lacks under-standing or resource in this respect, those organizations should put mechanisms in place to share their policies. For example, procurement can include a 'suitable D&I policy' and an intention (for large companies) to monitor and report on workforce diversity. Supply chain partners can also be encouraged to work together to improve workforce and supplier diver-sity by, for example, planning job swaps and two-way mentoring.

THE ENERGY SECTOR: EDF ENERGY

This energy company provides a publicly available Supplier's Guide to Diversity and Inclusion. The guide notes D&I is central to their vision, mission and ambitions, and sets out seven principles for working with EDF. Alongside these is reference to how that principle is embedded into EDF's practices and the expectations of EDF's suppliers in respect of that principle. Each principle is accompanied with a series of questions that a supplier organization is asked to consider, for example:

- 'Has your executive team committed to D&I?';
- 'Do you have a working environment that values individual difference?'

COMMUNITIES

Studies indicate that developing links with, and within, communities is a key aspect of widening participation in organizations (McBride and Mustchin, 2013 – see case study). Such activities can become embedded in organizational practice, such as the following recommendation:

> Some organizations include community work in social responsibilities strategies, others also seek to reach outside of their business for more philanthropic reasons, some realize that community work can help in product or service development or to provide career enhancing opportunities for their own people. An effective approach is one that understands the value of combining a number of these objectives. (BS 76005:2017: 32)

It is important to develop D&I action plans before any communities are involved, and that once started, 'effective engagement should be ongoing, planned and properly resourced' (BS 76005:2017: 33). A checklist of good practice ideas is provided in BS 76005: 33:

- public meetings in communities;
- workforce volunteering days;
- open days and site visits to promote careers within the organization;
- inclusion of engagement activities in annual reports.

THE HEALTH CARE SECTOR: A HOSPITAL EMPLOYER WITHIN THE NATIONAL HEALTH SERVICE (NHS), ENGLAND

This employer was located in a deprived inner-city area with high levels of unemployment. An explicit objective of the organization was to provide a 'Health Village' for the local community and support health gains through increasing economic activity amongst local people. A strategy for achieving this was attracting the unemployed and socially excluded into the organization in a variety of ways.

The hospital established pre-employment and volunteering schemes to attract staff to entry-level jobs. In partnership with the local authority, and using monies from a neighbourhood renewal scheme, the hospital set up an on-site job brokerage service that facilitated enquiries from members of the community. For example, if a woman had never worked or was a newly arrived immigrant wishing to work, they could join a community-based accredited programme provided by the hospital that promoted awareness of local health services, family health and introduced them to employment prospects in health and social care. The employer also trained staff working for sub-contractors as a recruitment avenue for direct employment in the NHS and provided a series of progression opportunities for its existing staff.

The employer believed their strategies enabled them to now be seen as 'the place to be'. Turnover had fallen by two percentage points in the previous year and the vacancy rate had fallen from 16 per cent to 10 per cent.

What activities should be included? The life-cycle of engagement

If D&I is to be an enabler of learning and growth, it needs to cover a whole range of activities, such as ensuring opportunities for learning and development, job quality, ethical management, health, safety and wellbeing, voice and representation. One way of addressing the life-cycle of engagement with organizations, be it employees and/or potential suppliers, is to conceptualize it as:

- 'getting in/starting a relationship';
- 'staying in/continuing the relationship';
- 'moving on/leaving the relationship' (BS 76005:2017: 2).

Framing normative activities within this life-cycle framework is an attempt to develop understandable, practical interventions (Tatli, 2011). It is also a way of sharing the responsibility for D&I across the organization so that D&I does not depend on the presence of diversity practitioners.

The life-cycle of engagement is embedded in the standard through the drafting of three chapters (see below) that identify the relevant objectives, policies, processes, practices and behaviours pertinent to that part of the cycle. To further embed this implementation across the broader stakeholder groups noted above, each recommendation needs to be:

- implemented in the organization;
- communicated with customers/clients;
- the subject of contracts with supply chain partners;
- a focus of engagement with communities (BS 76005:2017: 7).

GETTING IN/STARTING THE RELATIONSHIP

It is possible to set out practices designed to help an organization 'minimize bias in recruitment and selection such that it is fair and accessible and better able to attract and acquire a skilled, talented and diverse workforce' (BS 76005:2017: 7; see also Hoel and McBride, 2017). Normative recommendations can include reference to:

- job design;
- job requirements and candidate expectations;
- the candidate search and shortlisting process;
- selection process;
- appointment decisions and feedback.

More detailed recommendations are, for example, that managers can widen participation to entry-level jobs and graduate professions by the decisions they make and the diversity of pathways they create. Likewise, given that poor-quality jobs are not equally distributed between social groups, D&I needs to be taken into account when designing jobs and determining job requirements (FairWRC, 2015).

STAYING IN/CONTINUING THE RELATIONSHIP

Organizations are encouraged to 'communicate, consult, engage and influence stakeholders in valuing and increasing the diversity of people staying and developing within organizations and ongoing commercial relationships'(BS 76005:2017: 12). Normative recommendations include reference to:

- induction;
- appearance;
- job quality;
- working time;
- pay and reward;
- promotion;
- performance appraisal;
- support mechanisms;
- learning and development;
- relationships;

- voice and representation;
- health, safety and wellbeing.

When employees have a satisfactory work/life balance, for example, they are a healthier and more contented workforce, with business gains possible in terms of productivity, retention, reduced absenteeism and the reduced use of health care benefits, as well as the development of skills by other workers through temporary coverage or job enlargement resulting from the reorganization of work tasks (FairWRC, 2015).

Workplaces should be 'free from abuse, harassment, bullying and violence from any source' (BS 76005:2017: 16). For example, research has identified disabled workers (and those with learning difficulties and social/emotional disabilities in particular), gay, lesbian and bisexuals and younger workers as being at particular risk. In terms of sexuality, women, lesbians and female bisexuals have been found to be at particular elevated risk of bullying and harassment, thus emphasizing the need to analyze this using an intersectional focus which recognises individuals belong to multiple identity groups which may shape their risk of workplace bullying (FairWRC, 2015).

MOVING ON/LEAVING THE RELATIONSHIP

Organizations need to be sure that people are leaving for constructive reasons, rather than because of the prejudices of others. For example, older workers can be subject to prejudices, and there is a danger that some managerial interventions (eg performance appraisal) in organizations are used to manage older people out of the organization. Similarly, firms who employ diverse candidates need to ensure that those candidates are not leaving because they do not feel that they belong. Confidential exit interviews should be conducted to obtain feedback on policies aimed at valuing people, and statistical information about leavers monitored to identify potential exclusions or trends (FairWRC, 2015).

Organizations should check that any formal arrangements for leaving (such as redundancy or dismissals) adhere to recommendations for D&I and do not support patterns that may be detrimental to maintaining diversity. Succession planning needs to take account of 'the desirability of achieving and maintaining diversity at every level of the organization' (BS 76005:2017, 22).

The holistic nature of the human capital approach to D&I means that there are a number of issues for management to consider in the short and longer term regarding which stakeholders to involve (and when), and which activities to include and consider. Table 6.1 includes an indicative checklist which sets out some initial questions that managers may wish to consider in relation to D&I.

TABLE 6.1   Indicative checklist of D&I issues to consider across the life-cycle of employee engagement

	Getting in	Staying in	Moving on
Organization	Are you monitoring the applications and recruitment of staff in relation to D&I? Have you considered whether the way a job is designed might be deterring some individuals from applying?	What mechanisms do you have in place to ensure that employees have a satisfactory work/life balance; that they are free from abuse and harassment?	Do you know the impact on D&I of individuals moving on from the organization?
Customers/clients	Are your clients aware of your D&I intentions? Is there any potential for you to work with your clients to improve your recruitment process?	Are your clients making demands on your staff that are contrary to your D&I values? What mechanisms exist for you to be made aware of this?	Is it ever necessary to include customers and clients in redundancy, dismissals, resignations and retirement decisions to ensure that they are in-keeping with your D&I policy?
Supply chain	Are your suppliers aware of your D&I intentions? Do you know about the recruitment and selection processes of your suppliers, or about the diversity of their workforce?	How are you including D&I considerations in your procurement processes for sub-contracted staff?	Do you know about the processes of your suppliers in relation to redundancy, dismissals, resignations and retirement?

TABLE 6.1   *continued*

	Getting in	Staying in	Moving on
Communities	Do you have a strategy and action plan for engaging with the communities in which you are based that relates to the recruitment of the workforce?	Do you have a strategy and action plan for engaging with the communities in which you are based that relates to the wellbeing of the workforce?	Do you have a strategy and action plan for engaging with the communities in which you are based that relates to the retirement of staff?

The table shows D&I issues to consider at each of the three stages of employee engagement

Opportunities and challenges of adopting the D&I standard

Although a British national standard focused on D&I is relatively newly developed, and an international standard is under development at the time of going to press, initial experiences indicate a range of opportunities as well as challenges that organizations should anticipate when they come to move forward in this area of practice.

Opportunities

BROADER INVOLVEMENT OF STAKEHOLDERS

This standard has been explicitly written so that it can provide opportunities for the involvement of a broad number and range of stakeholders. This enables it to link internally to the engagement agenda, whilst also enabling it to link to communities and a broader corporate social responsibility (CSR) agenda – including influencing change in supply chains. Given the broad uptake of CSR, linking the standards to this approach could also make it easier to champion diversity work in non-traditional areas.

For example, championing sexual orientation equality and diversity work through the CSR agenda can be an effective way to negotiate a path through global and local tensions of difference (FairWRC, 2015).

PROVIDING THE OPPORTUNITY TO EVALUATE, REPORT AND COMPARE PROGRESS

The development of an explicit national standard, with a framework for valuing people through D&I and an integral framework for systematic performance evaluation, provides the potential for measuring (and then benchmarking) organizational progress against that of other similar operations/businesses as a way of encouraging ongoing focus and involvement.

MOVING FROM A FOCUS ON D&I TO 'THE WAY WE DO THINGS HERE'

As indicated above, the development of this standard around the life-cycle of engagement with organizations – whether as employee or supplier – enables the value of D&I to be embedded across an organization and associated business operations, and be part of everyday operations (Hoel and McBride, 2017), as opposed to only being the remit of the diversity practitioner (Tatli, 2011).

Challenges

ORGANIZATIONAL SIZE AND LIMITED ORGANIZATIONAL RESOURCES

Although the standard is written with large and small organizations in mind, the broad, comprehensive and formal approach may initially seem overwhelming and even irrelevant to many small and microbusinesses where a management approach to D&I is often piecemeal, informal and possibly unplanned. It is therefore important to emphasize that this standard does not require wholesale adoption where operation, reach and local context suggest that the letter of the standard does not apply. Instead, the standard speaks to a particular way of management thinking and acting which, where harnessed, should bring positive outcomes for the organization and its current and prospective stakeholders.

RESISTANCE TO POSITIVE ACTION WHERE DEEMED ESSENTIAL FOR SUCCESSFUL IMPLEMENTATION

In terms of a life-cycle approach, at the 'getting in' stage, positive action may be used to ensure widening participation for example through targeted recruitment and preparation or training of prospective job applicants prior to the selection process to enhance their chance of success. In contrast to positive discrimination, positive action is meant to provide a more equal playing field for groups frequently excluded of certain type of jobs or from the workplace altogether, rather than giving them any advantages during the selection process (Hoel and McBride, 2017).

Equally, during the 'staying in' stage, positive action may include preparation for promotion by means of workshop and/or training initiatives to enhance successful promotion and counteract self-doubt and defeatism. It is argued that, there is often an 'ongoing power struggle of competing approaches' to diversity and a number of actors wishing to define the limits and 'rules of the field' (Tatli, 2011) To avoid any backlash from competing actors or employees, such initiatives, albeit targeted at underrepresented or previously excluded groups or individuals, could be made open for anyone.

INHERENT TENSIONS OR CONFLICTS BETWEEN MANAGEMENT AND WORKERS

Although the standard builds on an approach that emphasizes the intrinsic value of all employees, underlying potential conflict between workers and managers associated with the labour process and the managerial prerogative are likely to surface around issues such as staffing and remuneration processes. Equally, whilst the standard promotes justice and dignity, such ideals may be compromised by strict adherence to (self-) imposed performance targets and lopsided understanding of flexibility and flexible working practices, paying little attention to the needs of workers (FairWRC, 2015).

These tensions could be exacerbated by the response of management. Without top management buy-in and long-term commitment, fundamental change in respect of D&I cannot be implemented. In addition, simply paying lip service to change is likely to back-fire and may undermine any progress in the longer term. Likewise, the success of the standard relies on line management commitment and competencies. This reiterates the importance of developing a management system to manage change. In the absence of planning and support, a lack of resources, competing priorities and lack of personal commitment to the ideals of the standard may all militate against successful implementation and uptake of the standard (Hoel and McBride, 2017).

Monitoring, evaluation and improvement

Another feature integral to the human capital approach to managing people – and a core element of BS 76000 – is the need to monitor and evaluate the impact of policies and practice and develop feedback mechanisms to support continual improvement. The standard uses the term 'performance evaluation' to encompass desired elements of monitoring, evaluation and improvement. It is recommended that performance evaluation is embedded in at least three ways:

1 The development of a systematic approach to 'measuring, monitoring, analyzing and evaluating performance in relation to diversity and inclusion' (BS 76005:2017: 3).

2 The use of internal audit, management review and continual improvement.

3 The measurement of performance across key areas of recommended activity (BS 76005:2017, 35).

Performance can be monitored in relation to each stakeholder group, for each component of life-cycle engagement. Good practice also includes performance evaluation of the leadership, management and behaviours required to embed D&I. When measuring the breadth and depth of the workforce affected by the measures being adopted, it is important to be aware of the contractual status of those included in the measurement.

One way of measuring the extent that inclusion goes beyond those directly employed is to consider the experience of those on non-standard or external contracts. For example, at the point of recruitment one process measure that is useful is the adoption by the organization of a broader set of candidate search and shortlisting processes and an appropriate outcome measure is the diversity of candidates and new recruits.

In addition, with specific relevance to engagement with the community as a feature of D&I, a process measure might be the percentage of candidate search and shortlisting processes linked with the community, and an outcome measure might be the percentage of candidates attracted through community links.

Summary

CEOs have identified diversity as an important issue (Deloitte, 2017). Developing a holistic approach to valuing D&I in the form of a standard provides an explicit means of prompting dialogue on these issues with a broad range of stakeholders and providing practical interventions that are 'progressive and inclusive and go beyond legal compliance' (Tatli, 2011).

Both strategic and operational actions provide the basis through which organizations can minimize the negative consequences of a lack of organizational diversity and progressively adopt a human capital approach to D&I. Emerging national and international standards provide an important source of evidence-based guidance to organizations committing to enhance and continuously improve their approach to D&I.

References and further resources

BEIS (2017) The Time for Talking is Over. Now is the Time to Act. Race in the workplace – The McGregor-Smith Review www.gov.uk/government/publications/race-in-the-workplace-the-mcgregor-smith-review (archived at https://perma.cc/XZ43-QCR9)

BSI (2015) BS 76000:2015 *Human Resource. Valuing People. Management System. Requirements and Guidance* https://shop.bsigroup.com/ProductDetail/?pid=000000000030298954 (archived at https://perma.cc/4T5X-8VC4)

BSI (2017) BS 76005:2017 *Valuing People Through Diversity and Inclusion: Code of practice for organizations* https://shop.bsigroup.com/ProductDetail/?pid=000000000030338898 (archived at https://perma.cc/2ECE-3EL9)

CIPD. Human Capital Measurement and Reporting, *CIPD* www.cipd.co.uk/knowledge/strategy/analytics/human-capital-factsheet (archived at https://perma.cc/V94T-3R9X)

Deloitte (2017) Rewriting the rules for the digital age: Deloitte Global Human Capital Trends www2.deloitte.com/content/dam/Deloitte/global/Documents/About-Deloitte/central-europe/ce-global-human-capital-trends.pdf (archived at https://perma.cc/EWE4-N44Z)

EDF Energy. Supplier's Guide to Diversity and Inclusion, *EDF Energy* www.edfenergy.com/sites/default/files/suppliers_guide_to_diversity_inclusion.pdf (archived at https://perma.cc/PG44-RL5H)

FairWRC (2015) *Diversity and Social Inclusion in the British Workplace: An outline of relevant discussions and contributions*, University of Manchester Press, Manchester

France Stratégie. The Economic Cost of Discrimination, *France Stratégie* www.strategie.gouv.fr/publications/cout-economique-discriminations (archived at https://perma.cc/5W4L-KBV6)

Hoel, H and McBride, A (2017) 'Getting in', 'staying in' and 'moving on': using standards to achieve diversity and inclusion, in Arenas, A *et al* (eds) *Shaping Inclusive Workplaces Through Social Dialogue*, Springer

ISO (2010) ISO 26000:2010 *Guidance on social responsibility* www.iso.org/standard/42546.html (archived at https://perma.cc/LP8D-RCFW)

ISO (2016) BS ISO 30400:2016 *Human resource management. Vocabulary* https://shop.bsigroup.com/ProductDetail/?pid=000000000030324720 (archived at https://perma.cc/EJF9-XPG5)

ISO (2019) ISO 27501:2019 *The human-centred organization – Guidance for managers* www.iso.org/standard/64241.html (archived at https://perma.cc/LN2E-R9Y7)

ISO [accessed 28 April 2019] ISO/IEC Directives, Part 1 – Consolidated ISO Supplement – Procedures specific to ISO, *ISO* www.iso.org/sites/directives/current/consolidated/index.xhtml (archived at https://perma.cc/2NUW-ZD5C)

McBride, A and Mustchin, S (2013) Creating sustainable employment opportunities for the unemployed, *Policy Studies*, **34** (3) pp 342–59
McBride, A, Hebson, G and Holgate, J (2015) Intersectionality: are we taking
enough notice in the field of work and employment relations?, *Work, Employment
and Society*, **29** (2), pp 331–41
Tatli, A (2011) A multi-layered exploration of the diversity management field:
diversity discourses, practices and practitioners in the UK, *British Journal of
Management*, **22**, pp 238–53

7

Occupational health and safety management

Martin Cottam

Introduction

One of the important obligations of any employer is in respect of the occupational health and safety of its employees, and others such as visitors to its premises to whom it owes a duty of care.

In the UK, and in many other jurisdictions, there is a legal obligation on employers to protect the health, and safety of their employees and others who might be affected by their business. There is also a widely held view that there exists a moral obligation on employers in this regard. It can also be argued that good health and safety management represents good business practice, as the costs of prevention are generally held to be less than the costs that accrue to organizations from injury and ill health, when taking into account the resulting impacts, including unplanned absences, business disruption, legal and insurance costs, and reputational damage.

More broadly, successful management of occupational health and safety (OH&S) contributes to the reputation of organizations, sectors and countries. Injury rates are frequently compared between organizations within a sector, and between sectors and countries. The London Olympics in 2012 was notable for having suffered no fatalities during the construction of its stadia and other facilities, an achievement that subsequent hosts have, to date, been unable to match. The collapse of the Rana Plaza factory building near Dhaka in Bangladesh in 2013, which killed more than 1,100 garment workers and injured around 2,500, raised public awareness of the working conditions, including exposure to health and safety risks, of workers in developing countries, employed in the global supply chains of major international brands.

Globally, data from the International Labour Organization indicates that there are over 2.78 million deaths per year as a result of occupational accidents, and over 374 million work-related non-fatal injuries/illnesses per year many resulting in extended absences from work. The economic burden of current OH&S performance is estimated to be 3.94 per cent of global GDP.

In March 2018, the International Organization for Standardization (ISO) published BS ISO 45001:2018 *Occupational health and safety management systems. Requirements with guidance for use*, its first international management system standard addressing OH&S management. This provides an important new tool both to help raise the profile of OH&S management, and to help organizations manage and where necessary improve their OH&S performance.

CHAPTER OBJECTIVES

This chapter sets out to:

- explain the background to the development of the ISO 45001 standard;
- describe the key elements of an OH&S management system, as expressed in ISO 45001.

Key terms

The following definitions of key terms are reproduced from ISO 45001.

Hazard:	Source with a potential to cause injury and ill health. ISO 45001 notes that hazards can also include sources with the potential to cause harm or hazardous situations, or circumstances with the potential for exposure leading to injury and ill health.
Injury and ill health:	An adverse effect on the physical, mental or cognitive condition of a person. These adverse effects include occupational disease, illness and death. The term 'injury and ill health' also implies the presence of injury or ill health, either on their own or in combination.
OH&S opportunity:	A circumstance or set of circumstances that can lead to improvement in OH&S performance.

OH&S risk: A combination of the likelihood of occurrence of a work-related hazardous event(s) or exposure(s), and the severity of the injury and ill health that can be caused by the event(s) or exposure(s).

Risk: The effect of uncertainty – an effect is a deviation from the expected – whether positive or negative. Uncertainty is the state, even partial, of deficiency of information relating to, understanding or knowledge of, an event, its consequence, or likelihood. Risk is often characterized by reference to potential 'events' and 'consequences', or a combination of these. Risk is often expressed in terms of a combination of the consequences of an event, and the associated 'likelihood' of occurrence.

Worker: A person performing work or work-related activities that are under the control of the organization. Note that persons perform work or work-related activities under various arrangements, paid or unpaid, such as regularly or temporarily, intermittently or seasonally, casually or on a part-time basis. In addition the term 'workers' includes top management, managerial and non-managerial persons. It is also the case that the work or work-related activities performed under the control of the organization may be performed by workers employed by the organization, workers of external providers, contractors, individuals, agency workers, and by other persons to the extent the organization shares control over their work or work-related activities according to the context of the organization.

Workplace: A place under the control of the organization where a person needs to be or to go for work purposes. It is important to note here that, for ISO 45001, the organization's responsibilities under the OH&S management system for the workplace depend on the degree of control over the workplace.

Background to the development of ISO 45001

Existing management system standards

The fact that ISO 45001, ISO's first international standard on OH&S management, was published as recently as 2018 may seem surprising when one considers that the principal ISO management system standards addressing quality management (ISO 9001) and environmental management (ISO 14001) were first published in 1987 and 1996 respectively. Indeed, there are over thirty standards within the ISO family of management system standards addressing many aspects of business management including risk management, business continuity management, asset management, information security management, energy management, and anti-bribery management.

In part, the explanation for this lies in the fact that when compared to quality or environmental management, stakeholders with an interest in the OH&S performance of organizations appear to have been less readily convinced as to (i) the role of management system standards and (ii) the value of any associated conformity assessment. This may partly stem from there being, in many developed countries, an extensive framework of health and safety legislation, the origins of which date back to the rapid industrialization of the 19th century.

Historically, this has led some OH&S practitioners to treat legislative compliance as being the prime requirement of OH&S management, a view which seems thankfully to be rather less prevalent today. The move from prescriptive to goal-based regulation may also have contributed to the increasing attention given to management systems, as providing the framework within which the organization discharges its duty to protect the health and safety of its workers, and takes the decisions required of it by a goal-setting regime.

National legislative frameworks have evolved, in part, to reflect national OH&S experience and culture, particularly in the way they express the relationship between employers and workers. The existence of this strong national dimension to OH&S has also meant that there has been a relatively slow progression from management system standards published at national level to an interest in an international OH&S standard, with the growth of global organizations and supply chains contributing to the change.

The emergence of ISO 45001 as the third key ISO management system standard, alongside the equivalent well-established standards for quality

(ISO 9001) and environmental (ISO 14001) management is likely to encourage more organizations to align their OH&S management system with the requirements of the new standard, and to consider third-party certification.

Development and use of standards in OH&S management

ISO 45001 is not the first OH&S management system standard; guidance standards on OH&S management systems have been in existence for many years. In the UK, one of the earliest pan-sector guides was the UK Health and Safety Executive (HSE) publication *Successful Health and Safety Management*, first published in 1991 and subsequently revised in 1997 and 2013, and generally known by its reference number HSG65. This was followed in 1996 by a British Standard which presented its guidance in two alternative structures – the management system model used in HSG65, and the plan–do–check–act (PDCA) model of the environmental management system standard ISO 14001.

The latter model was subsequently adopted, reflecting market preference for alignment of management system standards around a common structure to facilitate their application to integrated management systems combining the requirements of quality, environmental, and occupational health and safety management into a single organizational management system.

The initial British Standard was a guidance standard rather than a specification of requirements. Interest in third-party certification of OH&S management systems began to emerge in the late 1990s, and individual certification bodies developed proprietary certification schemes. Compared to the certification available for quality and environmental management systems, such proprietary schemes were an unsatisfactory solution as the variety of schemes caused confusion, hindered organizations changing certifier when required, and lacked the external oversight provided by accreditation.

The suitability of occupational health and safety management systems for voluntary certification was debated extensively in this period. Some stakeholders were concerned that such certification might encourage a 'tick box' approach to the way organizations designed and operated their management systems. Others worried whether requirements for certification would be passed down supply chains in a prescriptive manner and feared that this could create an administrative burden for small businesses – a concern that persists today. Ultimately, market forces determined the way forward as interest in certification grew, and the use of national guidance standards for certification proved the need to develop an international requirements standard, to provide the basis for globally consistent assessment and certification.

In this period the British Standards Institution (BSI), on two occasions, proposed to ISO the development of an ISO standard to provide the requirements specification for an OH&S management system, but on both occasions the ballot of national standards bodies failed to secure sufficiently strong support for the work to proceed. Following the second of these ballots a group of national standards bodies, certification bodies, and other interested parties came together on a voluntary basis and in 1999 and 2000 published British standards OHSAS 18001 and OHSAS 18002 respectively. In subsequent years, these became the principal reference standards for OH&S management systems and primary basis for the third-party certification, replacing the certification bodies' proprietary schemes. Several national accreditation councils, including the United Kingdom Accreditation Service began to offer accreditation for OHSAS 18001.

The subsequent growth of accredited certification, and other evidence of market demand, prompted a further proposal from BSI for the development of an ISO standard. A ballot in 2013 attracted the necessary support, and work to develop ISO 45001 began that year.

Following the publication of ISO 45001, OHSAS 18001 and OHSAS 18002, were withdrawn, meaning that organizations certified to these standards have until March 2021 to migrate their certification to ISO 45001 if they wish to maintain certification.

About ISO 45001

Alignment of ISO 45001 with other ISO management system standards

One of the key differentiators between ISO 45001 and previous OH&S management system standards is that ISO 45001 is based on the overall structure, and common high-level text which ISO has now adopted across the majority of its management systems standards, including ISO 9001 and ISO 14001. This structure and common text is commonly referred to as the 'high-level structure'. The intention of the high-level structure is to make clearer the similarities and differences between the requirements of standards within the ISO management system family, and thereby make it easier for organizations to incorporate the requirements of multiple standards into a single 'integrated' management system.

Comparing ISO 45001 with the previous British Standards Documents

While ISO 45001 builds upon, and is broadly consistent with, previous OH&S management system standards, there are also some differences. These are driven by the adoption of the high-level structure, including the requirements in respect of 'context of the organization' and 'risks and opportunities', and other differences including terminology and the requirements for the involvement of workers.

From a UK user perspective, some of the terminology adopted in the standard requires careful reference to the definitions. For example, the term 'worker' is used throughout the standard as the default term for those whose occupational health and safety the organization is seeking to manage. It is common in the UK to use 'worker' as a term which excludes some or all levels of management. In contrast, the definition of the term and its supporting notes in ISO 45001 make it clear that the term includes management at all levels, together with unpaid interns, volunteers, temporary and seasonal workers, and can extend to workers of external providers, contractors and agency workers.

Similarly, the definition of 'workplace', as a 'place under the control of the organization where people need to be or to go for work purposes' is broad – particularly as a result of the supporting note which states that 'the organization's responsibility for the workplace under the OH&S management system depends on the degree of control over the workplace'.

This note implies that the organization has some degree of responsibility for the occupational health and safety of workers, when they are present, as a result of their work, in locations which the organization does not control. An example of this is business travel where the organization has some influence on the health and safety of its workers via its travel policy, affecting such matters as the choice of airlines and hotels, and the way travel time and driving for business are managed.

Organizations with an existing OH&S management system based on OHSAS 18001 that they wish to adapt to comply with ISO 45001, will need first to take into account the differences in structure and language between the documents. Many of the requirements of the standards are similar although some new requirements are introduced in ISO 45001.

Based on this comparison, the organization can carry out a gap analysis of its existing system to identify where changes are needed to align with the new standard.

Application of ISO 45002-1 to organizations of differing size and complexity

The standard is capable of being applied to an organization of any size, operating in any sector(s). However, the wording of the requirements tends to be more obviously applicable to larger organizations than to small and medium enterprises (SMEs) as it tends to imply a formality of structure and process typical of larger organizations. So it is important to emphasize that the principles still readily apply to SMEs, and compliance to the standard, and, if desired, third-party certification, can certainly be achieved by SMEs.

Indeed, in some respects it may be easier to achieve the requirements of the standard in a smaller organization. An example of this would be internal communication on OH&S issues; in a very small single-site organization with just a handful of workers, communication can easily take place amongst the entire worker population through informal meetings and conversations, whereas for a multinational, multisite organization, more complex processes are required to communicate effectively with workers, as a structured cascade may be needed, as may translation of messages into local language(s).

One of the perceived barriers to the adoption of standards by smaller organizations is the belief that standards require the development and maintenance of documented procedures and the maintenance of records to a degree that simply adds bureaucracy to the working of smaller organizations. Such criticism might reasonably have been directed at some of the earlier management system standards which did mandate the creation of documented procedures to address specific aspects of the management system.

The approach in the high-level structure, however, is quite different; while there is a requirement for some specific information to exist, such as an OH&S policy, there is flexibility as to the format and medium in which such information is maintained, and an emphasis on the organization determining for itself what information is necessary in order for the OH&S management system to be effective. This allows much greater scope for organizations to tailor the extent to which they maintain 'written' information, according to their needs and circumstances. This creates the flexibility to consider using pictorial information, graphics, screenshots or videos, instead of or alongside more traditional text-based content.

Given that SMEs employ a significant proportion of the working population, both in the UK and internationally, and in order for ISO 45001 to help contribute to an improvement in global OH&S performance, it is important to ensure that it is accessible by, and intelligible to, SMEs. With this in mind, the BSI OH&S Standards Committee is developing guidance standards to support the application of ISO 45001, targeting the SME audience. Of these, a general guide (BS 45002-0) was published simultaneously with ISO 45001 followed by a series of topic-specific guides, the first of which are BS 45002-1, BS 45002-2 and BS 45002-3.

As well as using a simpler language than ISO 45001, these guidance standards aim to help smaller organizations understand how to apply the requirements of the standards in an SME context.

Strengthening the management of occupational health

One of the commonly identified shortcomings of organizations' efforts to manage occupational health and safety is that the system is more strongly focused on, and more effective at, addressing safety-related aspects than those related to health. There are a number of factors which contribute to this; the harm caused in safety-related incidents tends to be immediate and visible, whereas health-related impacts may occur long after the actual exposure to harm has occurred, and may be less visible. A further factor may be that health includes mental health, which society has historically been less comfortable addressing than physical health.

While supporting guidance to OH&S management system standards have often contained a reasonably balanced mix of safety- and health-related examples, organizations often appear to need greater guidance on the health component of their OH&S management than they do in respect of safety. To help address this, a British standard providing guidance on occupational health (BS 45002-1) has been developed to support the application of ISO 45001. The ISO committee responsible for ISO 45001 is also developing a guidance standard specific to the management of psychological risks to health and safety of workers (due to be published as ISO 45003 in 2021).

While much of what is required in respect of health is very similar to what is required in respect of safety, areas of potential imbalance can include the effectiveness of hazard identification in respect of health, and the extent of measurement and monitoring in respect of health issues. Leadership may also tend to focus less on health than on safety. The British standard provides useful guidance in all these areas.

It suggests that when identifying factors which may give rise to, or exacerbate, occupational ill health, it can be useful to consider potential worker exposure to different types of hazards, including:

- chemical hazards (eg fumes, asbestos, silica, dusts);
- physical hazards (eg noise, vibration, extremes of temperature, extremes of pressure);
- biological hazards (eg bacteria, viruses, fungal spores, enzymes, animal proteins, genetic material);
- ergonomic hazards (eg lifting, lowering, pulling and pushing, posture, repetitive movement);
- psychosocial hazards (eg job security, stress, bullying, harassment, excessive work demands, shift work, work relationships, lack of control).

It makes clear that the organization should also consider hazards that can be created by a worker's state of health for which health monitoring could be appropriate. This is different from health surveillance. Examples of this could include:

- pregnant workers;
- new mothers;
- vulnerable workers (eg workers with caring responsibilities, lone workers, night workers);
- young and older workers;
- workers with pre-existing health conditions;
- workers required to perform safety-critical roles (eg drivers, emergency response teams).

It also indicates that if there is a possibility that workers could be exposed to OH hazards that exceed legal limits, the organization should plan appropriate occupational health surveillance, eg skin inspections, hearing and lung function tests. Another important area for monitoring is sickness absence records. Both these types of record can be used to identify trends or clusters of occupational ill health. Another important area for monitoring is the application and effectiveness of risk controls, especially since the harm arising from a failure of controls may not manifest itself immediately.

Regarding leadership in respect of health, the British standard suggests that top management can demonstrate leadership by encouraging work/life balance, regular breaks, healthy eating, exercise, and by supporting health and wellbeing initiatives and campaigns.

The overall structure of ISO 45001

The overall structure of the standard follows the familiar PDCA cycle as illustrated in Figure 7.1. Important inputs to initial planning, and to the ongoing tuning of the system come from the organization's understanding of the context in which it is operating, both in terms of internal and external issues, and stakeholder needs and expectations. There is an emphasis on the role of leadership and on worker participation throughout the cycle.

FIGURE 7.1   Relationship between the clause structure of ISO 45001 and the PDCA cycle

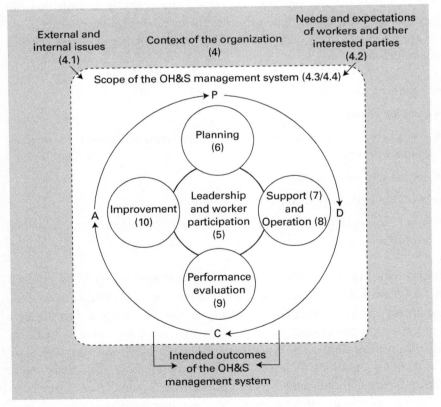

The figure shows how the PDCA cycle relates to the clause structure of ISO 45001

NOTE The numbers given in brackets refer to the clause numbers in ISO 45001

The PDCA cycle of OH&S management in ISO 45001

Understanding the context of the organization

The first section of the standard setting out requirements for the OH&S management system addresses the context of the organization, and reflects provisions introduced across all ISO management systems standards via the high-level structure. It requires the organization to identify the internal and external issues that affect its ability to achieve its desired OH&S performance, and the needs and expectations of workers and other stakeholders.

Making this the first requirement in the standard makes it clear that a management system needs to be appropriate to the circumstances of the organization, and that it needs to reflect, and evolve with, those circumstances. Another way of expressing this would be that the management system should serve as a risk management tool for the organization, which should be tailored to the risks and the landscape within which the organization is operating.

This means the organization should consider external factors such as the market and competitive environment in which it is operating, the legal, political, social and cultural context in which it is operating, and any technological changes, as well as its physical surroundings. These factors, and any associated trends, should be considered for their implications on the organization's OH&S management. For example:

- Will investment be necessary to meet the requirements of planned legislation?

- If new technology is to be adopted how will this potentially affect OH&S risks?

- How is the organization's current OH&S performance viewed by customers and other external stakeholders?

- Is emerging knowledge of hazards and risks likely to require action by the organization?

- What physical and environmental aspects of the surroundings of the workplace influence its OH&S performance, eg climate, weather, activities of neighbours?

Similarly, the organization should consider internal factors such as its structure and governance, policies and strategies, culture, formal and informal decision-making processes, human, financial and other resources, information systems, working conditions and working time arrangements, and employee relations. These factors, and any associated trends, should be considered for their implications on the organization's OH&S management. For example:

- Are there changes in the workforce demographic which may affect OH&S performance?
- How are trends in employee engagement impacting OH&S performance?
- How is the organization's financial performance impacting OH&S?
- What are workers' perceptions and expectations regarding the organization's OH&S performance?

Equipped with an understanding of the internal and external landscape relevant to its OH&S performance, the organization can ensure that its management system is relevant and appropriate to the context in which it is operating, and that it addresses emerging risks and issues.

The requirement for review of an organization's context is not a requirement of previous standards, and hence will be new for many organizations aligning an existing OH&S management system to comply with ISO 45001. But such a review is also a feature of other management system standards including ISO 9001 and ISO 14001, so there is scope either to carry out the review in common across all the standards, or to use reviews carried out for these other standards as an input to a review specific to OH&S. This provides such organizations with an important opportunity to consider how well the existing system suits the situation in which they are operating.

Planning and risk management

In planning an OH&S management system, it is important to define its scope. This may include the whole organization or a specific part of it, provided this has its own distinct management. Whether ISO 45001 is to be used as the basis for a self-declaration of conformity, or as the basis for third-party certification, it is important that the scope is clear, and that it is not misleading to stakeholders; this means that the scope should not exclude activities which have a material impact on the OH&S performance. There is little point, and even potential for reputational damage, if an organization applies ISO 45001 to office workers in its administrative functions but excludes from the scope of its management system the workers in its higher-risk manufacturing facilities.

Once the scope is decided, the organization establishes an OH&S policy, defines roles, responsibilities and authorities for OH&S matters, and reviews and addresses its risks and opportunities, and its legal and other requirements. Based on this it sets objectives and develops plans to achieve them.

OH&S POLICY

The standard requires that the organization's policy contains a number of specific commitments, namely to:

- provide safe and healthy working conditions for the prevention of work-related injury and ill health;

- fulfil legal requirements and other requirements;

- eliminate hazards and reduce OH&S risks;

- ensure continual improvement of the OH&S management system;

- ensure consultation and participation of workers, and where they exist workers' representatives.

There are also requirements in respect of the communication of the policy within the organization and its availability to interested parties.

ORGANIZATIONAL ROLES, RESPONSIBILITIES AND AUTHORITIES

The standard requires that roles, responsibilities and authorities within the OH&S management system are defined and communicated. It highlights that workers at all levels of the organization are responsible for those aspects of the OH&S management over which they have control. There is also a requirement to assign responsibility for ensuring that the OH&S management system conforms to the requirements of the standard, and for reporting on the performance of the system to top management.

RISKS AND OPPORTUNITIES

When addressing the theme of risk management, in line with the high-level structure, the standard consistently refers to 'risks and opportunities'. It can be tempting for readers with an OH&S background to immediately associate the term 'risk' with the health and safety risks associated with individual workplace hazards – for example the risk of slips, trips and falls. While such risks do indeed need to be managed, the standard is also asking the organization to think more broadly about risks to the achievement of its desired OH&S performance; in other words, including the internal and external factors and uncertainties which may impact what it is able to achieve. This means considering also factors which may indirectly, rather than directly, affect OH&S performance.

For example, weaknesses in succession planning may lead to key OH&S posts being unfilled, leaving gaps in the organization's OH&S capability. Similarly, changes in the characteristics of the resource pool from which the organization recruits may mean that its existing OH&S induction and training programmes become less effective. In both cases, the indirect effect may be that OH&S matters are less well understood, and that incident rates increase.

The standard also highlights that risk can be positive or negative and that deviations from the expected can be positive or negative in nature. It introduces the term 'opportunity' to highlight that organizations should be alert, and should respond, to circumstances or sets of circumstances in which they can effect an improvement in OH&S performance. Noting again that the standard takes a 'whole organization' view, this may be interpreted as asking the organization to consider the potential for OH&S improvement both at the level of individual hazards and more broadly.

One way of characterizing this would be to include consideration of OH&S in decisions in which it might not naturally be included. For example, if an organization is contracting and is consolidating activities from several sites into one, there may be an opportunity to configure the surviving site to provide a better and more ergonomic working environment than was previously available. Similarly, the introduction of technology enabling more effective virtual meetings may be considered in order to save the time and cost of travel, or to improve the organization's environmental footprint, but it can also offer occupational health and safety benefits.

In its requirements for the identification of workplace hazards and the assessment of the associated OH&S risks, the standard acknowledges that each organization needs to determine for itself the methodologies and criteria, according to its own circumstances and the hazards and risks it needs to manage. Where it is more specific is in setting out a large range of factors that the organization's chosen process(es) should consider. In so doing, the standard provides a useful checklist highlighting factors which experience tells us are sometimes overlooked in organizations' hazard and risk assessment.

It highlights, for example, the need to consider:

- not just the routine operation of equipment, but also its cleaning and maintenance, when different hazards may exist, and some risk controls may be disabled or ineffective;

- potential emergency situations;
- differences between how procedures envisage work being performed, and actual practice;
- the effect of leadership and culture in the organization;
- the effects of social factors such as workload, working hours, victimization, harassment and bullying;
- the potential impact of activities in the vicinity of the workplace but outside the organization's control, such as the activities on neighbouring sites;
- previous incidents inside or outside the organization.

In providing a fairly extensive list of such factors to consider, the standard does not require the organization to document the results of considering each of these factors for each individual hazards and OH&S risks. Rather, it requires the organization to design its process so that relevant factors such as these are considered.

LEGAL REQUIREMENTS AND OTHER REQUIREMENTS

As a voluntary standard, applicable to organizations across a wide variety of OH&S legislative regimes, the requirements of ISO 45001 in respect of legal requirements are for the organization to maintain a process through which to:

- determine and have access to applicable legal requirements;
- determine how these requirements apply to the organization and what needs to be communicated;
- take its legal obligations into account in its OH&S management system;
- maintain and retain information on its legal requirements.

The same requirements apply to 'other requirements', meaning requirements from other sources, whether imposed or voluntarily undertaken, such as commitments to, or of, a parent company or industry body, agreements with interested parties, employment agreements, codes of practice or other such specifications.

OH&S OBJECTIVES AND PLANNING TO ACHIEVE THEM

Finally, in the planning section, armed with an understanding of its context, the scope of its management system, its risks and opportunities, and its obligations, the standard requires the organization to plan the actions necessary to address its risks and opportunities, its legal and other obligations, and to establish OH&S objectives and plan the work necessary to achieve them.

Leadership and worker participation

As Figure 7.1 illustrates, the requirements for leadership and worker participation may be considered to lie at the heart of the OH&S management system, and to permeate all the activities of the PDCA cycle. There has been a strong emphasis in management system standards on leadership and the role of top management, and this was reflected in the previous British Standards. Where ISO 45001 goes further than other standards is in its requirements for worker participation.

The increased focus on, and strengthened requirements in respect of, worker participation in ISO 45001 are in no small part a reflection of the differing compositions of the groups responsible for the previous and new standards. The involvement of the International Labour Organization and the International Trade Union Confederation, amongst others, and the inclusion of a stronger labour representation within some national delegations meant that worker participation requirements were one of the most hotly debated aspects of ISO 45001.

From the labour side there were strong representations suggesting the standard should require the establishment of health and safety committees, provision of PPE at no cost to workers, and the provision of training during working hours. However, after much discussion, the consensus view was that a voluntary management system standard should not mandate such specific requirements, and alternative wording was agreed, including notes in the text acknowledging that these provisions may remove significant barriers to worker participation.

ISO 45001 requires that top management demonstrate leadership and commitment with respect to the OH&S management system, and specifies a number of ways in which this is to be done. This is more extensive than in OHSAS 18001. The core requirements included via the high-level structure include:

- ensuring that the OH&S policy and objectives are established and are compatible with the strategic direction of the organization;
- ensuring the integration of the OH&S management system requirements into the organization's business processes;

- ensuring that the resources needed for the OH&S management system are available;

- communicating the importance of effective OH&S management and of conforming to the OH&S management system requirements;

- ensuring that the OH&S management system achieves its intended outcome(s);

- directing and supporting persons to contribute to the effectiveness of the OH&S management system;

- promoting continual improvement.

OH&S specific additions in ISO 45001 include:

- developing, promoting and leading a culture in the organization that supports the intended outcomes of the OH&S management system;

- protecting workers from reprisals when reporting incidents, hazards, risks and opportunities;

- ensuring the organization establishes and implements a process(es) for consultation and participation of workers;

- supporting the establishment and functioning of health and safety committees.

It is notable that the main focus of the requirements on top management additional to those prescribed via the high-level structure is in the area of worker participation.

This theme is developed further in a section on consultation and participation of workers. Among the requirements which go beyond previous standards, it requires the organization to:

- provide mechanisms, time, training and resources necessary for consultation and participation;

- determine and remove obstacles or barriers to participation and minimize those that cannot be removed;

- involve non-managerial workers in determining the mechanisms for their participation and consultation.

It also sets out areas in which non-managerial workers should be consulted, and in which they should participate, the latter including identifying hazards and assessing risks, determining actions to eliminate hazards and reduce OH&S risks, determining competence requirements and training needs, and the investigation of incidents. Throughout the standard references to involvement of, or communication with, workers frequently extend this to 'and, where they exist, workers' representatives'.

Taken together, the sections on leadership and worker participation suggest a wish on the part of the standard writers to put a distinctly stronger emphasis in this standard on the need for, and benefit of, the strong and active involvement of top management in leading OH&S matters. It indicates that a significant focus of such effort should be directed at establishing a collaborative approach encouraging and supporting the involvement of workers at all levels.

Support

The standard addresses five elements which support the effective operation of the OH&S management system. These are resources, competence, awareness, communications and documented information. It requires the organization to:

- provide the necessary resources for the development, maintenance and continual improvement of the system, noting that these may be financial, human, technological, natural or infrastructure resources;
- determine the competence required by workers relevant to OH&S performance, ensure workers are competent, taking action to acquire and maintain competence as necessary, and evaluating the effectiveness of these actions;
- make workers aware of aspects of the OH&S management system including the policy and objectives, relevant hazards and risks, how they can contribute to effective OH&S performance and the consequences of not conforming to system requirements;
- establish and maintain processes for internal and external communication relevant to the OH&S management system;
- maintain and control documented information necessary for the effective operation of the OH&S management system.

One specific requirement defined in relation to awareness, but with implications also for workers' competence, is that workers are to have the ability to remove themselves from work situations that they consider present an imminent and serious danger to their life or health, and are to be protected from undue consequences for doing so.

Operation

This section of the standard addresses the processes of the management system that support the day-to-day operation of the organization. It requires that controls and criteria are established for the processes, to implement the actions determined during planning. It makes explicit mention of the possible need to adapt work to workers. It also highlights the need for coordinating relevant OH&S arrangements with other organizations in multi-employer workplaces.

This section of the standard also sets out a 'hierarchy of controls' through which the organization should address its OH&S risks. At the top of this hierarchy is elimination of the hazard, beneath it in order of effectiveness are:

- substitution of processes, operations, materials or equipment with less hazardous alternatives;
- the use of engineering controls, or reorganization of work;
- the use of administrative controls, including training;
- the use of personal protective equipment.

This is an area in which ISO 45001 is prescriptive, as it mandates the adoption of this hierarchy; the supporting guidance points out that it is usual to combine several controls to achieve the required level of risk control. This may involve combining controls from different levels in the hierarchy.

Management of change is also addressed in this section of the standard. This reflects much evidence from investigations suggesting that poor change management frequently contributes to OH&S incidents and non-conformities. The requirement is for a process for the implementation of both permanent and temporary changes that impact OH&S performance; this process must, by implication, include requirements for hazard and risk assessment of actual or proposed changes. There is also a requirement to review the consequences of unplanned changes, taking actions as necessary to mitigate any adverse effects.

Procurement is also addressed in this part of the standard, addressing the provision both of products and of services, the latter including both outsourcing and the use of contractors. Here the overarching requirement is to ensure that procured goods or services are controlled such that they do not undermine or compromise the organization's management system, or its ability to achieve its objectives and its desired level of OH&S performance.

The type and degree of control required will vary according to the risk posed by the products or services being procured. In the case of contractors whose work involves physical presence in the workplace, there is also a need to consider risks to the contractors' workers, from the organization's activities, and risks to the organization's activities from the contractors' activities.

Emergency preparedness and response is the final topic addressed in respect of operations. It highlights the role of risk assessment in identifying the potential emergency situations for which the organization should plan. There are explicit requirements for provision of first aid, training for the planned response, and for the testing and exercising of plans. In a standard which rarely mandates that specific information must be maintained in documented form, there is such a requirement covering the process for emergency planning and response, and the emergency plans themselves.

Other aspects covered in the requirements include communicating relevant information to workers, contractors, visitors, emergency response services and other stakeholders. There is also a requirement to take into account the needs and capabilities of these interested parties and, where appropriate, involving them in the development of the plans.

This is an appropriate moment at which to emphasize that, while a management system standard sets out its requirements under a series of distinct headings, the reality is that, in the operation of the management system, these elements overlap and/or combine together, and the success of the management system often depends not upon the effectiveness of the individual components but upon the effectiveness with which they work in combination.

As a simple example of this, consider the topics discussed earlier in this section, namely management of change, procurement, and emergency preparedness and response. One scenario in which this interaction occurs would be the bringing onto site of contractors to carry out construction or refurbishment work in one part of the facility. That work may render part of the facility inaccessible, and may mean that emergency egress arrangements need to be adjusted for the duration of the work.

The management of change process should identify this; the adequacy of the alternate arrangements should be assessed, and if satisfactory these should be communicated to workers, including the contractors, and potentially to visitors. It could be useful to test the revised egress arrangements with an evacuation drill before the construction or refurbishment work begins. In cases where the organization's premises are part of a multi-tenant facility, there may be a need to liaise with the landlord or site owner, and with neighbours to ensure they are not adversely impacted by the change in egress arrangements, and are aware of any need to adjust their own emergency arrangements.

Performance evaluation

This section of the standard addresses performance measurement and evaluation across the OH&S management system, and broadly places the onus on the organization to determine what needs to be measured and monitored and when, the appropriate methods for monitoring, measurement, analysis and evaluation, and how the results are communicated. The underlying requirement is that the results are suitable and sufficient to enable the organization to determine the effectiveness of the OH&S management system. The organization is required to retain documented evidence of its monitoring, measurement, analysis and performance evaluation.

There are additionally specific requirements for evaluation of compliance with legal requirements and other requirements, for internal audit, and for management review. The organization is free to determine the frequency and method by which it evaluates its compliance with legal requirements and other requirements, but must retain evidence of the result obtained, and take action if needed.

Internal audit is required to test the effectiveness with which the OH&S management system is implemented in the organization, and to test whether the management system meets the requirements of the standard. There are requirements for an audit plan, criteria and scope for each audit, objective and impartial auditing, reporting of results to relevant managers, workers and other interested parties, and action to address nonconformities. Documented information is to be retained evidencing the audit programme and the results.

Management review is the overarching review by top management of the OH&S management system. The review considers information on the organization's OH&S performance, and, importantly, trends in that performance. The review should consider the following aspects of the management system, taking improvement action where necessary:

- its suitability – how well the system fits the organization, and its internal and external context including its culture and the expectations of interested parties;
- its adequacy, in terms of how well it is implemented;

- its effectiveness, in terms of whether it is achieving its intended outcomes and level of OH&S performance.

There is a specific requirement that top management communicate relevant results from the management review to workers.

Questions that should be considered during management review include:

- Whether actions from previous management reviews have been completed, and whether they have proved effective.

- What changes have occurred or are anticipated to internal or external factors relevant to the OH&S management system, such as changes to legal requirements, changes to the organizations processes and/or the associated risks, changes to the expectations of interested parties.

- Whether the OH&S policy remains appropriate, and whether the policy commitments are being met.

- What is the performance, and what is the trend in performance, in key measures including:

  o results of evaluation of compliance with legal requirements and other requirements;

  o results of workplace inspections;

  o audit results;

  o incidents;

  o results of emergency drills, and any actual emergency situations;

  o consultation and participation of workers.

- Whether there are adequate and suitable resources to maintain the effectiveness of the management system.

- What opportunities there are for improvement.

Improvement

The standard addresses improvement at both micro and macro levels. At the level of individual incidents and nonconformities, it requires there to be processes for reporting, action to control and correct the situation, and to deal with the consequences. It requires workers and other relevant interested parties to be involved in evaluating the need for corrective action to address the root cause(s) and prevent recurrence (or occurrence elsewhere), and for the effectiveness of any action taken to be reviewed.

At the organizational (or system) level there is a requirement for the organization to continually improve the suitability and effectiveness of the OH&S management system, through actions to enhance performance, promote a culture that supports the OH&S management system, and communicating with, and promoting the participation of, workers.

Summary

This chapter has described the background to the development of ISO 45001, the first ISO management system standard for OH&S management.

It has explained the advantages this standard offers over previous OH&S management system standards, by virtue of its compatibility with other widely-used ISO management system standards such as ISO 9001, for quality, and ISO 14001 for environmental management, and by providing a basis for conformity assessment, either by the organization itself, or by others.

It has then described the main elements of an OH&S management system, as set out in ISO 45001, which follow the familiar PDCA cycle. Particular features of the standard have been described, including the emphasis that it places on leadership and the role of top management, and on the consultation with, and participation of, workers.

There are both financial and reputational benefits for organizations which manage OH&S effectively, and organizations with global supply chains increasingly seek assurance as to the OH&S management of their suppliers. ISO 45001 provides a framework through which organizations can gain assurance regarding their own OH&S management, or that of their suppliers, and through which an organization can work to improve its OH&S performance.

References and further resources

BSI (2018) BS 45002-0:2018 *Occupational health and safety management systems. General guidelines for the application of ISO 45001*: https://shop.bsigroup.com/ProductDetail/?pid=000000000030334815 (archived at https://perma.cc/9EG4-6GQD)

BSI (2018) BS 45002-1:2018 *Occupational health and safety management systems. General guidelines for the application of ISO 45001. Guidance on managing occupational health*: https://shop.bsigroup.com/ProductDetail/?pid=000000000030362021 (archived at https://perma.cc/65EC-7HCC)

BSI (2018) BS 45002-3:2018 *Occupational health and safety management systems. General guidelines for the application of ISO 45001. Guidance on incident investigation*: https://shop.bsigroup.com/ProductDetail/?pid=000000000030362017 (archived at https://perma.cc/95NY-XDVN)

BSI (2019) BS 45002-2:2019 *Occupational health and safety management systems. General guidelines for the application of ISO 45001. Risks and opportunities*: https://shop.bsigroup.com/ProductDetail/?pid=000000000030362019 (archived at https://perma.cc/3A4E-URUA)

BS OHSAS 18001:2007 *Occupational health and safety management*. Requirements: https://shop.bsigroup.com/ProductDetail?pid=000000000030148086 (archived at https://perma.cc/7EPQ-QQUL)

BS OHSAS 18002:2008 *Occupational health and safety management. Guidelines for the implementation of OHSAS 18001*. https://shop.bsigroup.com/ProductDetail?pid=000000000030328181 (archived at https://perma.cc/KF9L-NJMZ)

CIPD. Health and wellbeing at work: survey report, *CIPD* www.cipd.co.uk/knowledge/culture/well-being/health-wellbeing-work (archived at https://perma.cc/3V5D-A6SX)

HSE (2009) *Health and safety law: What you should know* (poster), HSE Books, London

HSE (2011) INDG244 (rev2) *Workplace health, safety and welfare: A short guide for managers*, HSE Books, London

HSE (2013) HSG65 *Successful Health and Safety Management*, HSE Books, London

HSE (2013) INDG417 (rev1) *Leading health and safety at work*, HSE Books, London

HSE (2014) HSG268 *The health and safety toolbox – how to control risks at work*, HSE Books, London

HSE (2014) INDG163(rev4) *Risk assessment – a brief guide to controlling risks in the workplace*, HSE Books, London

HSE (2014) INDG449 (rev1) *Health and safety made simple – The basics for your business*, HSE Books, London

HSE www.hse.gov.uk/ (archived at https://perma.cc/PU8E-XVZG)

ISO (2018) BS ISO 45001:2018 *Occupational health and safety management systems. Requirements with guidance for use*: https://shop.bsigroup.com/ProductDetail?pid=000000000030299985 (archived at https://perma.cc/LG73-PARY)

ISO (forthcoming) BS ISO 45003 *Occupational health and safety management – Psychological Health and Safety in the Workplace – Guidelines*: https://standardsdevelopment.bsigroup.com/projects/2018-02515 (archived at https://perma.cc/PP3X-5DHM)

Stranks, J (2016) *Health and Safety at Work: An essential guide for managers*, 10th edn, Kogan Page, London

Tolley (2017) *Tolley's Health and Safety at Work Handbook* 2018, 30th edn, Tolley, London

8

Moving on from the organization

Valerie Anderson

Introduction

This chapter will focus on the management and development systems that are needed when people move on from the organization, leaving for either voluntary and involuntary reasons.

In many cases an individual makes a voluntary decision to leave their employment for personal reasons such as career development, secondment opportunities or retirement. Involuntary 'triggers' for leaving an organization result from senior manager's decisions concerning down-sizing, out-sourcing and/or redundancy. They may also follow from incidents of employee misconduct.

Whatever the 'trigger' to move on, when someone leaves their organization the management of the transition process is important if the organization is to succeed in having the right workforce in the right place at the right time.

In relation to people joining and leaving the organization, attention is often given in standards documents to measures of workforce turnover and workforce retention. Reduced levels of turnover in organizations and the retention of important skills and capabilities are regarded as signals of organizational 'health' and good governance. However, a range of external factors such as employment levels in the area or industry sector; supply of requisite skills; labour mobility and migration trends, and competitor activity will affect the decisions of organizations and individuals about continued employment.

When someone leaves their employment it can be personally costly, both financially and emotionally. Organizational costs, both financial and in terms of training and change management, arise when people who have moved on must be replaced. Poor practice in the management process surrounding people who leave their employment can damage organizational reputation and lead to poor organizational performance. Correspondingly, the effective management of appropriate movement into and out of the organization may also signal sustainable organizational performance and good governance and management systems.

This chapter focuses on standards of practice, procedure, regulation and governance that can minimize negative consequences associated with the 'moving on' process and can provide a basis for the competent and equitable management of workforce exit. It identifies where standards are in place, puts forward ideas about where new standards would be beneficial, and highlights areas of good practice that organizations can implement to ensure that the 'moving on' stage can be as effectively managed as other stages in the employment relationship.

CHAPTER OBJECTIVES

This chapter sets out to:

- describe individual level and organizational 'triggers' that cause people to 'move on' from their employment;

- discuss how existing standards and regulations as well as guides of good practice can provide a guide for effective management practice in relation to those who move on from the organization;

- identify the challenges and the opportunities of implementing standards to manage processes of leaving the organization;

- propose ways of evaluating the success of management processes associated with employee turnover.

Key terms

Most of the terms associated with leaving the organization are well known. However, they may be differently defined and understood in different national contexts. The following terms (presented in alphabetical order) are used as follows in this chapter.

Dismissal: This term refers to the termination of employment for substantial reasons. These reasons may be economic, technical or organizational. Reasons for dismissal include employee misconduct, lack of capability, poor performance or role redundancy. Dismissal usually involves serving notice of the end of the employment relationship or making payment in lieu of notice. In certain circumstances (such as serious or gross misconduct by an employee), the dismissal may be made without notice. Many countries have legal or regulatory provision in place to protect individuals who believe that they have been subject to unfair or unwarranted dismissal.

Outsourcing: This term refers to an arrangement where an organization hands over activities, functions or processes that could be performed 'in house' to external process or service providers, resulting in the loss or transfer of jobs from the original organization.

Redundancy: This term refers to a form of dismissal that occurs when an employee's job no longer exists. This may be due to an employer deciding to reduce their workforce or to close the business. It may also occur when the work undertaken in the specific role is no longer needed, or when a decision has been made to outsource work to a third-party service or process provider.

Resignation: This term refers to a decision communicated by an individual, either verbally or in writing, that they intend to leave their job. Threatening to leave, or looking for work elsewhere is not the same as formally resigning. The intention to resign is usually accompanied by giving notice to the employer of the intention to leave. However, in some circumstances, it is possible to resign without notice. In some countries, if an employee feels forced to resign because of the actions of their employer, this may be regarded as 'constructive dismissal'.

Retention: HR standards such as BS ISO 30400:2016 *Human Resource Management. Vocabulary* refer to this term as: 'the observation, analysis and description of the extent an organization retains its workforce'. Retention may be measured as a proportion of a workforce with a specified length of service, typically one year or more, expressed as a percentage of overall workforce numbers. BS ISO 30400 refers to 'retention rate' as the ratio of the total workforce that is retained over a defined period.

Whilst a declining retention rate may indicate lack of worker satisfaction with their employer and signify problems such as a lack of organizational career opportunities, there are occasions when it may also be advantageous for both the workforce and the organization if some of the workforce take up opportunities outside their current employment. Senior managers may also decide to focus activities to ensure retention of only those employees that they considered are the best or most critically important performers.

Retirement: This event occurs when a person leaves their job at what they consider is the end of their active working life. In different countries a person may choose to retire at different ages and different tax laws and pension rules mean that a 'standard retirement age' is impossible to specify in a general publication. In some countries, retirement ages are different for males and females.

Eligibility for some form of financial (pension) support through social insurance schemes, either private or public, is often a 'trigger' for an individual's decision to retire and, although in many countries support for the old is mainly provided through the family, in most developed countries retirement with a pension is considered the right of many workers.

An individual may decide to take 'early retirement' before the age or tenure they need to be eligible for any pension support (see later in this chapter). In such circumstances, the individual must rely on their own savings and investments until such time that they qualify for social insurance payments. In some parts of the world, 'flexible retirement' is possible, where employees can change to flexible or part-time work to remain economically active.

Turnover: This term refers to a measure often used to observe, analyse and describe the proportion of the workforce (employees, contractors, and contingent/temporary labour) that leave their employment over a defined period, usually a year, and is calculated as a percentage of total workforce numbers. At its broadest, turnover assesses the rate at which workers are leaving the organization for both voluntary and involuntary reasons but it is possible to calculate turnover by categorizing voluntary and involuntary leavers (ISO/AWI TS 23378 *Human Resource Management: Turnover and Retention* – under development). An unforeseen high turnover ratio may lead to recruitment and training costs, and may indicate management and governance problems.

Existing standards

No standard has so far been developed that focuses on management systems and practices associated with 'moving on' processes, although many standards feature turnover and retention rates as useful metrics for organizational system effectiveness. For example, reduced turnover rates and improved retention rates may signifying positive outcomes of effective management practice, for example, BS 76000:2015 *Human Resource. Valuing People. Management System. Requirements and Guidance* and ISO 30409:2016 *Human Resource Management – Workforce Planning*. However, the following standards refer to the management of processes when employees leave the organization:

- ISO 27501:2019 *The human-centred organization – Guidance for managers*: This standard identifies that the wellbeing of the workforce is a business priority and gives guidance on how organizations might create a healthy workplace with benefits for retention and reduction in work-related injury and ill health. It further recommends that organizations provide people with meaningful work and with opportunities to use and develop their skills so that, regardless of gender, age, disability, or personal beliefs and orientation, workers might engage with and want to remain a part of the organization.

- ISO 45001:2018 *Occupational health and safety management systems. Requirements with guidance for use*: This standard provides a framework for managing risks as well as opportunities relating to the occupational health and safety of an organization's workforce, something that has relevance to issues of turnover and retention. Organizations have a duty to fulfil legal and regulatory requirements relevant to their sector, geographical and national locations as they pertain to the health, safety and wellbeing of members of their workforce. This standard sets out systems to implement good practice that may be in addition to statutory regulation. Key issues in this standard are:

o Identifying and managing risks that might have an adverse effect on the physical, mental or cognitive condition of any member of the workforce.

o Ensuring that risks about occupational disease, illness and death are identified and managed in a systematic way.

o Minimizing hazards that have the potential to cause harm or hazardous situations, or circumstances with the potential for exposure to hazards that could lead to injury and ill health of workers.

- BS 76005:2017 *Valuing people through diversity and inclusion: Code of practice for organizations*: This standard requires attention to management systems and policies that encourage the retention and progression of a talented, diverse and inclusive workforce. It indicates that redundancy policies should be reviewed to ensure that they do not reinforce inequality with respect to workers from minority groups and it recommends that the potential impact of redundancies on under-represented groups is assessed in advance. This standard also indicates the benefit of measuring and monitoring both dismissals and resignations to ensure no detriment occurs to maintaining a diverse workforce. BS 76005 indicates that organizations should develop a policy to remove inhibitors, such as cultural attitudes or workplace inflexibility, to those who want to stay at work. It recommends that employers provide a range of retirement planning processes and options available to the workforce, including opportunities for a meaningful transition from work to retirement involving part-time or casual work, flexible working arrangements, or access to less-demanding jobs with a reduced range of tasks.

- ISO 37500:2014 *Guidance on Outsourcing*: This standard is principally concerned with governance issues relating to outsourcing. This standard requires risk identification associated with outsourcing that includes attention to appropriate processes for 'migrating' systems, processes and people from the outsourcing organization to the provider.

In summary, existing standards leave scope for organizations to identify and develop their own forms of good practice to ensure that they manage the process and events surrounding people who leave the organization in an effective way. The remainder of this chapter outlines important regulatory issues as well as good practices relevant to the triggers of leaving events and processes.

Human governance and employee regulation

In many countries, commercial organizations are expected to comply with codes of corporate governance although these take different forms. Although codes of corporate governance are important, for the issues of employment, codes of human governance are more relevant. Codes of human governance also have application to public sector and non-profit organizations as well as to those operating in a commercial market. BS ISO 30408:2016 *Human Resource Management – Guidelines on human governance* clarifies the importance, for issues of turnover and retention, of the rules, systems, processes and behaviours that organizations put in place that set out how they are directed, controlled and held accountable. These have implications for activities connected with workers' transition out of the organization, particularly the extent to which they are fair and transparent.

Human governance requires organizational and managerial choices; it requires senior managers to make explicit their organization's stance towards issues of transparency, responsibility, accountability, employee participation and responsiveness to the needs of the workforce. Decisions about these managerial choices will vary in line with the unique goals and strategy of the organization. However, human governance decisions will have implications for the composition of the workforce and decisions about when and how people are likely to move on from the organization.

Although there are no standards specifically addressing workers' transitions out of the organization, it is important that the process is undertaken in a credible and competent way. Current standards provide only limited guidance for management systems and processes, and these will vary depending on the individual, organizational and national context. In different countries, different features of human governance are legally regulated. The detail of regulation is different in various country contexts. Figure 8.1 illustrates the areas that may fall within the remit of legal regulation.

In this chapter, both good practice and areas of regulatory influence are discussed in relation to 'moving on' processes. Organizations that are committed to good practice relating with the management of worker transition out of the organization will need to identify relevant legal requirements and other regulatory principles to which the organization subscribes. Managers will also need to determine how compliance with these legal and regulatory standards will be achieved. However, this chapter also identifies areas where organizations can go beyond the 'regulatory minimum', recognizing that the management of those who are 'moving on' is an important feature of sustainable organizational performance.

FIGURE 8.1   Areas of employment regulation

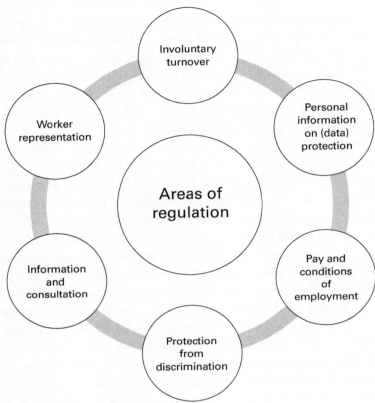

The figure shows areas of employment that are legally regulated

Standards, regulation and good practice

In this section of the chapter, the moving on processes associated with individually triggered decisions are outlined first before a discussion of involuntary turnover which results from organizationally triggered decisions.

Individually triggered decisions

There are two principal triggers that might stimulate an individual to decide to move on from their employment. These are resignation and retirement.

RESIGNATION

There are many reasons why an employee may decide to resign their position in the organization. For example, they may have accepted a new job with a different company, or they may wish to make a change to their career path. Once the decision is made, it can trigger uncomfortable situations in the workplace as the organization or local work team may feel 'let down'. In most parts of the world, legal or other regulations and standards should be observed for issues such as:

- Legal or collectively agreed minimum notice periods that may depend on the worker's length of service.

- Additional period of notice: the employer may have set out (in writing) a longer contractual notice period at the point at which the worker was recruited to their current role. This period should be honoured by both employer and employee.

- Pay in lieu of notice: although employees normally receive their normal pay and benefits during their notice period, in certain circumstances payment in lieu of notice may be given, although it is good practice to include this possibility in the contract of employment.

- Fixed-term contracts: in most parts of the world, no notice of the expiry of a fixed-term contract is necessary but, if the employee resigns before its expiry date, then they should give the correct amount of statutory or agreed notice.

In addition, good practices to avoid disputes arising that may have negative consequences for the reputation of the organization and may lead to ineffective moving on processes, summarized in Figure 8.2, include:

- Encouragement of the employee who has decided to leave to communicate their resignation in writing clearly indicating their intended last day of service.

- Communicating about the resignation to other members of the workforce to avoid the news spreading via rumour and informal channels.

- Involving the employee in the handover of their work and preparing for their departure. This may involve their assistance in finding and supporting their replacement.

- Arranging for an 'exit interview' where the employee can discuss the reasons for their decision to resign and provide feedback on the management systems and processes they have experienced during their

FIGURE 8.2   Good practice in resignation transition processes

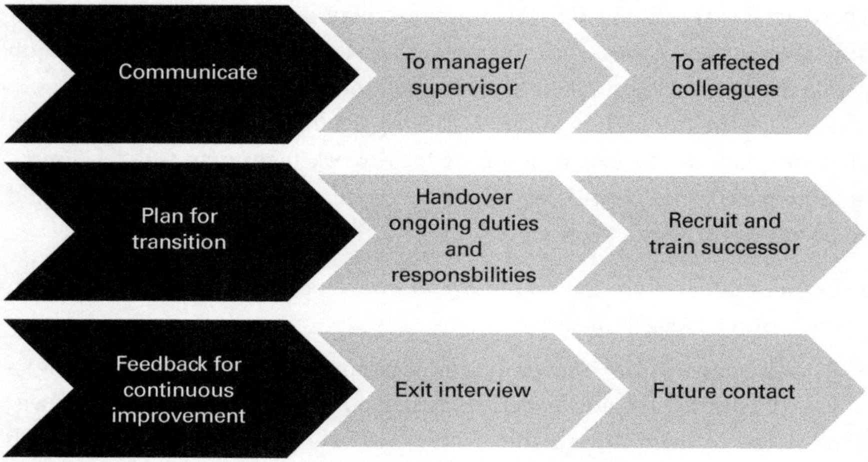

Communicate	To manager/ supervisor	To affected colleagues
Plan for transition	Handover ongoing duties and responsbilities	Recruit and train successor
Feedback for continuous improvement	Exit interview	Future contact

The figure shows good practice for organizations to follow when an employee resigns

period of employment. Exit interviews provide useful feedback to the organization and the following items of feedback are often sought:

o pay and benefits;

o quality of working life;

o relationships with managers, colleagues and other stakeholders;

o training and development and career advancement opportunities;

o organizational culture and work environment;

o job role and responsibilities;

o organizational leadership and management.

To summarize, good practice in systems to manage processes of resignation contribute to an environment of mutual trust in the organization. The transition of an employee as they leave their employment requires attention to both legal standards and to areas of good practice that are not currently subject to standards and regulation. In the period during the resignation process, it is possible for the organization to gain useful information relevant to continuous improvement of organizational management and development processes.

RETIREMENT

Work forms a big part of people's social, emotional and economic identity. Therefore, the decision to retire is a major life event. Historically, 'standard' retirement ages were set in many countries. However, in recent years this practice has been recognized to be both discriminatory and economically and socially unsustainable.

Excluding pension provision, there are few standards or regulations associated with retirement. However, effective management systems focused on preparation for and implementation of retirement can help to avoid unnecessary retirements and lead to positive reputational outcomes for the organization.

Age Scotland, a leading charity representing older people in Scotland, has developed a model to guide employers in good practice about becoming an age-inclusive employer (Age Scotland, nd):

- Scope: Identify areas of management practice that relate specifically to the issue of age-inclusivity.

- Aspirations: Identify which of these areas of practice have the highest impact on your organization.

- Current Reality: Assess the current reality as perceived by your workers.

- Gaps Analysis and Action Plan: Identify the largest gaps between aspiration and current reality and produce an action plan to address the areas which will have the biggest impact.

- Implement and Evaluate: Make appropriate changes to policy and practice and evaluate the success of these changes.

Financial support

Financial support for a person, once they have ceased work, is an important feature of the retirement process. As indicated previously, in some countries of the world, particularly in Africa and parts of the Middle East, the primary source of financial support for elderly people is the family. However, in North America, Europe and parts of Asia there are legal and social expectations that financial provision for those who have retired from paid work may come from one or more of the following:

- a state pension scheme, funded through some form of social insurance;

- an occupational pension scheme, organized and administered through the employing organization and comprising contributions by both employer and employee;

- a personal pension scheme, taken out either on a group or an individual basis.

Whilst the motivational value of pension provision may be limited for younger or contingent workers, research has shown that older, professional and higher-paid staff expect that a good employer will organize and maintain a good quality occupational pension; something that also has positive consequences for the reputation of the organization for both investors and for workers.

Pre-retirement good practice

Evidence shows that older workers in good health and with up-to-date training are equally productive as younger workers. Therefore, although most attention may be paid in organizations to pension provision, a range of other good management practices can enable older workers to continue to contribute their skills, knowledge and resources to the benefit of their employing organization. These may include making reasonable adjustments or offering retraining or redeployment where possible for health and/or disability, caring responsibilities or work/life balance reasons. These adjustments can have a positive impact on older workers' decisions to remain in employment rather than to retire.

Flexible retirement

This option involves the worker changing to flexible or part-time work in order to remain economically active. Options include:

- Part-time working: The worker reduces their regular hours of work, day of work or tasks, alongside their 'pro-rata' employment benefits. This enables the organization to retain the skills and capabilities of valued workers while enabling them to have more time outside the workplace.

- Job share: When two or more employees are responsible for one role between them.

- Flexitime: When the defined hours of work are altered on a regular basis so that, although a full working week is completed, workers have the flexibility to undertake other activities outside of the workplace.

- Compressed working week: When the worker commits to completing the hours for a certain number of days over a shorter period. Although this requires working more than the traditionally allotted hours per day, it enables the worker to maintain a strong connection with the organization.

- Career break/unpaid leave: Older employees may be attracted to the option of having a break rather than opting for immediate retirement and, following the agreed period, they may return to the workplace energized and with greater motivation.

- Additional planned unpaid leave: When the worker has additional unpaid leave, either on a regular occurrence (such as two weeks off every two months), or as part of their overall remuneration package (eg an additional 20 days of unpaid leave, taken with agreement across the year).

- Retirement pool: Where the organization and its willing retirees maintain contact, with the possibility that those retirees could return to work on a temporary basis. This enables the organization to cope if there is a surge in demand, or an unexpected reduction in staff.

- Fixed-term contract: This can occur when a worker's contract is for a fixed period, possibly to provide extra support on a seasonal basis or in accordance with demand as a final role before retirement.

Phased retirement

The transition from full-time work to permanent retirement can seem like a 'cliff edge' for both the worker and the organization, and an alternative phased or progressive process can involve the gradual reduction in the hours or days a worker spends at work, before their final point of retirement. This process differs from the flexible working arrangements outlined above in that an 'end-date', at which the employee agrees to completely transition out of the labour market or decrease their hours even further is agreed. In addition, the arrangement may make reference to a pension, particularly where an occupational pension has been accumulated.

To summarize, the decision to retire is consequential for both individual workers and their organizations. Although standards for financial provision and pension arrangements are often legally regulated, the effective management of these processes is not codified in current national or international standards. Good practice in systems to manage processes surrounding preparation for, and the decision to, retire contribute to organizational effectiveness.

There are a range of options for senior and operational managers to consider. Organizational management systems for retirement are only effective if managers and employees are aware of the options for flexible working and/or phased retirement. Clear processes and criteria for eligibility for alternative forms of working and clear rules must be in place and monitored to ensure equity of access. Good practice in relation to retirement processes also includes discussion opportunities for all workers, irrespective of age, about their personal development plans and future aspirations; retirement preparation support and pre-retirement training and counselling opportunities.

CAREHOME INC

CareHome Inc is a non-profit organization operating in residential care homes for elderly residents. It is a medium sized organization that, like many organizations in the care home sector, experiences high levels of staff turnover. CareHome Inc took the decision to commit to an 'age neutral' retention policy, with management decisions about retirement based on people's ability to do their job regardless of age.

The organization decided to set out a formal flexible retirement policy. This policy enabled workers in caring roles who might decide they no longer wished to apply to continue with the full range of duties to apply for phased retirement with reduced hours and duties. This resulted in an age-diverse workforce and one-third of workers in the organization are over 50, with the oldest being 77 years of age. The organizational benefits that have resulted from this policy are:

- a more stable workforce leading to a reduced turnover rate and reduced expenditure on recruitment;
- reduced levels of sickness absence;
- retention of organizational skills, capability and experience;
- better standards of client and customer care delivered by workers with life experience, patience and good levels of stress resilience.

Organizationally triggered decisions

In addition to decisions to move on triggered by individual and personal reasons, workers may leave their employing organization for reasons that are, to some extent, outside of their control. Involuntary decisions for a worker to leave their employment that are triggered by organizational decisions rather than the preference of the individual worker are generally referred to as 'dismissal'. In some cases, the decision to terminate employment is taken on an individual basis following misconduct or lack of capability. In other cases, the work of groups of workers are affected by decisions to restructure or otherwise change the work processes of the organization resulting in redundancy or outsourcing decisions.

Such instances are stressful for all involved and good management systems and practices are required to limit their negative consequences and achieve the objectives that originally prompted the strategic or operational decisions.

DISMISSAL FOR MISCONDUCT OR LACK OF CAPABILITY

The regulatory framework relating to dismissal varies in different country contexts and is continuously evolving. Practice varies across different national jurisdictions. In Europe, employees are entitled to a minimum notice of termination (except in cases of gross misconduct), but this is not necessarily the case in other parts of the world. However, good practice in relation to dismissal involves organizations in collecting relevant information, engaging in a sequence of decision points and making informed judgements based on the legal and organizational policy framework that is in place.

In Europe, for employees on permanent or indefinite terms of employment, there must be real and serious grounds for dismissal. Employees also have the right to receive a written explanation of the reason for their dismissal.

Before making a decision to dismiss an employee, good practice (that is legally enforceable in many countries) suggests that the outcome must be reasonable. This is usually defined as a decision that:

- is for a fair and valid reason;
- follows a proper investigation and procedure;
- is based on the organization's genuine and reasonable belief on the balance of probabilities.

In determining whether a reason for dismissal is fair and reasonable, it is relevant to differentiate between misconduct (about which a worker might be warned and given the opportunity to improve) and gross misconduct, which is considered so serious that workers who commit such acts will be subject to immediate dismissal without warning. Therefore, in order to operate effectively, good management practice involves setting and communicating standards for performance and conduct, which may be included in company rules.

Good practice, often also set out in employment regulations, is that organizational rules should be made clear to employees; usually in writing through a personal copy or written information about how to access them – for example, on the organization's intranet or in their handbook. In many countries, employees are entitled to a written statement of employment information. This may include information about disciplinary rules and procedures.

It is good practice to give special attention to workers without recent experience of working life (for instance, young people or those returning to work after a lengthy break), and workers whose language or reading ability is limited or who have a disability such as visual impairment. In such circumstances, they should be clear about the rules and the importance of the rules for their continued employment.

INVESTIGATIONS PRIOR TO DISMISSAL

If the decision to dismiss an employee is made, it is good practice to show the reasonable grounds for genuine belief that misconduct has occurred. This requires a fair investigation of the matter to collect all relevant information. Evidence such as witness statements, written documents and physical evidence is necessary. Whenever possible, the investigator should not be involved in the issue being investigated. In some instances, the organization may determine that it is appropriate to initiate a period of suspension with pay pending an investigation, but it is good practice to ensure that this period is as brief as possible and is kept under review.

Once the investigation is concluded, it is good practice to give the worker involved the facts of the case and allow them to put their response forward. An appeal process against formal decisions also provides evidence of fairness and equity in treatment of all workers that may be subject to some form of disciplinary action in the workplace.

In some countries, poor performance is not an acceptable reason for dismissal, but in other countries dismissal for lack of capability is considered fair and reasonable. Capability refers to skill, aptitude, physical and mental abilities, health, flexibility and qualifications of the worker in relation to the duties they are contractually obliged to perform.

Carelessness, wilfulness and negligence are not the same as competence, and constitute misconduct rather than lack of capability. Therefore, when an employer has concerns about the capability of a worker, it is good practice to determine wither the incompetence may be remedied (perhaps through additional training and support).

Decisions about a potential lack of capability through ill health requires a series of steps and decision points which might lead to consideration of redeployment, retraining or some form of flexible working prior to reaching the conclusion that a dismissal would be considered to be the only option available.

In summary, management processes relating to the dismissal of workers for reasons of misconduct or capability are subject to different standards included in regulatory frameworks in most countries and as set out in rules and policies in many organizations. Fairness and consistent standards of practice are vital for the effective management of dismissal cases, so good practice in processes relating to dismissal are essential. Such good practice provides the basis for effective operational performance and offers workers confidence that they will be treated in an appropriate way.

FAMILY CONSTRUCTION LTD

Family Construction Ltd is a family-run small company with 10 employees, including the founding manager and his daughter. They employ two 16- and 18-year-old apprentices and three 24–25-year olds. In addition, they employ experienced workers involved in construction and administration.

Although for many years they managed the company without the need for written rules, one or two incidents where misunderstanding about expected codes of behaviour occurred led them to decide to set out their disciplinary rules. They consulted with their experienced staff about the features they should adopt and developed a user-friendly format with the following characteristics so that the rules:

- are simple, clear and in writing;
- are displayed prominently in the rest-room/changing area;
- cover issues such as absences, timekeeping, health and safety and use of equipment;
- set out examples of conduct that would lead to disciplinary action in the form of warnings (eg lateness);
- set out examples of misconduct that would normally lead to dismissal without notice (eg working dangerously, fighting).

Redundancy

In any organization, decisions about the size, structure and most efficient use of the workforce are the responsibility of senior managers. However, if these decisions are communicated and implemented poorly there can be negative consequences for the skills base of the organization, its climate of employment relations and its ability to manage the change processes involved.

This section focuses first on redundancies caused by decisions to restructure parts of the business or to lose staff in response to changing environmental or economic conditions. The next section then considers job redundancies caused by decisions to transfer production or services to a third party through an outsourcing process. Redundancy management is a matter of employment regulation in many parts of the world, although the extent to which regulations are applicable depends on the size of the number of redundancies that are planned and or the size of the organization. In some circumstances, if the number of job roles to be lost is small and redundancy management can occur on an individual basis. On other occasions, group or collective redundancies may be necessary and these instances are often subject to greater regulation at national level.

Important stages in any redundancy procedure are consultation with employees or their representatives, selection of workers whose posts will be made redundant, and financial provision and arrangements for training or job-search support for those workers whose employment will be terminated. As regulatory expectations vary country by country, this section sets out the main features of good practice in these areas.

CONSULTATION

In the European Union, employees in organizations employing more than 50 people have the legal right to be informed and consulted about the organization's economic and employment situation and any decisions that might lead to significant changes in work organization, including redundancies or transfers. However, regardless of the size or type of organization, when senior managers are considering options to reduce the size of the workforce, consultation with employees or their representatives is an important feature of good practice, within a timescale that allows people to propose alternative decision options and to prepare themselves for the possibility of employment termination through redundancy.

SELECTION CRITERIA

A second feature of good practice, also required by law in some countries, is that selection criteria for those being made redundant are objective, fair and consistently applied. These must also be agreed in advance with worker representatives where such consultation processes are in place. Senior managers should determine the selection criteria, but they may also decide to manage part or all of the redundancy process through non-compulsory (voluntary) selection criteria.

Compulsory selection criteria

These might include attendance or disciplinary record, skills and experience, standard of work performance and capability. Where organizations have diversity or inclusion policies, their redundancy selection criteria should not be directly or indirectly discriminatory. In addition, where standard of work performance is a criteria then such decisions must be evidence-based; for example, from an organizational appraisal or performance management scheme.

An appeals procedure against selection for redundancy is a further feature of good practice and is required as a feature of employment regulation in some countries.

Non-compulsory selection criteria

Voluntary redundancies occur if senior managers decide to invite employees to volunteer for redundancy, in which case enhanced redundancy payments may be offered as an incentive. To avoid unnecessary loss of organization-ally critical skills and experience, good practice in this area is that senior managers make clear that they will determine the authorization of specific voluntary redundancy agreements.

Early retirement may occur when senior managers decide that an alternative to redundancy might be the opportunity for workers to apply for early retirement (see earlier in this chapter). This may involve the organization in a longer-term financial commitment to early retirees in the form of enhanced pension payments.

FINANCIAL PROVISION AND OTHER SUPPORT ARRANGEMENTS

Loss of employment through redundancy can be a life-changing and difficult time for those affected and lead to a range of financial worries and conse-quences. In many countries, a financial payment to workers whose jobs are redundant provides some financial predictability whilst they seek alternative employment. The length of time in which such 'protective awards' are made may vary depending on the number of people to be made redundant. In addition, workers whose jobs will be lost to redundancy decisions should be offered retraining and support to search for alternative employment.

Workers affected by redundancy may be entitled to redundancy pay, pension payments and/or social insurance scheme benefits. This features as a part of employment regulation in Europe, for example, but in the USA there is no statutory right to redundancy unless workers are represented by a union and where a collective-bargaining agreement is in place between the union and the employer that contains provisions in regard to redundancy payments.

Whatever arrangement is in place, this information should be communicated clearly to affected workers. Most payment provision, where it is in place, involves a calculation of the employees' length of service and age. The International Labour Organization (ILO) provides a comparison of the severance payments and redundancy provision in different countries (ILO, nd).

Other support arrangements that feature as good practice or feature in codes of regulation include:

- Alternative employment: Workers affected by redundancy can be offered suitable alternative work in their current organization or in an associated business unit. In such circumstances, sufficient information about the alternative employment is needed to make such a decision. This information should include pay, status, working environment, hours of work and location. A trial period in the alternative job role without detriment to eligibility for redundancy pay may be appropriate.

- Time off for training, or to look for new work: Employees who are 'under notice' of redundancy should be given time off to look for new employment opportunities. This is a legal requirement in some circumstances in some countries. However, employer contact with other local employers or employment agencies to assist workers in their job search, and training in how to identify appropriate jobs and present their applications in the most effective way is a further feature of employment good practice in redundancy situations.

COMMUNICATION

In many parts of the world issues of consultation, selection and financial provision for workers who will be required to leave the organization are subject to standards of regulation. However, the process of giving individuals the bad news that their job role is to be made redundant does not feature in current standards. The person with responsibility for communicating decisions on an individual basis may be the line manager or another person with a less close working relationship with the individual.

Good practice in relation to communication with an individual about the loss of their job includes ensuring that the communicator is:

- fully informed and understands why the redundancy decision is necessary;
- permitted to communicate information about the decision with the affected individual(s);
- trained to undertake difficult conversations about job losses;
- given sufficient time to have the conversations;
- supported by the organization through practical advice on the procedural and emotional demands of communicating with individuals about planned job losses;
- fully informed about any new developments in the organization that may affect the response of individuals whose jobs are likely to be lost through redundancy.

REDUNDANCY AGREEMENTS

Although there may be occasions when an ad hoc approach to redundancy is appropriate, good practice in employment relations includes the establishment of an organizational policy and procedure for redundancy management which is clearly communicated to all employees and worker representatives. This is a legal requirement in some countries. The redundancy policy may include agreements about the following issues:

- a commitment to keep employees or their representatives as informed as fully as possible about the likely need for redundancies;
- consultation arrangements and timescales in the event of a possible decision to make redundancies;
- the number and descriptions of roles at risk of being made redundant and the timescale over which redundancies will be achieved;
- the redundancy selection process;
- the method of calculating the redundancy payments to be made to those who will be dismissed and any groups of staff who will not qualify for redundancy payments;
- the support arrangements to be put in place; for example, reasonable time off with pay to undertake training or seek alternative work and assistance with job-seeking.

ENERGY PLC

The rapidly changing business environment in the utilities sector led Energy plc to undertake a strategic review and consider future changes to the structure of the organization and changes to the services offered. The organization wanted to re-focus resources to ensure business development in priority areas. As part of the strategy, Energy plc introduced a Voluntary Severance Scheme with the option to consider applying to leave the organization on a voluntary basis and with goodwill on both sides, subject to the operational requirements of the organization.

In developing this scheme, the recognized trade unions were consulted and some guiding principles were established to ensure:

- a fair, objective and confidential process of calculating the additional benefits to be paid to those whose application for voluntary severance is agreed;

- transparency in identifying eligibility criteria for application to the scheme;

- a clear and simple process for applications for voluntary severance;

- a clearly agreed date by which employees whose applications are successful must have left their employment;

- clarity that the voluntary severance scheme would not involve early access to pensions funds;

- clarity about the settlement agreement to be made in the case of voluntary severance.

Outsourcing

Outsourcing occurs when activities previously performed 'in house' are transferred to external process or service providers. The decision to outsource services or processes can lead to redundancies as, although some of the affected job roles may be transferred to the new organization, some roles may become redundant. In these cases, redundancy management processes and good practices as outlined earlier in this chapter become necessary. Outsourcing decisions are an increasing feature of management discussion in all countries, both in the public and private sectors.

In some cases, outsourced services or processes are transferred to third-party organizations based in the same country, but an increasing trend is for outsourced services to be provided 'offshore' (referred to as offshore out-sourcing). Most outsourcing client organizations are based in North America, Europe and Japan, and the range of countries where organizations offer outsourced services and processes continues to expand to include countries in the same regions, but countries located in the 'global south' regions of the world increasingly provide offshore outsourced processes and systems.

Where outsourcing occurs and members of the workforce are transferred to an outsourcing provider, then regulations and employment laws pertinent to different national jurisdictions must be enacted. This means that there will be a requirement for organizations to implement systems and processes that enable the effective management of groups of employees that may have different terms and conditions.

KEY TERMS FOR OUTSOURCING

As the trend towards outsourced service and process provision has increased globally so a number of new terms have arisen connected with the management of those who leave the organization for this reason. These include:

- Affected worker: Any worker (employed by the incoming or outgoing organization) affected by the transfer including those who remain behind with the outgoing employer or those already working for the incoming employer.

- Due diligence: The investigation of a business process by a potential outsource provider to determine the costs, liabilities, benefits and risks (including what are referred to as 'employer liabilities') associated with transferring the service or process provision.

- Employer liability information: Information which the outgoing employer must provide about transferring employees to the incoming employer.

- Incoming employer/transferee: The employer who will be taking over the service or process delivery after the transfer takes place.

- Outgoing employer/transferor: The employer who hands over the service or processes when the transfer takes place.

TRANSFER ARRANGEMENTS

In many countries, the workers of the outgoing organization automatically become employees of the incoming employer at the point of transfer. However, this assumption does not apply in all countries. In Australia, for example, employees do not automatically transfer in the event of outsourcing, and so effective management of redundancy procedures (see earlier in this chapter) is required.

In some countries, both the outgoing and incoming organizations have a legally regulated duty to inform and consult with employees or their representatives about the implications of their decisions. In other countries, eg the USA, transfer arrangements are not legally regulated. However, where outsourcing transactions involve organizations in countries where there are regulatory requirements, then these must be observed.

Whatever the regulatory standards in place, transfers can be stressful for all those involved and effective management systems for outsourcing will have positive consequences for cost effectiveness and employment relations. Productivity, efficiency and customer satisfaction can be affected unless the transfer process is implemented in an effective way.

INFORMATION AND CONSULTATION

When considering decisions about outsourcing it is good practice for organizations to put in place arrangements for information and consultation with employees and/or their representatives. It is also good practice to communicate in writing to those who may be affected by the decision:

- information about the transfer – indicating when it will occur and why it is necessary;
- the implications for affected workers, such as a change in location, risk of redundancies and so on;
- any implications for workers in the services provider organization;
- information about measures the incoming employer is considering taking in respect of affected employees.

Where employment transfers are likely, good practice in management systems will be implemented over four stages: due diligence; pre-transfer; during the transfer; and post-transfer. The major features of good practice are depicted in Figure 8.3.

INFORMATION ABOUT TRANSFERRING EMPLOYEES

Once the decision to transfer workers is made, the incoming and outgoing employers must agree an implementation process. In some transfer situations this may be difficult, but it is good practice for both employers to discuss:

- the identity and age of the employees who will transfer;

FIGURE 8.3   Good practice for outsourcing transfer processes

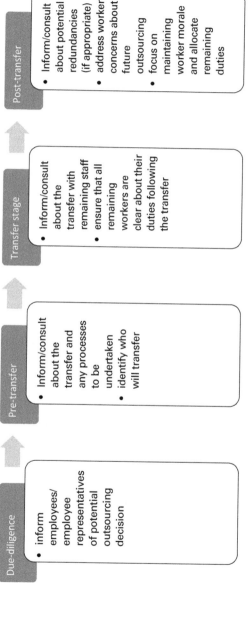

Due-diligence
- inform employees/ employee representatives of potential outsourcing decision

Pre-transfer
- Inform/consult about the transfer and any processes to be undertaken
- identify who will transfer

Transfer stage
- Inform/consult about the transfer with remaining staff
- ensure that all remaining workers are clear about their duties following the transfer

Post-transfer
- Inform/consult about potential redundancies (if appropriate)
- address worker concerns about future outsourcing
- focus on maintaining worker morale and allocate remaining duties

The figure shows good practice over the four stages of outsourcing the transfer process

- their employment terms and conditions, for example, pay, commission and bonus entitlements, holidays, job title and function, and sick pay provisions;
- information relating to any disciplinary, grievance or legal actions or processes taken over an agreed period;
- information about any collective agreements.

TERMS AND CONDITIONS

Following a transfer, providers of outsourced services often find they have employees with different terms and conditions working alongside each other. They may wish to change/harmonize terms and conditions. Such decisions are outside the scope of this chapter although information relating to terms and conditions will feature as part of the employee consultation process indicated in Figure 8.1.

In some countries, transferred employees benefit from protection against negative changes in their terms and conditions if the reason for their transfer was the outsourcing decision. Occupational pensions are rarely transferred. Therefore, it is likely that the transferred worker will transfer to the occupational pension, where one is in place, of the incoming employer.

The challenges and opportunities of moving on

As this chapter has indicated, the prevalence of employment regulation in different parts of the world has led to a general trend towards standardization in matters of human capital management, with implications for workers' transitions out of their employing organization. However, there are many regulatory differences across the world. Efficient and consistent operational management practices when workers move on from the organization are important.

Good practice in areas of employment transition out of the organization can minimize the likelihood of corporate scandals relating to sexual harassment; unequal pay and unfair pensions provision. In addition, employment relationships that feature in what has become termed the 'gig economy' have led to increased interest in the need for fair and consistent management standards that apply to all stages of the employment relationship, including the management of transition out of the organization, whether for voluntary or involuntary reasons.

Two challenges face those who would like to achieve greater standardization in these areas. First, it is difficult to specify generic and standardized practices for the moving-on process that are appropriate across different national and institutional boundaries. Although the development of a global economy provides for increasing conformity across national boundaries, in the areas of retirement, dismissal, redundancy and so on, legal regulation and organizational contexts make a 'one-size-fits-all' approach impossible.

A second challenge for those who wish to standardize practices in these areas is that of balancing the benefits of standardization with the increasing requirements for organizational flexibility. Therefore, while standards in this area offer potential benefits to organizational reputation, process efficiency and operational effectiveness, standardized and uniform practices are difficult to implement where organizations are committed to individual and organizational flexibility and change.

However, in a context where patterns of legal regulation vary widely in different countries and regions of the world, the development of standards in these areas provides the opportunity for organizations to 'fast-forward' the development of their human governance systems and to establish a benchmark against which organizational practices can be measured, evaluated and continually improved. Specifically, in areas of voluntary turnover, such as retirement and resignation, standards offer opportunities for enhanced and sustained organizational performance that are unlikely to conflict with wider legal and employment regulation.

Evaluating governance and standards for moving on

Evidence about the effectiveness of practices relating to moving on can be difficult to quantify, but this data comprises useful organizational information and should include both soft (qualitative) and hard (quantitative) evidence of the impact of turnover and its management. Appropriate assessment measures are turnover, retention, monitoring and reporting on equal opportunities, diversity and inclusion levels of employment; and other key performance indicators developed to meet organizational and business development plans and strategy.

Organizations that are committed to effective management systems for worker transition processes will require a systematic approach for measuring, monitoring and analysing management systems and activities associated with 'moving on' events. This may involve conducting regular internal audits of practices surrounding both voluntary and involuntary transition practices as a feature of continuous improvement.

Organizational information with relevance to moving on processes include:

- assessments of compliance with legal and other regulatory requirements;
- the results of internal and/or external audits;
- absence and retention data;
- return on investment data from outsourcing or redundancy processes.

Important questions to address include:

- How quickly are 'outgoing' skills and capabilities identified and replaced?
- What proportion of people with crucial capabilities are leaving the organization (and why are they leaving)?
- How responsive are organizational processes to ensuring the workforce has sufficient skills and capability to meet new/future business opportunities?
- How successful are knowledge-sharing processes between those who are moving on from the organization and those who will remain?
- How effective are team leaders, supervisors or people management processes associated with resignation, retirement, and involuntary turnover?
- What proportion of people leave the organization as a result of a lack of internal career development opportunities?
- To what extent is turnover affected by productivity, accident, safety, and risk management outcomes in the organization?
- How successful is the organization at retaining people who work in priority areas?

Summary

Workers move on from the organization, leaving for voluntary and involuntary reasons. Whatever the trigger for the decision to leave the organization, the event itself can be traumatic for the person concerned and their work colleagues. Financial and emotional as well as organizational costs result from resignations, retirements and dismissals. Poor practice in these areas can damage organizational reputation and lead to poor organizational performance.

Good practice in these areas contributes to sustainable organizational performance, good governance and effective management systems. Standards of practice, procedure, regulation and governance minimize negative consequences and provide a basis for the competent and equitable management of workforce exit.

This chapter has described individual level and organizational 'triggers' that cause people to move on from their employment. It has discussed existing standards and regulations, as well as guides of good practice that can provide a guide for effective management practice in this area, acknowledged areas of challenge, and identified opportunities for organizations to develop their management processes for workers who transition out of their employment. It has also briefly outlined guidance for assessing the success of management processes associated with employee turnover.

References and further resources

ACAS www.acas.org.uk (archived at https://perma.cc/U7T4-J9LB)

Adams, B. 26 [November 2017] 6 simple steps to revitalizing your candidate experience, *ERE Media* www.ere.net/5-simple-steps-to-revitalizing-your-candidate-experience/ (archived at https://perma.cc/T76T-G5SC)

Age Scotland. [29 March 2019] Age Inclusive Matrix, *Age UK* www.ageuk.org.uk/scotland/services/age-inclusive-workplaces/age-inclusive-matrix-hr-support-for-an-age-inclusive-workplace/ (archived at https://perma.cc/4WMN-D78G)

British Standards Institution (BSI) (2015) BS 76000:2015 *Human Resource. Valuing People. Management System. Requirements and Guidance* https://shop.bsigroup.com/ProductDetail/?pid=000000000030298954 (archived at https://perma.cc/2GK4-H6P2)

BSI (2017) BS 76005:2017 *Valuing People Through Diversity and Inclusion: Code of Practice for Organizations* https://shop.bsigroup.com/ProductDetail/?pid=000000000030338898 (archived at https://perma.cc/V6XF-5P4D)

ILO. 29 March 2019] Employment Protection Legislation Database, *ILO* www.ilo.org/dyn/eplex/termdisplay.severancePay?p_lang=en (archived at https://perma.cc/9MYT-QD2B)

Incomes Data Services (IDS) (2010) *Employment Law Unfair Dismissal Handbook*, Thompson Reuters, London

IDS (2011) *Redundancy Handbook*, Thompson Reuters, London

IDS (2011) *Transfer of Undertakings Handbook*, Thompson Reuters, London

ISO (2014) ISO 37500:2014 *Guidance on Outsourcing* www.iso.org/standard/
56269.html (archived at https://perma.cc/75N7-WVJL)

ISO (2016) BS ISO 30400:2016 *Human resource management. Vocabulary*
https://shop.bsigroup.com/ProductDetail/?pid=000000000030324720
(archived at https://perma.cc/V8A9-CKTT)

ISO (2016) BS ISO 30408:2016 *Human Resource Management – Guidelines on
human governance* https://shop.bsigroup.com/ProductDetail/
?pid=000000000030284701 (archived at https://perma.cc/M9WY-ZTQ5)

ISO (2016) ISO 30409:2016 *Human Resource Management – Workforce Planning*
www.iso.org/standard/64150.html (archived at https://perma.cc/2BYU-9VWJ)

ISO (2018) BS ISO 45001:2018 *Occupational health and safety management
systems. Requirements with guidance for use* https://shop.bsigroup.com/Product
Detail?pid=000000000030299985 (archived at https://perma.cc/X57D-MC48)

ISO (2019) ISO 27501:2019 *The human-centred organization – Guidance for
managers* www.iso.org/standard/64241.html (archived at https://perma.cc/
57AV-7RKS)

ISO (forthcoming) ISO/AWI TS 23378 *Human Resource Management: Turnover
and Retention Technical Specification* www.iso.org/standard/75372.html
(archived at https://perma.cc/UE8W-NAZ9)

9

Cross-national, cross-sectoral and cross-functional issues

Alaa Garad

Introduction

This chapter will discuss the utility of standards in human capital management and development (HCMD) where coordination between organizations (as in an industry sector, say safety or aviation, health standards) is necessary and where outcome assessments involve different professional functions and competencies. As organizations look to the future digital transformation is of prime importance, accelerating cross-border operations, scalability and increasing use of low-cost equipment and software.

This chapter considers the implications for integrated management systems in relation to human capital management (HCM) standards, especially for collaboration in the areas of assessment, safety, mental health, wellbeing and performance management.

CHAPTER OBJECTIVES

This chapter sets out to:

- investigate the issues and challenges related to human capital that arise from cross-functional, cross-sectoral and cross-national perspectives;

- discuss the impacts of new technologies such as artificial intelligence (AI) and Industry 4.0 on HCMD.

Key terms

In this section, key terms related to contemporary human capital issues are briefly described and defined.

AI:	This term refers to the development and application of computing technologies to perform in areas hitherto requiring human intelligence. Examples of these involve decision-making, facial recognition and interpretation, learning from prior experience and adapting to new stimuli.
Industry 4.0:	This is a term often used by practitioners to refer to the fourth industrial revolution. This follows previous revolutions such as mechanization (Industry 1.0), mass production (Industry 2.0) and automation (Industry 3.0). Industry 4.0 is the label given to the gradual combination of traditional manufacturing and industrial practices with increasingly technological functionality. Industry 4.0 provides the potential for large-scale machine-to-machine communication to leverage increased automation, improved communication and monitoring, self-diagnosis and analysis as the basis for productive and service efficiency.
Internet of Things (IoT):	This refers to a system of interrelated computing devices, mechanical and digital machines, objects, animals or people that are provided with unique identifiers (UIDs) with the ability to transfer data over a network without requiring human-to-human or human-to-computer interaction (IoT Agenda, nd).
Machine Learning (ML):	This is an application of AI that provides systems with the ability to automatically learn and improve from experience without being explicitly programmed. ML means that computer programs can access and use data autonomously (Expert Systems, nd).

Robotic Process Automation (RPA):	This term refers to the use of software with AI and ML capabilities to handle high-volume, repeatable tasks that previously required human input. These tasks can include queries, calculations and maintenance of records and transactions. RPA allows computer software configuration and robotic processes to emulate and integrate human actions within digital business process systems.

Standards discussed

In this section, the following standards, which have the greatest relevance to cross-national, cross-sectoral or cross-functional organizational issues are:

- ISO 30414:2018 *Human resource management – Guidelines for internal and external human capital reporting*;
- ISO 10667:2011 *Assessment service delivery – procedures and methods to assess people in work and organizational settings (Parts 1 and 2)*.

These standards are outlined below.

ISO 30414

As discussed in Chapter 1, This standard focuses on the cross-organizational measurement of the cumulative knowledge, skills and abilities of an organization's people. It provides guidance on metrics to examine the impact on an organization's long-term performance and competitive advantage achieved through maximizing productivity and efficiency. Applied appropriately, this standard can provide the basis for cross-sectoral comparison of performance management and measurement.

The standard is guided by the principles of human rights at work, and is grounded in the value of human capital (people) as the basis of the ability and opportunity of the organization to create long-term and sustainable value. It aligns with the human governance standard (ISO 30408) and establishes guidelines on human capital data capture, measurement, reporting and analysis. The guiding principles are:

- recognizing the importance of the human capital contribution to organizational success;
- focuses on metrics that are in consonance with the organization's leadership direction, proportionate, practical and material to an organization's business and operating model, regulatory, political and social contexts;
- relevance for organizations in all sectors, of all types and sizes, and internationally;
- transparency of reporting in terms of opportunity and risk for internal and external stakeholders.

In the context of cross-functional or cross-national working, there are many potential benefits of a standardized approach to human capital reporting, which include:

- improvement of human resource management (HRM) processes using standardized and agreed data, which describes the value in a broadly comparable sense, alongside individual case-based solutions;
- a greater understanding of the financial and non-financial returns that are generated as a result of investments in human capital;
- access and understanding of an organization's human capital; and its present and future performance for internal and external stakeholders;
- provision of data facilitating the improvement of HRM processes using standard measures and data capture.

This standard is almost the only standard that takes into account three associated elements of risk, namely employee life-cycle risks, compliance risks and workforce planning risks.

In the first of these, six forms of risk can affect cross-sectional, cross-functional and cross-national working. For example, in various industries, risk is minimized in the hiring process if sufficient attention is paid to the scrutiny and selection process applied to candidates from a broad pool to ensure they meet pre-defined standards related to essential and preferred skills and qualifications, and are assessed and examined to ensure that claims made are validated through the selection process.

A further risk in the employee life-cycle relates with succession risk and the potential loss of talented people without having qualified and ready successors in place. To overcome this risk, a transparent scheme of succession planning provides an effective risk minimization process.

INTERNATIONAL HOTELS AND RESORTS GROUP

Due to high turnover in the luxury hotels and resorts sector, International instituted a succession scheme. This involved identifying the competencies of the jobholder, and using this as the basis for the identification of a list of successors. The first successor on the list is defined as ready for immediate succession, if required. The second may require a six-month period of preparation, and the third may require a year to be fully prepared.

There are other risks associated with the employee life-cycle, such as remuneration risk and risks related to termination process. Both issues could be potentially damaging to either the employee or the organization if not addressed carefully and in compliance with appropriate laws and regulations, as well as taking into account human rights and other human factors. Compliance risk concerns the likelihood of violating, either intentionally or unintentionally, labour laws and other regulatory and practice-relevant conventions. These areas are potentially damaging although often underestimated, and should be the centre of focus in all organizations and across all sectors.

The third element addresses workforce planning risks that might be addressed by making sure that the supply of talent to the organization is in line with identified strategic workforce requirements at an organizational level.

BS ISO 10667

This standard focuses on the practices of assessment services providers and their clients. According to BS ISO 10667, good practice is achieved by:

- defining appropriate practice for assessment procedures and methods;
- ensuring equity in the application of assessment procedures;
- enabling appropriate evaluation of the quality of assessment service provision.

In contemporary organizations, there is an increasing demand on engagement with assessment services. Standards provide a useful approach to benchmarking that can support the achievement of successful outcomes in selection, recruitment and management practices of service providers to support organizational strategic objectives.

This standard provides guidance appropriate to organizations of all sizes and types about methods to assess individuals, groups and organizations in their specific occupational arena. This is particularly relevant where working relationships between clients and service providers require clarity about their respective obligations and responsibilities before, during and after any assessment processes. It also provides guidance on the rights and responsibilities of others involved in assessment procedures, including those who are recipients of the assessment outcome and results.

BS ISO 10667 comprises two parts:

- requirements for the client;
- requirements for a service provider.

Contemporary human capital issues

Cross-national and cross-cultural issues

Organizations operating in a global context face a number of challenges in order to adapt and sustain their business practices in a dynamic and sometimes volatile business environment. In the international context of human capital, the cross-cultural environment, internationalization characteristics and the opportunities presented by a multinational management staff have the potential for significant impact on diversity and organizational performance.

In global workplace settings, people reflect a diversity of societal cultural backgrounds and this presents both opportunities and challenges for those involved with HCMD. In particular, employees of multinational companies represent different cultural backgrounds that can present challenges due to cultural differences in relation to understanding, implementation, and evaluation of the organization's goals and strategy.

The difficulty of specifying standardized practices that might 'travel' across cultural and company/business unit boundaries are well-known. Differences are evident in the expectations of standardization processes in different countries, reflecting, in part, the different characteristics of their national culture, history, and economic context (Ernst, 2013). Distinctive understandings of the employment relationship that are prevalent in different parts of the world lead to different policies applied in different ways.

However, in the volatile and dynamic environment in which global business is conducted, standards against which evaluation of human capital processes can be benchmarked are increasingly necessary to ensure coherent and consistent strategy and operational execution. This is particularly pertinent in areas such as diversity and inclusion.

The development process of international standards by the Human Resource Management Standards Committee (TC 260) highlights the challenges of developing consensus on guidance for practice and standards of excellence. Nonetheless, as more countries participate in these processes, culturally and contextually relevant documents are developed that provide a basis for coherent approaches to HCMD that are relevant and applicable across national and regional boundaries.

Organizational innovation

Technology endows today's knowledge workers with what may be termed a real-life superpower: the ability to process enormous amounts of data in real time, increasing productivity while cutting out time-consuming manual labour. Those who focus on knowledge work also highlight the potential for the elimination of many repetitive jobs with the promise of empowering workers to focus more on cognitive and tailored processes devoted to specific audiences, clients or markets.

The combination of critical thinking abilities with the availability of decision-making data sets offers potential for radical changes to assumptions about the meaning and value of work. Technology has become a 'hygiene factor' in many organizations: smartphones, computers and other digital systems being increasingly seen as an essential part of day-to-day labour. According to Waite (2018), future managers' effectiveness is dependent on their ability to use technology intelligently and prudently as a feature of training, development and retention of valued workers.

Large organizations, in particular, are identifying the importance of methods for 'reskilling' employees to cope in this different context. A key principle, outlined in many chapters of this book, is that workers' workplace learning and growth opportunities provide the most effective route to innovation, collaboration and sustained organizational advantage.

Employee empowerment

In the context of rapid advances in technology, many changes are occurring in national and international labour markets. In many parts of the world there are growing proportions of females in the workplace and, as health improvements are achieved, so the workforce in many parts of the world is ageing. Part-time and insecure forms of working are also more prevalent.

As this trend continues economists predict that some job roles will be replaced by new technologies (Waite, 2018), machine technology, AI and robotic technology. In addition to sectors such as manufacturing and retail, other sectors such as construction, health care, insurance, financial services, office management and education expect that many job roles will be automated in the near future.

In this context, the basis of employee empowerment is expected to shift. Englemann and Schwabe (2018) argue that in this context the basis for frequently changing areas of responsibility, agile, smart or mobile learning will become prevalent that can enable workers to optimize their skills. Such developments require workers to develop and optimize their problem-solving skills as a feature of achieving efficiency benefits as situation-dependent specialist knowledge forms the basis for effective knowledge work.

Cross-sectoral issues

Further challenges facing organizations that operate in the globalized and interconnected business environment are critical issues that affect business sustainability, such as the widening gap between the employed and the unemployed and territorial and cultural conflicts. The ability to respond in a timely and appropriate way to issues as they are recognized requires new levels of cross-sectoral collaboration. This presents challenges relating to balancing priorities, managing multiple stakeholders and identifying pathways of action that replace competition and avoidance with accommodation and compromise.

In this part of the section, some of the cross-sectoral challenges are outlined before the opportunities presented by human capital and other standards are discussed.

CHALLENGES TO CROSS-SECTORAL COLLABORATION

A key cross-sectoral issue is leadership development. Regardless of the specific sector, effective leadership is required to ensure effective deployment of human capital resources and experience, particularly taking into account different demographic profiles in specific industries and sectors, as well as different approaches to assessments of risk, time, and scale.

Standards in the human capital field assume that effective leadership will incorporate recognition that robust and sustainable practices, policies and problem solutions will come from designing with (and not just for) the communities most affected by them.

A number of potential benefits can arise from cross-sectoral collaboration, including:

- lower production costs/cheaper labour costs;
- increased creativity/innovation;
- logistical streamlining;
- improved quality of services and products;
- better margins and revenues;
- enhanced customer loyalty;
- better levels of organizational and sectoral resilience.

However, effective cross-sectoral leadership involves a human-centred approach and engagement of key stakeholders in decision-making and implementation processes. This co-creative capacity to map, plan and implement a system with the involvement and commitment of those most affected, addresses important power dynamics, such that stakeholders can engage with and commit to the co-designed solution. However, achieving this process requires leadership that can build trust and enable participants to address tensions as a feature of developing an appropriate and shared culture. Difficult issues must also be addressed in balancing competitive advantage within sectors with collaborative benefits.

The concept of competitive advantage is familiar with organizational decision-makers, but remains an elusive feature in the objective of gaining market share. The value chain is an important feature of achieving competitive advantage (Tanwar, 2013), but changes to the global environment now focus attention on ecosystems of technology, talent and information. As a result, sustainable performance is often associated with networking and collaboration. Alliances, joint ventures and other collaborative arrangements are increasingly evident in the business.

Although some alliances may be no more than fleeting encounters, lasting only as long as it takes one partner to establish themselves in a new market, others may be the prelude to a more sustained relationship between two or more organizations' technologies and capabilities. There are a number of implications of this trend for standards and standardization in relation to:

- provision of people assessment;
- performance management and measurements;
- internal marketing.

Cross-functional issues

Further development in contemporary business organizations, both large and small, is the increasing requirement for cross-functional team working. Cross-functional teams are typically composed of individuals who have functional eg marketing, engineering or IT roles, but who also work collaboratively on issues or projects that require a diversity of resources.

Access to technology also provides a basis for remote cross-functional teams to be established for specific projects, with time and resource benefits as well as the potential to benefit from diversity as a feature of the optimization of human capital. Organizations in public, private and third sectors are increasingly team-based; relying on project teams, taskforces, committees, working groups and so on. Such processes provide the basis for increased knowledge sharing and learning.

Human capital standards issues are relevant to these developments requiring attention to:

- hierarchy/organization structure;
- lack of communication, 'silos' and learning (dis)abilities;
- pay and reward structures to achieve a balance between roles considered 'core' and other support roles;
- worker empowerment and organizational culture;
- high-performance cross-functional work processes and practices.

Industry 4.0 and AI

As indicated already, AI refers to the capability of a machine to imitate intelligent behaviour, and Industry 4.0 is the term used to refer to the potential for large-scale machine-to-machine communication leading to increased automation, improved communication and monitoring, self-diagnosis and analysis as the basis for productive and service efficiency. There are 75 standards published by national and international standards bodies addressing issues related to robots and robotic devices in the workplace, home and care delivery. Yet this is considered the infancy stage of the machine's era.

In relation to HCM, technology-enabled communication incorporating ideas, information, databases, archives and software (PD IEC/PAS 63088) present important issues affecting the dynamics of the workplace and labour market. Since the inception of computer technology, HR functions have become progressively automated. However, changes in the global business environment make urgent the need to integrate the different systems that have been developed for different areas of HR work. Waite (2018) estimates that process automation remains the focus for 45 per cent of large companies.

The implications of such process automation are briefly considered below:

- The role of the machine in recruitment and induction: AI tools are increasingly likely to be used to source candidates from social media, data banks and other sources. ML algorithms will undertake screening and RPA may feature in employee onboarding processes across systems and organizations for physical access, seat allocation, hardware, physical card, asset allocations, travel arrangements, manuals, FAQs and contact points.

- AI automation of payroll functions to enable synchronized data flow, error detection and remediation: This is likely to take forward existing functions relating to 'self-service' capability for payroll query resolutions.

- AI tools are likely to feature increasingly in talent management decision-making, recommending and assigning development opportunities based on inputs from competency mappings, succession planning and performance management processes.

- ML-based algorithms have the potential to measure and track 'employee sentiment', predict employee engagement levels, and predict turnover risk. This could help organizations identify possible attrition for top talent and plan interventions.

In summary, Bughin, Chui and Manyika (nd) predict that ML, when combined with robotics, may increase global productivity growth by 0.8–1.4 per cent, while automating nearly 50 per cent of current work. This raises issues of a potential mismatch between the education provided for students and the qualifications and experiences sought by employers (Flynn, Dance and Schaefer, 2017). There are legal and ethical issues associated with these developments, particularly around work values, leadership and management culture and life-long learning and development. These are illustrated in Figure 9.1.

FIGURE 9.1   Impacts of Industry 4.0

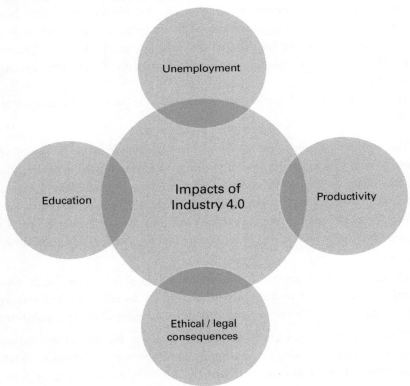

The figure shows the impacts of Industry 4.0 on HCM

Industry 4.0 requires significant review of HCM and the nature of 'good work' by employers. The World Economic Forum has set an agenda for the future of human capital in the era of Industry 4.0 that focuses attention on education and training to build and maintain a skills set that is appropriate for this context. The increasing pace of technological change and globalization opens up new opportunities. However, it also foregrounds the priority for organizational leaders to align company practices, public policy with education and training systems.

Areas that organizational leaders and HCM specialists might address include:

- personal competences: the ability to learn and to act in a reflective and autonomous way;
- value systems: the ability develop an appropriate attitude and ethical value system;

- agility and personal flexibility with respect to hours of work, place of work and role responsibilities;
- a values-driven leadership style
- collaborative working to integrate smart working reflecting diversity in culture, educational background and geographical location;
- social/interpersonal competencies: to communicate, cooperate and establish social connections and structures with other individuals and groups;
- intellectual competencies: a mindset open to building and maintaining networks of experts to resolve problems in a cooperative and collaborative way;
- action-related competencies: the ability to analyse, evaluate and implement new ideas.

Summary

This chapter has discussed future-orientated as well as cross-national, cross-functional and cross-sectoral issues. These all foreground the importance of coordination within and between organizations, networks and supply chains. These are areas where standards can be beneficial but work is still required to develop them. ISO 30414:2018 *Human resource management – Guidelines for internal and external human capital reporting* represents a good start.

Among the long list of factors that impact human capital, digital transformation is of prime importance as it occurs at a high speed and can easily cross borders enabled by technology, scaling and the relatively low cost of equipment and software. Further research is needed to identify the impact of these issues, and the impact that standards can have on coherent and agile performance by organizations and industries.

References and further resources

British Standards Institution (2017) PD IEC/PAS 63088:2017 *Smart manufacturing. Reference architecture model industry 4.0 (RAMI4.0)* https://shop.bsigroup.com/ProductDetail?pid=000000000030350369 (archived at https://perma.cc/Y25T-TQHG)

Bughin J, Chui, N and Manyika, J. An Executive's Guide to the Internet of Things, *McKinsey* www.mckinsey.com/business-functions/digital-mckinsey/our-insights/an-executives-guide-to-the-internet-of-things (archived at https://perma.cc/7UZV-4292)

Englemann, A and Schwabe, G (2018) *Enabling Workers to Enter Industry 4.0: A Layered Mobile Learning Architecture, Proceedings of the 51st Hawaii International Conference on System Sciences* http://hdl.handle.net/10125/49892 (archived at https://perma.cc/QB7M-TCFF)

Ernst, D (2013) America's Voluntary Standards System: A Best-Practice Model for Asian Innovation Policies?, *Policy Studies*, **66**

Expert System. What is Machine Learning: A definition, *Expert System* www.expertsystem.com/machine-learning-definition (archived at https://perma.cc/H9FY-868C)

Flynn, J, Dance, S and Schaefer, D (2017) Industry 4.0 and its potential impact on employment demographics in the UK, in *Advances in Manufacturing Technology XXXI*, ed. J. Gao *et al*, IOS Press

IoT Agenda. Internet of Things, *IoT Agenda* https://internetofthingsagenda.techtarget.com/definition/Internet-of-Things-IoT (archived at https://perma.cc/VB35-WYXW)

ISO (2011) ISO 10667:2011 *Assessment service delivery – procedures and methods to assess people in work and organizational settings (Parts 1 and 2)* www.iso.org/standard/56441.html (archived at https://perma.cc/G995-6T4A)

ISO (2016) BS ISO 30408:2016 *Human Resource Management – Guidelines on human governance* https://shop.bsigroup.com/ProductDetail/?pid=000000000030284701 (archived at https://perma.cc/NP64-MFQF)

ISO (2018) ISO 30414:2018 *Human resource management – Guidelines for internal and external human capital reporting* www.iso.org/standard/69338.html (archived at https://perma.cc/4AD6-3XXL)

Moore, M. What is Industry 4.0? Everything You Need to Know, *Tech Radar* www.techradar.com/uk/news/what-is-industry-40-everything-you-need-to-know (archived at https://perma.cc/DTT7-92TQ)

Tanwar, R (2013) Porter's Generic Competitive Strategies, *IOSR Journal of Business and Management*, **15** (1), pp 11–17

UI Pat. What is Robotic Process Automation?, *UI Path* www.uipath.com/rpa/robotic-process-automation (archived at https://perma.cc/BS42-6XDA)

UKAS www.ukas.co.uk (archived at https://perma.cc/K2FJ-XRYX)

Waite, S (2018) How Emerging Technology Is Empowering Knowledge Workers, *Forbes* www.forbes.com/sites/forbescommunicationscouncil/2018/02/28/how-emerging-technology-is-empowering-knowledge-workers/ (archived at https://perma.cc/756M-U9V8)#599ad1cd295f

10

Assessment and accreditation

Angela Mulvie

Introduction

For many organizations, no matter their size, sector or purpose, working with external quality standards provides a number of opportunities to review operational practices including those dealing with the management and development of staff. Such standards play an important part in organizational life, providing both an ethical and 'quality assured' basis for activities undertaken (Chartered Institute of Personnel and Development (CIPD), 2018).

Where human capital management (HCM) standards are used, these will impact specifically on the way in which an organization's human resources are dealt with through the cycle of attraction and recruitment of staff, their retention and development, and the way in which they move on from their role and how this is managed. This takes place against a backdrop of employment legislation which has shaped human resource management (HRM) and human resource development (HRD) practices for many years. Assessment against such HCM standards will provide an opportunity to review not only how HRM and HRD functions are operating, but also how this compares to other organizations' employment practices, both within a specific sector and geographically.

The standards themselves, which are devised and refined regularly by specialist professionals in a relevant field, are considered to be 'leading edge' in that they reflect good practice in that particular area of operation. In its most simple application, the assessment/certification process can provide extremely valuable insights into what is going on inside an organization, how well internal processes and systems are operating and with what results, and what might need to be changed to make improvements.

A key issue for any organization is the wide range of standards (and quality awards) which currently exists both within the UK and internationally, making the choice of which one(s) to work with difficult. Many of these standards extend beyond employment and HR-related issues, such as those relating to quality management systems, the management of customer service, the application of specific environmental factors, and so on.

This degree of complexity can also extend to the assessment process itself, where organizations seek accreditation against a standard as a means of demonstrating that requirements meet or indeed surpass what is required. It is therefore important that not only those tasked with the conduct of an assessment (the assessors), but also those who are preparing for the event (the client), know and understand what is involved.

The journey towards final certification, accreditation or recognition can be challenging and often requires a number of changes to be made to how things are done, both during preparations for the final assessment, or a result of feedback from that process following a final decision by an assessor. The outcomes achieved from the assessment journey itself may therefore be valuable in terms of making changes to operational and employment practices. During that journey it is possible to consider what the concept of 'good practice' actually looks like, using that as a comparator for what exists within the organization under review at that time, and to analyse what problems/issues are impacting on the delivery of operations and services. The value of a robust and well-conducted assessment process cannot therefore be emphasized enough.

This chapter focuses on the steps required via the assessment process, to achieve final certification for some of the HR standards under consideration in this text. It explains in general terms the principles behind assessment, and considers the use of both traditional and emerging methods. These changes to the way in which decisions are made about whether or not organizations match appropriately with the requirements of a particular standard are often the result of changes to the standards themselves, where these have been updated to capture and reflect current trends and applications in a particular industry/sector.

This chapter also reviews some of the bodies which support the assessment process and considers how their work is quality-assured, so that a high-quality review is undertaken. This includes consideration of what needs to be done to recruit, develop and retain competent assessors.

CHAPTER OBJECTIVES

This chapter aims to provide the reader with an understanding of the following issues:

- the principles that underpin a sound assessment process;
- the stages involved in an assessment process;
- timescales that need to be followed;
- costs and other resources that require consideration;
- the roles played in the assessment process by the different stakeholders participating;
- what 'evidence' looks like and how it should be prepared for analysis and consideration;
- what the concepts of maturity and readiness mean in terms of both preparation for assessment and maintenance of the standard thereafter;
- the outcomes that might be achieved from the assessment process and how these should be dealt with going forward;
- other factors that need to be taken into account;
- what quality assurance of the assessment process itself takes place.

Key terms

When dealing with external standards and awards, several variations in the use of terminology are evident. Whilst many practitioners and academics will use these interchangeably, it is important to differentiate between a standard, a model and an award (Mulvie, 2018).

The following terms are important in considering where and how an assessment process is undertaken.

Accreditation: This term is often used interchangeably with 're-cognition' but implies a more formal approach. Used in many different fields, accreditation is a process whereby formal approval and certification is given, usually by an awarding body, to demonstrate some authority or credibility in that area or sphere.

It is this last definition which we need to consider in particular when describing the assessment process for HCM standards. That process can be both resource intensive and require a period of time for both the preparation and conduct of a formal review.

Audit: This term is often used by awarding bodies themselves and the specialists developing the standards, as well as those working as assessors and organizational stakeholders who are helping to prepare for a formal review. The term, which is often synonymous with that used within the field of finance and accountancy, is sometimes also considered when describing the assessment process. It implies a careful review of information and evidence by an authorized person to check and officially verify against facts.

However, the thinking around assessment of quality standards is changing to reflect a less regimented approach and the use of more flexible and holistic methods (see later in this chapter). This is reflected in the terminology applied, whereby less use is being made of the term 'audit', and more use made of approaches which reflect feedback which includes some degree of advice and guidance.

External quality award: This term is used to describe an award which is given in recognition of an organization achieving certain agreed levels of activity in its field of operation. The award is given by the organization which 'owns' it, eg the Best Companies Award.

External quality model: This term is used to describe a way of operating which is based on a specific way of doing things, built on both good practices and ongoing research to ensure the currency of the model. Sometimes 'external quality framework' is used interchangeably. An example of an external quality model would be the European Foundation Quality Model (EFQM).

External quality standard: This term is used to describe an external set of rules or principles to which an organization must adhere to receive accreditation. It provides an accepted way of doing things relevant to the organization operating in its sector/industry. An example of an external quality standard would be one sitting within the ISO 9000 family of standards.

The assessment journey

Principles underpinning the formal assessment process

Given the large number of standards and quality awards available in the marketplace, we might assume that variations exist in the assessment methods used for different standards. However, several key principles are evident no matter the content of the standard or the award under consideration. It is this similarity of purpose that gives the assessment process credibility, although variations in style and approach may arise depending on the certification body and the specific content requirements of the standard itself.

In an educational context, students are assessed during and/or also at the end of that learning experience by both formative and summative assessment. As a result of a formative assessment process, initial and ongoing decision-making about what is under review can lead to changes being made to procedures being applied as a result of feedback. Summative assessment, on the other hand, takes place at the end of the learning journey whereby students are graded, often through the application of examination methods, or at least by completion and grading of final assignments, by overall consideration of the standards they have reached. It is a more formal summary of progress against specific requirements and often results in a specific grade being allocated. 'Evidence' has to be found and checked against requirements.

Many of the assessment methods used to measure organizations against an agreed employment-related standard reflect both formative and summative assessment when the client is 'on the journey' towards final decisions being made, as well as at that end point when the assessor(s) makes a decision to award (or not) certification and provide(s) feedback accordingly. A key difference however between assessment within an educational setting and that which occurs in a workplace is the requirement in many cases to provide a great deal of written evidence of actual systems and procedures operating, to demonstrate how such systems are actually being managed and applied.

The journey towards final assessment and the various stages involved are critical to the end result. The client organization working with the standard requires to address several issues which have a number of practical considerations. These might include:

- organizational stakeholders' understanding of the requirements of the standard and what these mean when being applied;
- what business rationale pertains for pursuing the certification/accreditation and whether this can be positioned well with those key influencers whose decisions may impact on a successful outcome;
- where and how the organization sits against the standard at the start of the process;
- what key areas need to be addressed to ensure success at the end of the journey and how will feedback from the assessor be received and acted upon;
- what the resource implications are for the organization that is pursuing certification;
- what training might be required for those involved in the preparation of the organization to ensure success;
- what competitors are doing around working with this standard, when the benchmarking element is under consideration.

Where such a list prevails, there is value in the organization preparing a project plan for the journey about to start, and liaising closely with the relevant awarding/certification body to ensure that relevant information is made available on which to base decisions. Most, if not all, awarding/certification bodies work alongside the client organization on its journey to ensure a clear understanding of requirements. However, it is also important to note that in doing so, objectivity and rigour must be maintained to ensure that the standard of the assessment process itself remains high and that it is conducted in an effective manner.

This raises the issue of how assessors can, and indeed do, adopt both an advisory and assessment role during their working relationship with the client organization.

Mulvie (2018) provides a review of how these differences have been handled with regard to the Investors in People (IiP) framework and its development both in the UK and internationally.

THE CHANGING APPROACH TO ADVISORY AND ASSESSMENT SERVICES

Historically, the two roles of advice and assessment applied to the IiP framework were kept entirely separate by the different agencies managing the process. In the early 1990s, IIP UK became the employer-led organization which remained the custodian of the IiP standard for several years. The standard (and therefore assessment activity) was delivered at that time through a local network of regional quality centres, which had geographical coverage of the whole of the UK. Internationally, IiP was delivered both in terms of advisory and assessment services by the International Quality Centre.

For many years, the management of IiP remained in government hands, first within the Department of Employment, and thereafter under the auspices of the UK Commission for Employment and Skills (UKCES) following its incorporation in April 2008. In late 2009, IIP UK was transitioned across into UKCES, who took formal responsibility for IiP activity in April 2010. UKCES had been formed from a merger between the then-Sector Skills Development Agency and the National Employment Panel (UKCES, 2016).

The Commission had a strong remit to enhance training and upskill the national workforce through the work of the Sector Skills Councils, employer-led bodies established for a number of different industries. The merger aimed to cut administrative costs and help to rejuvenate what was seen to be a 'flagging brand'. A refreshed delivery network was also established, along with a new business model.

In 2015, as part of a further spending review, the government announced the closure of UKCES during 2016 to enable the prioritization of funding for core adult skills development. It was also agreed that by 2016/17 IiP was to become completely self-funding, and in 2017, IiP activity was taken into a new IIP Community Interest Company (CIC) within the Department of Education, for the purposes of managing the standard. At the same time delivery centres across the UK were rationalized, including that for the international work of IIP. This self-funded, self-managed CIC is now focusing on re-energizing both the national employment agenda and international employment practices through the provision of sound IIP services.

As part of that process, the traditional advisory and assessment services, which had been delivered as separate services, are now linked together with early assessment activity using a self-managed model via the client. This includes a self-completed online questionnaire to take the 'temperature' of employee viewpoints. This approach to combining advisory and assessment services is mirrored by many other certification bodies who provide guidance to the client organization on the understanding and expectation that they will undertake much of the preparations themselves.

The type of advice therefore at this early stage can take the form of initial site visits, and training courses for those involved in the preparations. This type of 'internal champion' training can prove very useful as well as being resource sensible, as it builds expertise in-house and provides a framework for action within the client organization.

The concepts of good practice, best practice and excellence

When considering the value of an assessment process and the elements it comprises, it is important to think about how we might define 'good' and 'best' practice as well as the term 'excellence'. These terms are often used interchangeably, both within the field of quality management and HRM, and also when describing quality standards and awards and their assessment. Yet there are subtle differences which it is helpful to take into account when considering that assessment process for such standards as both the client organization and assessor(s) need to be in agreement on what such terminology constitutes with regard to the standard under scrutiny.

The Advisory, Conciliation and Arbitration Service (ACAS) suggests that good practice in an employment context extends beyond just ensuring that legal rights and responsibilities are met, so that employees' levels of motivation and engagement are also taken into account when recruiting and retaining staff. Employees require support from their employing organization at different times in their careers; this support can take many forms and cover more than just financial compensation for work undertaken, for example in the form of learning and development opportunities.

In the context of working with, and also developing, HCM standards, the concept of good practice implies what might be expected beyond minimum legislative requirements with regard to employing and managing staff. In the UK, the legal framework of employment law has existed for many years and is updated depending on directives coming from the European Union. This situation may change depending on the outcomes of the process referred to as 'Brexit'.

Best practice on the other hand implies an accepted way of doing things which is considered at the time to be superior to any alternative available. It suggests a way of going well beyond legal or indeed ethical requirements. The term also implies that comparisons can be made with agreed standards being used in the marketplace. The concept of benchmarking is well established when we are considering quality standards, as working with these enables some type of comparison to be made with others in the same field of operation.

The application of standards therefore ensures that such comparisons are possible and indeed may become one of the reasons for pursuing certification as it provides the organization with some degree of comfort that it is operating to well beyond acceptable standards, which in turn may help with positioning in its marketplace against the competition. The scoring mechanisms inherent in both IiP and the EFQM frameworks enable such comparisons to be an outcome from the assessment process itself. As the more recently introduced British Standard series 76000 becomes established, more client organizations may look to consider how they compare with this standard against their competition.

The term 'excellence' is often understood as an approach or methodology that surpasses anything else available. The term has wider connotations than the concept of best practice. The search for excellence in the way in which organizations operate was first introduced in Peters and Waterman's seminal work (1982) which investigated what made organizations successful in their field. Whilst their work did not focus on the use or application specifically of standards of operation, it did highlight three key factors, namely people, customers and action, as critical to the success in high-performing businesses.

The eight themes of success identified through their research included having a management philosophy which guides everyday practices, which is an underlying element of any quality system. Many of the quality standards being used by organizations today demonstrate to the external world how well the organization is performing, whilst at the same time providing a framework internally for the management of strategy and delivery of operations.

Porter and Tanner (2004) describe business excellence as an approach which ... *'focuses on improving the organization's effectiveness, efficiency and responsiveness to customers' and other stakeholders' needs by actively harnessing peoples' skills and competencies in the pursuit of achieving sustained improvement to organizational performance...'*. This suggests a strong focus on providing the customer with a high-quality service, which can only occur when all employees and managers are working to optimum standards. Optimum use of staff is achieved through the application of sound HRM and HRD policies and procedures based on HCM standards.

Many of the different 'excellence' frameworks, models and standards that have emerged over the last thirty years or so, enabling organizations to compare themselves with others in their marketplace, have become widely used. In the international marketplace, some of these are also used. However, their application in the same way as in the UK, from an assessment perspective, is challenging as local legislative and cultural employment requirements also apply.

This strong focus on becoming 'world class' is inherent therefore within many standards being used, including those within the HCM arena. Such a focus on finding excellence in business practices and the value attached to this has been the subject of much debate and research in what is referred to as the 'culture-excellence' school. Collins (2001) suggests that greatness is defined by how financial performance grows well beyond market average over a sustained period, often because the company focuses on their specific field of competence. This implies that a commercial advantage may be gained from pursuing external standards, something which may need to be explored during the assessment process.

The stages involved in the assessment process

No matter which standard is being considered, there are several generic stages that are usually followed. Whilst these may demonstrate slight differences between certification bodies, the general principles attached to assessment have relevance across a number of areas. These comprise the following elements:

- The ownership of working with the standard rests with the client organization; however, the decision-making process around the final assessment phase – ie whether or not the standard is met rests with the assessor(s).

- The responsibility for the production of information and evidence to satisfy the assessor(s) rests with the client organization.

- The degree of effort to be placed in the preparation phase may differ from one organization to another depending on the resources being invested in the whole process.

- There is an expectation of some form of evidence checking; this may be done through different methods including written documentation, face-to-face interviews, surveys, videos and so on.

- The choice of method of evidence collection will be a joint decision between the certification body and the client organization, although the former will give guidance on this.

- The assessment process may require the appointment of one or more assessors and the resource requirement attached to the assessment process will depend on the size and geographical spread of the operation.

- The length of time for an assessment will depend on a number of variables, including the overall readiness of the client organization for the external visit.

- The use of feedback from the assessor(s) is well established and forms an integral part of the whole process of working with standards and awards no matter their focus.

Impartiality of the assessor(s) is a key feature, whilst at the same time they must remain helpful and supportive. This is a critical part of assessor training, no matter their area of interest and focus. PD IEC/PAS 63088I summarizes its approach to the assessment process by encouraging the following stages:

1 Initial contact is made with the British Standards Institution (BSI) to explain what is needed, and the standard which is being aimed for.

2 A proposal is issued to the client organization detailing the costs and time involved in a formal assessment.

3 An assessment team is allocated with a dedicated client manager.

4 Training workshops are offered to ensure that client organizational staff are ready for certification.

5 An optional pre-assessment can be undertaken to identify any omissions or weaknesses that require resolution.

6 The assessment is undertaken – the stages involved will depend on the particular standard being pursued.

7 A certificate of registration is issued, clearly outlining the actual scope of the certification.

Whilst this list depicts a highly practical focus to the assessment process, there appears to be limited attempt in the quality management and HRD literature to highlight such a real-world focus when considering how, when and why to work with external standards. Indeed, this is still an underdeveloped area of research. Yet as Anderson (2017) points out, standards have become a ubiquitous part of organizational, professional and social life both within the UK and internationally.

In the context of standardization in the HR field, both the development and application of some of the HCM standards under discussion in this text is at an early stage. Indeed, their take-up to date, apart from the IiP framework, is limited. However, the development of this range of HR standards provides a strong basis for encouraging organizations to pursue best practices in the fields of HRM and HRD. The process of assessment for such standards will generally follow the steps and stages highlighted above and be based on tried and tested ways of doing things to ensure objectivity and impartiality are maintained at all times.

Some possible resource implications of assessment

Any organization contemplating working with external quality standards of whatever type needs to consider carefully the resource issues, as the journey towards final assessment and certification/accreditation can be lengthy and take a considerable amount of time and effort. Identification of possible resource implications of working with any type of standard is necessary at the start of the process. As with any project plan, amendments to that initial costing may be required on the way.

Resource implications will obviously include financial costs, but other things such as time and management input must also be considered. The following are some of the main cost factors to take into account. These might be classified as 'internal', ie associated with the preparations being undertaken in-house before the final assessment visit; and 'external', ie relating to that external visit.

Internal cost factors include:

- establishment of a project team to manage the process with key players identified once a decision is made to pursue certification – some discussions and agreement from a strategic perspective on this will be required and involve members of the senior management team (see later in this chapter);

- purchase and distribution of copies of the standards under consideration;

- training of the project group to enhance their knowledge and understanding of the specific standard(s) under consideration – this might include either in-house training or attendance at external programmes, with associated costs;

- preparation of documentation and portfolios of evidence, and printing of these;

- checking of these against requirements and making adjustments, following such things as a pre-assessment, should this be pursued as part of preparation;

- ongoing liaison with certification body personnel to ensure appropriate progress is being made.

External cost factors include:

- initial gap analysis costs, should this be undertaken as a preliminary to the journey towards certification;

- arrangements for the final assessment visit – this will include the actual price of the assessment (based on the size of the operation and number of locations) as well as travel and accommodation costs for the assessor(s);

- the cost of making any necessary adjustments to systems and procedures as a result of feedback from the formal assessment visit;

- the costs of maintaining compliance once certification is fully granted;

- the cost of adjustments to business logos, etc, and printing costs once certification is achieved.

Whilst this list is not exhaustive, there are several things to consider, not least the issue of maintaining the standard once it is achieved. This cost is sometimes ignored in the pricing strategy adopted by the organization, but should be factored into any future work with standards. Increasingly, certification bodies are building these costs into their initial proposals to ensure that clients have a clear understanding of what will be involved going forward. In summary, organizations must look beyond the initial achievement costs as outlined above.

Each certification body will have its own pricing strategy, but there are often similarities across the different bodies working in the assessment marketplace. Most, if not all, bodies work on a day rate based on the size and geographical location of the organization. For example, for a company of 250 employees across four sites within the UK, a price for five days of assessment activity, including report writing, might be charged. Decisions would be made by the assessor(s) as to how to gather evidence in a cost-effective way across these several locations. Use might be made therefore of telephone interviews, focus groups, surveys and so on to gather employees' views as well as consideration of relevant documentation. Where assessments are undertaken internationally, then additional travel costs, eg flights and hotel accommodation, cost of visas and so on will need consideration.

THE EXPERTISE OF ASSESSORS

A further cost to the certification body itself will be the payments needed for assessors. Their training and development is normally part of the contractual arrangements made with individuals who often have a strong consultancy background and specific industry knowledge. In that sense they may be deemed to be 'subject experts' in their field, although a broader business background is often sought in terms of expertise.

Having a competent assessor pool to draw upon is critical for the success of the certification bodies providing their services. For example, for assessing against BS 76000 assessors need to have experience of evaluating a management system. For assessment against BS 76005, assessors need knowledge about current diversity and inclusion (D&I) agendas, whilst for PD 76006 a background in learning and development would be necessary.

Although assessors will generally work on a self-employed basis and be contracted to the certification body, for the purposes of the client organization these individuals are employed by the certification body and their costs are built into the overall price. What must not happen is for assessors to seek further work on their own behalf with the client organization following an assessment, as this would cause conflict of interest problems.

The roles of the different stakeholders involved

Preparing for an assessment involves many different stakeholders, each of whom have different roles to play. These include people from the client organization as well as the certification body involved in the assessment process. Managing client relationships throughout the assessment journey is important, in particular keeping communication channels open to ensure a good outcome without compromising impartiality and objectivity. The certification body will normally nominate someone as the client's point of contact to ensure that things run smoothly. By allocating an assessor early on, that relationship can be built up over time and the assessor can become a useful source of information in the early stages.

An important staff group within the client organization will be the senior management team who will need to lend support to the project. Often in-house specialists such as a quality manager or HR specialist will be involved, depending on the nature of the standard under consideration. For more technical standards relevant personnel will need to be available to advise on outcomes – eg for ISO 14001, someone involved in the environment, health and safety function will need to provide expertise. What will be critical here is the level of support from the senior team, who may wish to look beyond the initial costs of external assessment and consider the strategic value of achieving certification (see later in this chapter).

Another key group to consider when preparing for an assessment are the employees themselves. To ensure the success of any project, it will be important to include employee representation from the start of a project. Staff co-opted onto a project team can provide valuable insights, and participation in a certification project may be seen as a career development opportunity, if supported by the employing organization. Although there is an argument for training up in-house expertise, some organizations will engage external consultants to help support them towards final assessment. This will normally be done outside of the certification body, and compensated accordingly.

The nature of evidence – how to prepare this

A triangulation of diagnostic activity, with self-assessment and third-party assessor evidence, lies at the heart of a robust assessment process. All three elements are important in the preparations and the final outcome. The type and quality of evidence produced is influential in any final assessment decision.

A critical element in the assessment process is the type of evidence which is required to be shown to the assessor(s) to demonstrate the operation of key practices, and the existence of systems and processes to support this. A key difference between some of the British human capital standards and those which sit outside that framework, eg IiP, is the requirement to produce written evidence to support an assessment. Increasingly there is a focus on evidence gathering which tests people's understanding of what is in place and how it works, rather than just looking for evidence of 'compliance'. This has become the approach taken by IiP in recent times to ensure that what is really being tested during an assessment is how things work as far as staff and managers are concerned.

The inclusion of a sample of contractors and volunteers, if appropriate, during an IiP assessment is also useful, as it highlights just how these workers are included. However, by maintaining a requirement for documentation in the human capital standards there is an argument that this ensures structure and format which can be seen as valuable.

For example, there is an expectation with BS 76000 that certain practices will be in place such as having a staff appraisal process that works well and is used in a way that supports both the individual employee and the business. With PD 76006, there is an expectation that a range of learning methodologies will be in place and working. These might include a process for new starts (eg induction or a buddy system) which helps new employees learn about and become integrated into the organization that they have joined. Such a formal induction process is compared with more informal methods of helping people to settle into their new role. Both formal and informal evidence would be appropriate.

To prepare the evidence for a formal assessment, the client organization and its representatives must carefully scrutinize the relevant standard and its content and check this against what is already in place and working. This is where a 'gap analysis' at the start of the assessment journey can be very useful to highlight shortfalls against requirements. Such an initial gap analysis can be undertaken by the client organization itself or by the certification body as part of early preparations. Dealing with the findings of such a gap will become the main focus of the project team.

At that early stage, it is useful to consider what specific policies and procedures should be in place, against current activities, and to look beyond legislative requirements, to enable comparison of this against good practice encouraged by bodies such as the CIPD. A portfolio of evidence once amended can be compiled for consideration during the formal assessment visit.

A further consideration of the client organization in planning for an assessment is the timescales. For example, Stage 1 of an assessment might be a review of documentation, followed up later by the site visit. The timing of this latter element will depend on the outcome of the former. Some time may be required to amend or change evidence provided.

No simple guidelines can be given on how long it might take for an organization to achieve certification, as this depends on a large number of factors. However, in general terms the whole process may take up to a year or longer. What is critical to such timescales is the degree of currency and embeddedness of evidence, both of which need to be taken into account during both preparations and at the actual assessment visit.

The outcome(s) of the assessment process

At the end of the formal assessment visit, several decisions are possible. A final report will be issued highlighting strengths and weaknesses found, and providing guidance on next steps. That report becomes a key document for the client going forward, to ensure continued certification or achievement of accreditation where shortfalls have been identified. The client organization is hoping for certification based on the premise that it meets all elements of the standard. It may be that only partial compliance is evident, however with the proviso that certain amendments will be made to systems and procedures, over an agreed timescale. The quality of that report and the guidance it contains is therefore very important to the client organization.

A critical outcome of the assessment process will be the feedback provided, the way in which it is delivered, and the requirements being placed on the client organization moving forward. The quality of such feedback and the amount of detail it provides will therefore be of greatest interest to the client who wants to know what else needs to happen, and where via benchmarking it sits in its marketplace.

A further issue is the internal quality assurance of the certification body over how the assessment was conducted. Feedback from the client organization to the certification body is built into the whole process to ensure that both the assessor(s) and the body itself know and receive guidance on any changes they need to make to how things are done. It is often at this stage that the balance required between advice given and objective judgement is called into question.

In addition, certification bodies have a role to play where a standard is breached following the granting of certification. Appropriate action is necessary to 'deregulate' the organization and remove the certification. Whilst this rarely occurs, client organizations need to be aware of not bringing any standard into disrepute by discontinuing their good employment practices.

Some key human capital standards

As mentioned earlier, there are numerous quality standards and awards in the marketplace with a strong HR focus. Two of the major ones in use not only in the UK but globally are the EFQM and IiP. Whilst these two are usually referred to as frameworks rather than as standards in the traditional sense, and therefore are outside the scope of the human capital standards studied in this text, they are still worthy of mention because of their longevity, and their acceptance as adding value to the workplace (eg Bourne *et al*, 2010).

Both of these frameworks are updated regularly to ensure their currency and applicability to their marketplace. Additionally, both have a wide application to the workplace and a global reach that is a key factor in their acceptance as adding value to a business. The assessment process attached to each reflects a focus on self-assessment at the start of the journey, and a greater degree of flexibility in the presentation of evidence which moves beyond just a focus on documentation.

This has led to the argument in some quarters to maintain alignment with these two 'older' standards, rather than focus on the more detailed HCM standards under consideration in this text. Their slow uptake to date may not be so much an indication of competition in the marketplace from these other two frameworks, but rather a delay which is due in large part to more information and visibility being required on their content, application and the value they add to organizational life. As we might expect, it will take some time for these more recent standards to be able to demonstrate this.

In making choices about which HR-related standards to work with, organizations should consider the principles on which each is based and how such values align with their own employment practices. Where assessment is undertaken against these human capital standards, the values and the principles underpinning them must be known by the assessor(s) and considered during the assessment process to ensure that the organization under review is adhering to not only legal requirements but ethical ones as well. The following provides a brief overview of such principles when considering three key HCM standards.

BS 76000

This standard, which is often viewed as an 'umbrella' standard, shares the rigour associated with awards such as ISO 9001, a long-standing quality standard with international reach. Introduced in 2017, BS 76000 provides a framework for organizations to value their people for the mutual benefit of both parties. Built on the premise that people are an organization's biggest asset and should be treated as such, the standard is based on key principles each of which is of equal importance:

- All stakeholder interests, including those of staff, are integral to an organization.
- That organization is part of a wider society and therefore has a responsibility to operate in a fair and socially responsible way.

- The most senior managers in an organization should be committed to valuing their people.

- Those who work for the organization have rights over and above those which are legislated for; such rights must be respected by the organization.

An assessment against this standard will look at how these principles are being applied, against a backdrop of prescriptive evidence requirements.

BS 76005

This British standard builds on BS 76000 by focusing on how organizations value their people through a strong emphasis on D&I. It considers how objectives are developed alongside behaviours and measures that extend beyond minimum rights as stated in employment law. This D&I agenda has grown in importance in recent times in the UK workplace. Developed as a Code of Practice, working with this standard helps organizations to develop a management system that embeds these concepts beyond legislative requirements.

By working with this standard, the following benefits might ensue:

- Risks from equality issues may be reduced or eliminated, as compliance with the legal framework will be required.

- It should be easier to attract and retain staff by making the organization more adaptable.

- The organization will be encouraged to adapt sensitively in different social marketplaces; such commitment to these principles should also help to win tenders and new business.

- Levels of motivation, job satisfaction and engagement should increase.

An assessment against this standard will examine how these principles are applied, against a backdrop of prescriptive evidence requirements. To date a number of formal assessments have taken place against this standard.

PD 76006

As learning and development have grown in importance in recent years with the acceptance of HRD as a specialist field of both study and operation, having a specific standard against which to measure practices can provide the basis for guidance and recommendations on the planning, supporting and evaluation of organizational learning and development. It can help organizations consider how they provide learning and development at both organizational and individual levels.

As new methods of learning delivery such as e-learning are developed and traditional classroom approaches feature less in learning and development practices in organizations, working with such a standard will help an organization to really consider how best to invest in staff development.

This standard is structured around five key elements:

- individual level learning and development;
- common learning methods;
- organizational level learning and development;
- learning roles and responsibilities;
- assessing and evaluating learning and development.

Arguably, where organizations pay attention to these principles, a number of organizational benefits will arise such as:

- success in attraction, retention and development of talent, making it more adaptable and sustainable;
- improvements in decision-making by employing better talent;
- assisting individuals to fulfil their capabilities leading to greater job satisfaction and levels of engagement;
- enhancement of the planning, delivery and evaluation of learning and development.

Again, an assessment against this standard will therefore need to look at how these principles are being applied, against a backdrop of prescriptive evidence requirements contained within the standard.

The strategic implications of formal assessment activities

In order to effectively optimize and institutionalize assessment activities, strategic attention and positioning is necessary from the top of the organization to ensure acceptance of working with a range of standards, including those in the HCM arena. Whilst the ongoing debate about the value of the HR function and its place at the top table continues, a role for HR to be involved in working with these external quality standards is increasingly becoming apparent.

Traditional and emerging roles within assessment

As noted above, the ways in which formal assessments are undertaken have moved in recent years from a highly structured approach to a more fluid and flexible attempt to take account of individual organizational issues, without losing sight of the need to be objective and fair in the judgements being made. Yet that search for more flexibility in assessment activities does raise issues and concerns.

Anderson (2017) considers that the application of the IiP framework raises particular issues around content and level of detail when it is applied on a global basis, often through different licensed providers whose style and approach may differ geographically as well as culturally. The globalization of the IiP framework has developed via a network of licensed companies which are deemed competent to undertake both advisory and assessment services. Not all licence holders are authorized to undertake assessment activities, however, and so an allocation of an IiP accredited practitioner is made, often from the UK, to undertake the assessment. Some of these practitioners are themselves based in overseas locations, but work on a contracted basis for the UK operation (the IiP CIC).

Perhaps the greatest change going on within the field of quality standards assessment is consideration of how to place less focus on paperwork, and ensure a greater emphasis on demonstrating actual practices in situ. This requires assessors to be knowledgeable and experienced and able to interact with a range of personnel across an operation, including members of the senior team.

The role of technology in the conduct of assessments

A further recent development within the field of assessment is the use of digital platforms to assist with data collection and presentation. This is certainly the case with the IiP framework, where assessors are expected to carry out much of their work using such an approach. Preliminary research on an organization may include review of open access web-based information, social media reports, and so on.

Assessors now work with an initial online employee survey, calculating outcomes from that, uploading reports using specific templates, and generally handling data in this way. This requires some degree of IT knowledge and experience, and the training of assessors includes this type of support.

As client organizations themselves become greater users of technology, so certification bodies must embrace new approaches to collecting and managing data, although all legal requirements must pertain. A key reason for this move towards greater use of technology is to better manage costs and resources.

The role of certification and accreditation

Murthy (2017) suggests that standards, conformity assessment and accreditation are the three pillars on which most quality infrastructures are built. He considers that certification represents a 'written assurance by a third party of the conformity of a product, process or service to specified requirements', and contrasts that with accreditation as the 'formal recognition by an authoritative body of the competence to work to specific standards'. In other words, certification arises from third-party endorsement of an organization's systems or products whilst accreditation is an endorsement of that certification.

Both national and international accreditation bodies exist in their various fields to promote the highest standards of operation (Mulvie, 2018). In the UK, the only national accreditation body is the United Kingdom Accreditation Service (UKAS) which is responsible for determining, in the public interest, the technical competence and integrity of those organizations which offer testing, calibration, inspection and certification services. Indeed, the whole concept and ethos of quality assurance is supported by the work of objective, external entities. This implies that UKAS is the legitimate gatekeeper of standards and competence, ie it audits the auditors.

Established as a non-profit, self-funding body independent of government, it is licensed under a Memorandum of Understanding by the Department for Business, Energy and Industrial Strategy (BEIS). As its sponsor, BEIS recommends the use of UKAS-accredited conformity assessment services wherever possible. The reason for this is to ensure that the market has assurance that the conformity assessment bodies themselves operate to acceptable standards (BEIS, 2017).

Accreditation by UKAS ensures that the assessment bodies undertaking such services are competent, impartial and ensure integrity in the application of their services. As noted above, a key feature of what UKAS does is its value in 'checking the checkers' – that is, it provides quality assurance to the processes of both accreditation and certification.

UKAS has 'members' instead of shareholders; these members represent those who have an interest in all aspects of accreditation – national and local government, business and industry, purchasers, users and quality managers, and include the Chartered Quality Institute, the UK body which represents those working in the quality profession. This Institute has its own examination and membership categories with a membership base comprising quality management specialists, as well as those interested in the field of business excellence and continuous improvement.

Why organizations seek certification and accreditation

For many suppliers, being certified means that each time they work with new customers they do not need to be assessed as part of the business 'pitch', as they can demonstrate that they already have achieved quantifiable and known standards of performance in terms of the services and goods they are providing. A series of different national accreditation symbols relating to a variety of different sectors and services ensures that improved choices can be made around which is the best supplier to use. This, in turn, can impact on the supply chain that may be used.

Because UKAS has an involvement in a number of international groups, the need for multiple assessments across different geographical boundaries is reduced, thus helping to reduce trade barriers. UKAS is involved in international groups such as the European Cooperation for Accreditation, the International Accreditation Forum and the International Laboratory Accreditation Cooperation. Such relationships provide for mutual recognition.

By using an accredited assessment service, clients can have faith in the quality of that service. However, not all certification bodies are accredited with UKAS and are not required to be so. What is critical is their ability to manage their own internal quality assurance processes well.

Summary

The process of formal assessment against any standards, whether these have a HCM focus or a wider, more technical application, is challenging. New approaches to assessment are emerging with greater use of technology and less reliance on paper driven systems. The recruitment and retention of competent and experienced assessors is critical to the successful delivery of sound assessment services.

Client organizations wishing to be assessed have a range of options regarding which standard to work with, and how they prepare for the process. Working with the relevant certification body will ensure they are on the right track from the start of the assessment journey and should lead to a satisfactory outcome.

Whilst an ongoing dilemma between the provision of advice and assessment on the part of assessors persists, internal quality assurance methods used by certification bodies go a long towards ensuring that those involved in the delivery of assessments conduct themselves in a professional and ethical manner. However, limited information exists about who is actually certified in the marketplace to deliver assessments. The marketplace of assessment activity is complex and further research may be needed to inform assessment practices and ensure that all those involved in this work know and understand their role.

One way to help with this might be to ensure the uptake and application of HCM standards to certification bodies themselves, to encourage best practices in the field of assessment.

References and further resources

ACAS www.acas.org.uk (archived at https://perma.cc/NN4K-H8HU)

Anderson, V (2017) HRD standards and standardization: where now for human resource development? *Human Resource Development International*, 20 (4), pp 327–45

BEIS (2017) Conformity assessment and accreditation policy in the United Kingdom www.thenbs.com/PublicationIndex/documents/details?Pub=BIS&DocID=300785 (archived at https://perma.cc/QCR9-Z4AF)

Bourne, M *et al*. The impact of the Investors in People standard on people management practices and firm performance, *Cranfield Management School* http://dspace.lib.cranfield.ac.uk/handle/1826/4305 (archived at https://perma.cc/952P-WC37)

BSI (2015) BS 76000:2015 *Human Resource. Valuing People. Management System. Requirements and Guidance* https://shop.bsigroup.com/ProductDetail/?pid=000000000030298954 (archived at https://perma.cc/DQ53-ZFH6)

BSI (2017) BS 76005:2017 *Valuing People Through Diversity and Inclusion: Code of Practice for Organizations* https://shop.bsigroup.com/ProductDetail/?pid=000000000030338898 (archived at https://perma.cc/LJ6U-S5F6)

BSI (2017) BS PD 76006:2017 *Guide to learning and development* https://shop.bsigroup.com/ProductDetail/?pid=000000000030350673 (archived at https://perma.cc/MV8Y-K35R)

BSI (2017) PD IEC/PAS 63088:2017 *Smart manufacturing. Reference architecture model industry 4.0 (RAMI4.0)* https://shop.bsigroup.com/ProductDetail?pid=000000000030350369 (archived at https://perma.cc/YG87-3GC3)

BSI www.bsigroup.com (archived at https://perma.cc/3KPQ-D355)

CIPD (2018) HR and standards factsheet, *CIPD* www.cipd.co.uk/knowledge/strategy/hr/standards-factsheet (archived at https://perma.cc/5QHW-A79U)

Collins, J (2001) *Good to Great*, Random House Business, London

Council for the Curriculum, Examinations and Assessment www.ccea.org.uk (archived at https://perma.cc/6FZ5-5WSD)

International Organization for Standardization. ISO 14000 family – Environmental management, *ISO* www.iso.org/iso-14001-environmental-management.html (archived at https://perma.cc/5K8C-XLJA)

Mulvie, A (2018) *Working with External Quality Standards and Awards: The strategic implications for human resource and quality management*, Routledge, Oxford

Murthy, J (2017) What is the difference between accreditation and certification, *pbctoday.com* (archived at https://perma.cc/9CL2-EVBJ) www.pbctoday.co.uk/news/planning-construction-news/accreditation-and-certification-difference/32133/ (archived at https://perma.cc/8ZYK-KVYR)

Peters, T and Waterman, R (1982) *In Search of Excellence: Lessons from America's best-run companies*, Harper & Row, New York

Planning, BIM and Construction Today www.pbctoday.co.uk/news/category/publications/pbc-today/ (archived at https://perma.cc/N5HH-DRQN)

Porter, S and Tanner, L (2004) *Assessing Business Excellence*, 2nd edn, Elsevier Butterworth-Heinemann, Oxford

UKAS www.ukas.com (archived at https://perma.cc/QH9M-MBAK)

UKCES. Annual Report and Accounts 2015/16, GOV.UK https://assets.publishing.service.gov.uk/government/uploads/system/uploads/attachment_data/file/539723/56365_HC382_WEB_V0.2.pdf (archived at https://perma.cc/UAL7-554A)

11

The future of standards affecting human capital management and development

Wilson Wong

Introduction

This chapter explores where the drivers for standards and standardization may lie in national, organizational and professional economies, affecting the nature of work, the workforce and the workplace in the near term. As the technologies of measuring the value of human capital continue to mature, the value people create will become more tangible, opening up a need for new standards for human capital using new technologies, processes or (re)design.

CHAPTER OBJECTIVES

This chapter sets out to:

- discuss a variety of drivers shaping the future of work;
- provide a view on the development of technologies and drivers that may disrupt current ways of working;
- look at the impact of these drivers on the way people live, work and interact;
- identify the challenges and the opportunities for standards and standardization in these particular future contexts.

Key terms

Most of the terms will be in general use, but may be differently defined and understood in different contexts. For clarity, in this chapter the following terms (presented in alphabetical order) are used as follows:

Artificial intelligence (AI):	This term refers to the development and application of computing technologies to perform in areas hitherto requiring human intelligence. Examples of these involve decision-making, facial recognition and interpretation, learning from prior experience and adapting to new stimuli.
Business model:	This refers to the value proposition of an organization to its stakeholders and its operation to ensure its sustainable success. This requires identifying the business context, eg competitors and substitutes, sources of revenue, target markets, products and services, business intelligence such as market research for shifts in tastes and trends, evaluation and redesign.
Ecosystem:	In the business and management context in which this term is used in this chapter, it refers to the complex system or network of organizations, including suppliers, distributors, customers, competitors, government agencies, and so on, involved in product or service delivery. Ecosystems involve both competition and cooperation as each entity affects and is affected by the others. Ecosystems involve constantly evolving relationships and, as in a biological ecosystem, flexibility and adaptability are needed in order to survive.
Future of work:	This is a broad umbrella term encompassing approaches to the nature of work, the shape of workplaces and workforces in the future.
Futures:	This is the study of alternate futures (the possible, the probable and the preferred) and the study of the drivers (eg legacies, technologies, worldviews and mythologies) shaping these futures.
Human capital:	This term describes the value of the workforce: 'the knowledge, skills, abilities and other capabilities which describe individual capacities' (Ployhart *et al*, 2014).

Identity:
: In this chapter this term refers to a 'sense of self' constructed from, among other things, a person's memories, ambitions, desires, values, hopes and beliefs.

Organization design:
: A systematic approach to reviewing and intentionally developing an organization's ways of working, systems and processes (eg workflow, procedures, structures, systems and layout).

Principles:
: This refers to fundamental truths or propositions that serve as the foundation for a system of belief or behaviour, or to a chain of reasoning of a person, a plan, an organization or a nation on which policies, processes, laws, decisions and institutions are built.

Standardization:
: This term refers to the development, publication and application of guidelines, specifications and rules by a consensus of relevant stakeholders in order to ensure compatibility, interoperability, safety and consistency.

Strategy:
: A high-level plan or approach designed to bring about one or more goals under conditions of uncertainty.

The future of work

In this section some important trends affecting the future of work are discussed. These include digitization, the data economy, the emergence of new business structures, changes to peoples' sense of identity, emerging social trends and concerns, global demographic changes and patterns of migration and issues of cybersecurity.

An important general purpose technology that has and continues to disrupt and alter the way we live is information and communications technology (ICT). Under ISO/IEC JTC1, there are hundreds of standards ensuring interoperability in concepts, data management, user interfaces, information hardware and software, including automated processes, AI and sustainability. These processes of ICT standardization have shaped the ecosystem for ICT and the manner it is deployed. And yet, as these standards indicate, the potential of ICT to shape the way we live, work and play is really only at the early stages. There are standards already in development looking to the implications of the evolution of ICT both as an enabler and as a catalyst.

As the public and private, the social and the economic merge, it may be helpful to take stock of how ICT is shaping our world and consider where standards may extend their scope in years to come.

ICT has changed the skills required in modern organizations and changed the expectations of users and consumers. ICT makes 24/7 servicing of users possible, and we see this in retail, banking, education, publishing, media and entertainment. However, there are darker overtones to this changed information ecosystem. Take, for example, 'newsfeeds'. ICT has made the entry barriers to broadcasting negligible and there are thousands upon thousands of purveyors of 'content', from the digital feeds of traditional media companies to 'reality' shows and individuals with their vlogs, blogs, and real-time feeds on social media. News is now a commodity and the number of followers and hits the metrics required to get advertising income.

The key is differentiation, and this favours the novel and the extreme. The 'democratization' of newsfeeds via social media made possible with ICT in a user-driven economy has enabled minority tastes and voices to find and influence newsfeeds that reflect those minority attitudes and tastes. On the one hand, this creates new markets, but these communities of particular interests also encourage a culture of instant gratification ('likes' and retweets), instant reactions to quite complicated and nuanced issues (eg migration), single-issue campaigns (eg crowdfunding for someone to have surgery) and consequently, fragmented identity politics.

Digitalization

Digitalization, the foundation of present-day computing, is not only integral to business processes and standards, providing real-time data analysis and feedback on operations, it is transforming whole industries. The realization that big and small data when cleverly manipulated at scale are invaluable to competitive advantage and that data can be commoditized to support new business models could only have come about because of the integration of telecommunications and computing.

The transformation of analogue to digital of any content to bits and bytes is not new. The word processor replacing the typewriter displaced the typing pool. But the process of digitalization coupled with improvements in ICT, materials, analytics and robotics continues to transform other activities.

Examples in the healthcare industry include:

- the use of sensors and devices to submit personal data for analysis
- personalized medicine based on your individual genome profile;
- far less demand for centralized outpatient clinics;
- fewer staff needed to do scheduling of appointments.

In logistics, everything is mapped and scheduled so that resources are optimally deployed with real-time data on the health of both the vehicle and the workers in that team. There is sophisticated real-time engagement with the whole supply chain, from inputs from several suppliers to engaging with the clients so that they know the precise time a service is being delivered.

In education, learners can gain immediate access to bite-sized pieces of information to deal with a particular issue, while also accessing the context via virtual means that also provides some community support from those who've completed those bits of learning and successfully applied them. There may even have been the opportunity for them to monetize their experience as tutors for newbies as a means of rewarding learning while earning something to fund more learning. This bitty transfer of knowledge has its risks, but the immediate application of learning encourages both individuals and organizations to engage in learning and development.

In advanced manufacturing, the digitalization of production processes has led to real-time data feeds from materials to production with autonomous machines. Remotely controlled factories can be possible (UKCES, nd). In a modern brewery in Europe I counted only a dozen technical staff monitoring a 50,000 litre overnight run. Human labour only touched the product at the start when the ingredients were loaded and when the human tasters did their taste tests. The brewery is working on sensor technologies to see if the taste tests can be automated as well. This was a smart plant that was clean, relatively quiet, and lightly staffed.

Digitalization coupled with new manufacturing technologies, materials, advancements in robotics and rising demand for individualized/customized products is disrupting the economies-of-scale, lowest input cost mantra of mass manufacturing. Factors such as speed to market, sustainability and instances of inhumane treatment of workers in offshore factories have encouraged localization and decentralization. Additive manufacturing (also referred to as 3D printing) is still in its early stages, but holds the promise of delivering decentralized, complex processes to make customized products locally.

The data economy

ICT and sensors also enable real-time data on operations. Unsurprisingly, application of this technology is shifting to the workforce and the rise of workforce data and analytics. With platforms enabling thousands of people globally to offer their skills to willing payers on a seamless platform, and willing organizations under pressure to get greater efficiencies and finer workforce cost control, it isn't difficult to see more diversity in workers' relationships with employing organizations.

The modern knowledge economy is focused on the exchange and commodification of data. Currently, there is a surfeit of data (of variable quality) and not enough is cleaned, ordered, analysed and used. Media headlines usually showcase how data is misused to harm individuals (eg social media trolling), when corporations circumvent regulation (eg VW's emissions scandal) and where democracy is undermined (eg the manipulation of Facebook data by Cambridge Analytica).

Under the proper governance, data holds the potential to enable the paradox of personalized services at scale, support better decisions, provide insights to accelerate innovation and research, support better policy formulation and provide 24/7 convenience to users with a smart device. But as we have already seen in the case of Cambridge Analytica, data is being weaponized against citizens to manipulate their choices and opinions. There are also concerns about opaque algorithms that sift out certain groups of job applicants that seem more efficient and without any accountability for built-in bias.

We still don't know how to regard the hundreds of organizations collecting, holding and analysing our data. As Facebook realized, by creating an ecosystem to encourage app builders to tap into its user data, it enabled personalized manipulation of citizens everywhere. It enabled a kind of surveillance and profiling of individuals, which few users are aware of or even comprehend.

The open data movement wanted all of society to share the benefits of (publicly-collected) data to be shared more transparently so the many can harness the potential of data to benefit society. While the Open Data Charter is open to all organizations, this is largely operationalized by governments and public agencies where publicly-funded datasets are made available under a transparency agenda. The ambition is that open data can also spur innovation, allow cross-fertilization of ideas across disciplines, encourage interoperability of datasets collected and support the growth of the knowledge economy. The irony is that those countries leading the charge see open data as a side project, a silo that makes the ambition of using insights from data for better government and governance more difficult. The report from the World Wide Web Foundation (nd) clearly states that the open data culture in government working is far from the norm.

But given the dangers of data being owned, commodified and manipulated by large corporations, a regulatory backlash is underway, supported by data regimes like that under the EU General Data Protection Regulation (GDPR). It may be necessary to push back against some to the principles of the open data movement so that data is restricted within agreed boundaries–narrow purpose, time-limited or a closed group.

Deconstructing work with different business structures and ecosystems

The use of data as a commodity (made possible through digitalization) will intensify the need for more and more collaboration in order to increase the effectiveness of the gaze on every aspect of that digital economy, including the actual economic value contributed by individuals and teams in the workforce. Companies increasingly assume the role of platforms or nodes in networks coordinating the sharing of data within their partnerships. The impetus for innovation will require inputs and expertise from many disciplines oftentimes not found in any one organization or family of organizations. There will be more co-opetition and co-creation with many partners.

This kind of inter-organizational working is already seen in the aviation industry; for example, the Boeing Dreamliner global development chain. Networked, multi-stakeholder models of social innovation necessary for solving systemic problems will become more familiar to the hierarchical, protectionist architecture of most corporations. According to a UKCES study (nd), 40 per cent of global CEOs expect the majority of innovation in the future to be co-developed with others outside their organization.

There will be difficult adjustments for those moving to a networked way of working. Jon Larry Husband described this as a 'Wirearchy' (Husband, 2013) – 'a dynamic two-way flow of power and authority, based on knowledge, trust, credibility and a focus on results, enabled by interconnected people and technology'. Just as the hierarchical model of management fitted the industrial age, Husband and others argue that the networked economy (Castells, 2010a) means accepting the equal voice of all the players not because of their position or their role but the fact that they have a contribution to make. Labour is, therefore, more engaged and less 'commodified', with the quid pro quo that they will expect to be respected for all that they bring.

As a design principle, Wirearchy means that information flows differently in networked organizations than in traditional hierarchical structures. Knowledge in a networked context flows horizontally, based on connections and collaborations, rather than in official vertical streams. Problems that involve formal meetings and memorandums in hierarchical organizations can instead be solved, for example, with a wiki, tweet, blog post, social network or web conference. ISO 30401 on knowledge management systems, for instance, helpfully suggests that while formal processes are important, the sharing of information (and knowledge), inter alia, is a function of the cultural norms and behaviours in organizations.

Kässi and Lehdonvirta (2018), in their analysis of data gleaned from five online English language labour platforms (Upwork; Amazon Mechanical Turk; Freelancer.com; PeoplePerHour and Guru.com) between July 2016 and July 2018, observed that the Organization for Economic Co-operation and Development (OECD) countries accounted for 80 per cent of the online jobs posted, but only about 20 per cent of the workers. According to the Oxford Internet Institute (OII) Online Labour Index, the share of tasks normalized by GDP share puts Estonia, Australia, Israel, Canada and New Zealand as the top five, while the share of workers responding to these tasks normalized by the share of working age population has Ireland, Latvia, Greece, United Kingdom and New Zealand as the top five.

The rise of distributed workers, the large flows of digital data from sensors as the Internet of Things grow, the need to work in constantly reforming teams, the increasing sophistication of simulation, visualization and integrating technologies will mean much of the human capital will be distributed, measured (to a degree) and yet as a whole, the value of it will be unknown. That means that current business processes for innovation and product/service development will change, as the human capital is increasingly outside the control of the organization(s).

While this holds the promise of empowered labour, at least of the highly skilled variety, with more open, social-collaborative, non-routine forms of work, governments and organizations will have to consider the implications of such distributed ways of working on their intellectual capital and innovation programmes.

Identities and localities

Crudely, a person's sense of self is shaped by how one's physical and psychological characteristics interacting with the external environment and actors forms a unique identity or identities – that is, this configuration of physical, psychological, and interpersonal characteristics defines just that one individual. Identity, the sense of self, is constructed from, among other things, one's memories, ambitions, desires, values, hopes and beliefs. Identity also involves the making of meaning from what's around oneself. One's experiences and inputs (eg education) shape that identity by formulating opinions and ways of analysing what one encounters. The digitized networked society in which most of us now operate is a potent influence in identity formation.

In life, we inhabit a variety of roles, as a parent, a lover, a local councillor or school governor, a friend, a technical expert, a professional, a business owner, a citizen of a country, a religious adherent, a runner, an anarchist and so on. Each is mediated by the norms of the group, the place, the institution; and those in turn the factors shaping those norms on that society. The norms are negotiated within and in relation to groups.

ICT, by providing exponential conduits for social networks to form independent of place/space, means that identities can be influenced and affirmed by people far removed from the usual local networks. We have seen how extremist videos are able to recruit members worldwide. We can see how Facebook networks can influence opinions about abortion, LGBT+ rights and so on. By finding groups that share or affirm our views, and forming an in-group, the networked society is providing a powerful voice for particular positions and causes. This is the age of the globalized campaign, and this has been harnessed by the environmental movement, ideological causes (eg al Qaeda; ISIS; Arab Spring) and in gender/sexual politics (#MeToo; LGBT+).

However, it is also a means of organizing and bringing legitimate attention to local issues that may not have received political attention and official recognition. Both in the United States and in Britain, the political upheavals of the Trump phenomenon and Brexit have been, inter alia, a result of many grassroots voices coming together to challenge orthodoxies about the benefits of globalization. These groups have used social media to highlight the hitherto voiceless 'losers' of globalization and the failings of liberal democratic institutions in addressing local ills.

What Trump and Brexit have highlighted, via the power of democratized media channels, is that the institutions upon which liberal democracies depend – an independent judiciary, press, accountable politicians and various governance checks and balances by experts and technocrats – require lots of financial resources, time, expertise and knowledge of the system to access. Gaining a voice via these institutions is, therefore, privileged. Social media, blogs, vlogs and the internet have provided at scale a means for individuals to get a voice. It is Foucauldian, in that these media enable multiple points of resistance by many actors, in many places, with multiple frames of reference, simultaneously whilst inviting the gaze of everyone else, including the establishment, to in turn formulate resistances and attempts to establish re-control.

What is clear is that ICT has facilitated a networked society and allowed a flowering of seemingly contradictory trends and voices: religious fundamentalism/extremism vs challenge to religious institution's role in 'modern' societies; strong-men leaders vs decentralized governance; individual choice/freedoms vs greater group conformity; globalization/open borders vs localization/nationalism/anti free-movement. The liberation promised by ICT, like any technology, can be harnessed for any cause, by anyone, and that Pandora's Box will shape not just politics but impact how we (and the various technologies) develop in the future.

The challenge of fragmented identities for standards on human capital in attracting, measuring, developing, managing and retaining talent is that shared norms cannot be assumed. The management of diversity and the supporting technologies for inclusion of difference will become more and more important, especially as many organizations will have workforces on a variety of non-employment arrangements. The measurement of human capital will be a big and important industry.

Social trends and concerns

In this section, the term 'Big Tech' is used to refer to major technology companies such as Apple, Google, Amazon and Facebook, who have disproportionate influence on the business and social environment. An important social concern with implications for work and social life is the ways in which Big Tech companies are applying AI. Google's Project Dragonfly to develop a censored search engine for China, its involvement in a US government AI weapons programme, selling facial recognition technology to governments worldwide by Microsoft and Amazon and developing opaque algorithms that perpetrate bias from faulty data and assumptions have all received media coverage putting tech companies, including behemoths like

Baidu and TenCent, under the spotlight. The unease by many is how technologies that can ultimately be used for military and surveillance purposes is going to be propagated and deployed.

There is industry-wide recognition that while many of the AI projects are legal, there are ethical dimensions which need to be explored. One approach is to set out company principles for ethical AI. Think tanks like the Future of Life Institute have developed the Asilomar Principles to guide scientists. The reality is that given the stakes and the sheer potential of the technology, there is a power asymmetry. Realistically, only the Chief Executive Officer or a Senior Vice President can stop something. Industry voluntary codes are all very well, but not even Big Tech's own employees have the confidence that they will be consistently and transparently applied. A very visible demonstration of this was the shutting down by Deep Mind of the independent review body in November 2018 set up just two years earlier to scrutinize the sensitive use of National Health Service data in England.

The other concern about leaving important ethical debates to Big Tech is the impossibility of defining what ethical frame to apply. For instance, there is an inherent tension between doing what's right (a rules-based, 'what's correct' frame) and another moral imperative to do that which is good (virtue ethics, of knowing the right thing to do, in the right way, at the right time). Some Big Tech firms support a more the-ends-justify-the-means approach that focuses on solving real-world issues and needs, thereby using the technology to maximize the common good. This seems to be the approach taken by some of the Chinese Big Tech. But who decides on the nature of that common good is problematic – for example, when Chinese government authorities use facial recognition technology to monitor minority groups, like the Uighurs, with the ultimate goal of predictive policing.

Notwithstanding the real issues in AI, International Organization for Standardization (ISO) standards are already tackling the governance of AI use by organizations, the robustness of neural networks and the trustworthiness of AI including the issue of bias built into decision-making AI.

Global demographics and migration

In a networked world, where most news flows seamlessly across borders (subject to automated content filters), the physical also matters. Economies are now so interconnected that the movement of people within and across borders have implications for policies. In many countries, the migration of people within and across borders is a highly emotive issue, raising issues of security, sovereignty, otherness and the more unattractive identities of xenophobia and racism. But migration is also an important source of vital human capital to address skills shortages in many economies.

According to the medium projections of the UN Population Fund (UNFPA), world population in 2050 will breach the 10 billion mark and, based on a continuation of current trends of slowing fertility rates, reach 11.2 billion by the end of the century. UNFPA statistics show that fertility in the early 1970s was 4.5 children per woman. By 2015, this was 2.5 children. Should fertility not fall as expected in the medium projection, the planet may be supporting 16.5 billion by 2100 (UNFPA high projection variant).

The huge growth in the world population is really a measure of success of improvements in primary health programmes globally, advances in medicines and treatment options, education, the spread of human rights and improvements in living standards generally. These have reduced infant, child and maternal mortality. These factors have also contributed to longer average lifespans. Average life expectancy has risen from 64.6 years in the early 1990s to 70.8 years in 2017. Although fertility levels have declined, they have not fallen at the same pace as mortality levels. The world population will continue to grow for decades to come. Part of this is that the factors shaping health continue to improve, life expectancy is rising faster than the fall in fertility and, importantly, there are more women of reproductive age today. This will contribute to a relatively large number of births, even if those women have fewer children on average.

Although population growth is, today, largely attributable to population momentum, after 2060 it will almost exclusively be driven by fertility levels in the world's least developed countries. The population of the world's least developed countries is projected to double (some say triple) by the middle of the century. In high-income and rising-income countries, there is slow population growth or no population growth at all. Whereas the former continue to have large, growing, populations of young, working age people, the latter will have large, growing populations of older persons. This has implications for sustainable development, and patterns of migration. The developed countries with low fertility, a shrinking working age population and a high percentage of older citizens may still need skilled migrants to sustain services even with heavy use of automation. And some countries will have more working age citizens than jobs.

Migration is a complex phenomenon involving mobility of skilled and unskilled labour, international students, enforced displacements due to for example persecution, refugees, resettlement, enforced migration and modern slavery, remittances, public opinion/policy and so on. The UN International Organization for Migration (IOM) counted 258 million migrants in 2017, of which 25.4 million were official refugees, and $466 billion in remittance to low and middle-income countries, some three times the total of official development aid programmes.

In addition, the world is seeing high levels of urbanization and accelerating migration. 2007 was the first year in which more people lived in urban areas than in rural areas, and by 2050 about 66 per cent of the world population will be living in cities. The rise of mega cities, especially in the emerging economies, brings new economic centres of gravity from the clustering/agglomeration effects of having skilled labour, capital and interactions together, all amplified by the real-time information used to regulate the life-blood of the city – utilities, mobility, air quality. The dense urban population centre will also suffer inequality, security, cost of living, and likely environmental degradation. All these quality of life issues in cities will invite new technologies and new standards.

These macro-trends have far-reaching implications. They, together with other drivers like technology, will influence economic development and economic policies, employment patterns, income distribution/security, poverty patterns and social protections. The UN sustainable development goals like universal access to health care, education for all children, decent housing, sanitation, potable water, food security and affordable sustainable energy will all be impacted. This factor is important because to address those development goals, policymakers in all countries – developed and less developed – must understand the number of people under their jurisdiction, where they are, how old they are, and to prepare for likely future flows of people.

Cybersecurity

The digitization of almost everything into bits and bytes coupled with a reliance on networks, cloud computing, distributed databases and the constant exchange and transfer of data means that corruption, interception and abuse of data is a constant concern. Most national governments fund agencies to ensure there is a data ecosystem that looks after national security in the cyber world. The recent news about Huawei and the potential for backdoors in their 5G telecommunications systems, compromising national security, highlights the vulnerabilities of critical digital infrastructure in modern economies. The reliance on a steady stream of data to operate interconnected processes is a trade-off for speed, efficiency and convenience.

For example, when you use an app to purchase something online, you establish your identity to the seller by logging in and this is matched to a remote database which may require additional security checks. The item you wish to purchase is constantly monitored as inventory in another remote warehouse, and once availability is confirmed and your order is logged against stock, you are then asked to pay. Using your credit card, your identity and your account data is checked automatically across several databases (spending patterns, limits and so on) before an automated system approves the payment, whereupon this is communicated to the payment systems for the seller which is another third party. The data is then sent to have your order packed and shared again so it can be despatched and delivered by yet another party.

All this exchange of data and verification protocols aim to ensure that there are several security hoops to prevent fraud, preserve data integrity and trust in the system. Standards like the ISO 27000 family of standards on information security management systems recognize the centrality of looking at human behaviour and motivation in securing sensitive data by organizations.

In November 2018, British Airways reported that more than 500,000 customers had their names, postal and email addresses, and card details including the crucial card verification value (CVV) hacked. Cathay Pacific revealed soon after that that it had been covering up a data breach from March 2018 that affected 9.4 million people. Hacked data included passport numbers and Hong Kong ID card numbers, as well as credit card details, names, nationalities, birth dates and historical travel information. This has clearly impacted the trust and reputation of both global brands.

The UK Cyber Security Breaches Survey 2019 reported that about a third of businesses surveyed had a cyber attack in the previous 12 months, and for small or micro businesses the most severe breaches were identified by staff rather than antivirus software. This highlights the people risks in maintaining secure data management. The challenge to national agencies is that sophisticated cyber actors including nation-states can and do exploit vulnerabilities to steal information and money. The threat to reliable delivery of essential services is increasing as our systems become more and more interconnected. These actors can operate from anywhere in the world using the connectivity between cyberspace and physical systems. As we move to a world with 5G and having everything connected to the internet (Internet of Things), the vulnerabilities will increase exponentially.

Standards for the future

While we monitor some of the above trends and drivers, the key to resilience and long-term success is preparedness and accountability. The anticipation of potential disruptors is important when you consider how the drivers and trends above can interact in multiple ways, providing risk/opportunity points in many different configurations and sometimes having an interacting, cascading effect.

The section above on cybersecurity illustrates how systems can cascade. Risk registers and logs are often of limited value for this very reason. Sometimes a large risk emerges from a cascade of risks considered minor. Similarly, in examining disruptors, we must acknowledge that long-term processes do not always play out the way we anticipate. In fact, many new products have been used in ways quite different from the original intentions. For example, the encryption used in Blackberry devices was deployed to thwart police intelligence gathering of protests during the Arab Spring in Egypt.

Platforms (*Economist*, nd) are analogous to standards, being anything on which other things can be based or built on. The more who use the platform, the greater the multiplier network effects. In the physical world, a highway or a successful film can be a platform. A highway enables new economic activity to be built around it, generating growth and wealth. Disney's myriad animations were realized physically in the Magic Kingdom where children and adults can meet their favourite Disney characters in real life – and around each animation, an entire merchandising industry to extend the experience. Finally, with better and better technology, we see merchandising evolving to games and immersive experiences of virtual reality where the player can put themselves in the centre of the story. This blurring of realities is part of the power of platforms to engage and then retain users.

The network effect of the platform while supported by the advent of industrial standards really only came into its own with the rise of ICT in the 1980s and 1990s. Bill Gates of Microsoft realized very early on that whomever controlled a successful operating system, eg Windows or MS-DOS, wielded considerable power, and profit. If Microsoft could encourage other developers to adopt the operating system in developing applications, once a critical mass of adopters and users was reached, the effect would be exponential – and beyond the developmental costs of the platform, further licensing would be marginal or pure profit.

Another example of a cascading disruptor is the smartphone ecosystem. Apple invited developers to create apps on mobile devices to support the iPhone. This was only 13/14 years ago, but has completely changed the way we live, work and play – from ordering a meal (either for delivery or pickup) to shopping or to engage services (house cleaning, movers, gardeners or even professional advice). We no longer book a taxi and patiently wait for an available vehicle from one firm – instead we book a cab ride on an app and expect one to be available within minutes. To accommodate a 24/7 global network of contacts we share notes, life experiences, photos and repost content on WhatsApp or Weibo. On social networking sites, we get to know everything about a person who is very far from us. Video calling is near costless, and allows us constant contact globally.

Google's open Android platform, which is at the heart of more than 2 billion devices and thousands of apps, is acknowledgement of the network effect of platforms. The core building blocks of the Android ecosystem are kept stable with incremental improvements, thus allowing the apps to evolve and innovate in endless permutations of functionalities, while all the time drawing in interfaces with other applications on time, location, identity, meta-tagging of user created content (eg, comments, tweets, contacts, photographs and videos) and so on.

This networked architecture of ICT is already cannibalizing the vertical, hierarchical structure of the industrial paradigm. The by-passing of horizontal layers with a few (networked) platforms can be scaled up at virtually no cost, lowering transaction costs:

- for users (think of the platforms cannibalizing physical real estate agencies or supporting C2C sales, such as eBay or Gumtree);

- for start-ups (think of any of the apps you use on your smartphone that sit on and piggyback the main operating platform while interacting with other functionalities covered by other apps);

- for social enterprises and communities (think of the LinkedIn communities supporting each other with crowd-sourced wisdom and shout-outs for advice).

This ecosystem initiated by Apple has clearly made our lives easier, but it has impacted our lives in a negative way as well. The stickiness and attention-seeking nature of apps coupled with a fear of missing out does increase stress, and arguably reduces the need for face-to-face interaction with those around us. Various studies indicate that the average user spends 3–4 hours a day on their smartphones, which means that most of us are probably engaging far more with/on our phones than any person close to us. Of course, there are health apps that collect physiological data and monitor calorie intake/output, helping us maintain our physical health and psychological wellbeing.

Another form of cascade is the use of ICT to crowdfund. Crowdfunding is now normalized and is beginning to cannibalize angel funding for early start-ups. The advantage of crowdfunding is in how it pulls together thousands of people, each contributing relatively small sums of financing in pursuit of an entrepreneur's dream project. Crowdfunding simultaneously engages a wide community on an upcoming product or service. As each has a stake, albeit tiny, they are the potential early adopters and advocates and, if sufficiently large in number, create another network effect for a virtuous circle for that innovation.

DISRUPTORS AND HUMAN CAPITAL MANAGEMENT AND DEVELOPMENT (HCMD)

This level of systems interconnectedness will challenge the current approach to standards development and approaches to HCMD. This is partly addressed by the use of joint working groups where a blend of two domains of knowledge is required. In the domain of HCMD, these disruptive factors have many consequences for the expectations of those involved with work organizations.

In the workplace, citizens and workers increasingly expect organizations to provide flexibility in work arrangements. This reflects the increasing occurrences of self-management, co-working, collaboration and global working. The implications of these are that individuals increasingly bear the responsibility for their skills development and self-management.

More and more people are self-employed on fixed-term, project-based or even weekly-demand work arrangements. In the UK, the number of self-employed has grown steadily from 3.3 million (12 per cent of the labour force) in 2001 to 4.8 million (15.1 per cent of the labour force) in 2017, with around 4 million working without employees (ONS, 2018). The US Bureau of Labor Statistics (BLS) survey in May 2017 found 5.9 million (3.8 per cent of workers) had contingent jobs. This was a likely under-count, as the statistic largely excluded those with alternative work arrangements (BLS, 2018):

- 10.6 million independent contractors (6.9 per cent of total employment);
- 2.6 million on-call workers (1.7 per cent of total employment);

- 1.4 million temporary help agency workers (0.9 per cent of total employment);

- 933,000 workers provided by contract firms (0.6 per cent of total employment).

Being networked is crucial to securing the next 'gig', so individuals have to have reserves of resilience and a range of skills from technical to self-promotion. A highly-skilled minority will enjoy considerable bargaining power, while contingent, commodified labour do not. Where there are functions that can be easily and cheaply automated, these roles will decline including those of middle management which can be replaced with surveillance technologies and project outcomes for the contingent workforce. Even highly skilled technical roles will change as more and more of their traditional roles are automated.

While contingent work has always been part of the employment landscape, the continued growth of workers in such precarious, temporary arrangements, the stagnation in wages in entry-level and lower skilled jobs and the increased use and reliance of organizations on such arrangements raise questions about worker welfare, exploitation, long-term employability. Knowledge and skills quickly become redundant, with wider impacts on job quality and with social impact on communities and regions. The relationship between labour and capital, the drive for cost efficiencies and flexible arrangements (both supply and demand sides) is altering the understanding and expectations of what constitutes 'work'.

Maintaining the wellbeing of your human capital is no longer the purview of trendy tech start-ups. Turnover of your workforce generally has a detrimental effect on productivity, affecting not just operational sustainability but also the morale of those left in the team. Retention strategies now include wellbeing and wellness, a recognition that deterioration of the workforce's wellbeing can impact the bottom line. As the evidence grows, so will the call for standards around sustainability, health, safety and wellbeing. These standards, without dictating a one-size-fits-every-situation frame, will become the hygiene factors of workplaces that employees will be attracted to.

When looking at wellbeing, there are some areas that spring to mind – workload management, physical fitness, stress, mental health, job design for satisfaction and stimulation and a culture of openness without fear of stigma are all key management responsibilities. There remains a pervasive reluctance of many employers to build proper retention strategies that include well-being, citing cost as a factor, and also that it is the employee's responsibility to watch out for their own wellbeing.

According to the government-commissioned review of mental health and employers (Stevenson and Farmer, 2017), poor mental health is said to cost the UK economy between £74 billion and £99 billion per year, with direct costs to employers ranging from £33 billion to £42 billion. With new metrics on the workforce such as cost of hire and cost of turnover, it will become more evident to employers just how much avoidable loss of good staff costs their businesses.

New configurations of work and organizing people, responsibilities and accountabilities include flatter structures – agile project working with 'scrums', 'squads', 'chapters', 'guilds' and 'tribes'. These have the advantage of being less defined by function, seniority and levels of authority, so that there is more ownership of the customer's issues by nimble multi-function teams. However, shifting discretion and authority so that it is more proximate to the customer/user does challenge many existing management standards written under the assumption of hierarchies to ensure leadership, compliance and a clear chain of command for intervention.

At the same time, standards ensure consistency, and, perhaps more importantly, interoperability. Industrial standards establish clear parameters based on accepted norms for a process or product quality/safety that have to be replicated consistently. With more devolved, decentralized decision-making, many of these standards will have to revisit their implicit assumptions. Standards developers are already cognizant of these, and hope management standards will at least evolve to take on more diverse and contemporary assumptions about forms of organization.

In many areas of work it is clear that standards as a basis for seeking compliance is insufficient. A clear understanding of human behaviour and motivation is necessary to ensure that the parameters laid down in the standards are met. The happy situation is that the technologies of people management are evolving. While enlightened management talks about negotiation, worker voice and discretion, surveillance technologies are simultaneously collecting oodles of data points on their workforce via wearable devices. Organizations are already collecting physiological, behavioural and performance data in real-time and having algorithms analysing the data to provide insight into the state of the organization's human capital to feed into operational decisions and for the senior stakeholders.

As part of the evolution, you see the development of principles-led standards like BS 76000:2015 *Human Resource. Valuing People. Management System. Requirements and Guidance*, which lays out an approach to human capital management. It is a management systems standard under ISO and therefore follows a particular 'industrial' rubric. While the mechanistic plan–do–check–act (PDCA) approach is far from ideal for guiding the management of people, with all their idiosyncrasies and diversity, by shoe-horning a set of principles that establishes an ethical frame, the standard integrates professional judgement to the management of people.

The principles underpinning BS 76000 are:

- 'People working on behalf of the organization have intrinsic value, in addition to their protections under the law or in regulation, which needs to be respected.'

- 'Stakeholders and their interests are integral to the best interests of the organization.'

- 'Every organization is part of wider society and has a responsibility to respect its social contract as a corporate citizen and operate in a manner that is sustainable.'

- 'A commitment to valuing people who work on behalf of the organization and to meeting the requirements of the standard is made and supported at the highest level.'

- 'Each principle is of equal importance.'

Future standards will evolve to accommodate workplaces where people will have robots as co-workers and algorithms as managers. Human–machine interfaces will become more and more important to standards guiding all manner of processes. We can already see some of the big drivers shaping that future.

Externalities

In this section, the familiar PESTLE tool is used to encourage organizations to look at the external environment as part of the discipline of ensuring the organization's strategy and value proposition remains relevant. In ISO management standards, organizations are asked about their business, what they think is the value proposition and what can affect the relevance of their offerings, be it products or services.

As previously highlighted in this chapter, there are many drivers and actors looking for opportunities to disrupt the status quo and build new businesses. This section particularly highlights the legal, technological and economic externalities that have important implications for the future of standards.

Political externalities

Political actors, decisions, events or underpinning conditions can impact an organization's ability to ensure its operations are sustainable, secure and viable. A wide spectrum of political risks may affect businesses, and before (additional) investments, it pays to look at:

- analysis (understanding risks);
- assessment (how could it impact your business?);
- management (should critical 'red flags' light up, what contingencies should I plan for/rehearse?).

While domestic assessments are helpful (and here I am reflecting on Brexit and the politics affecting Britain's relationship with the European Union and the 27 members), political risk analyses are usual when considering activities outside the home country, for example when you are outsourcing key functions and need to understand the full extent of counterparty risks. When setting up overseas, the business will have assets or personnel exposed but also need to understand political risks on the expected profits and the market stakes of exporters, contractors, and licensors.

Any organization will have to engage with government agencies, ensuring proper registration and compliance with the local regulation the environment, health and safety, employment, industrial relations, tariffs, import/export restrictions, available tax concessions and subsidies/grants and consumer rights. A key consideration is whether rule of law is the norm, with appropriate judicial and enforcement mechanisms, where there are disagreements with the local partner or government-linked organizations.

Risks to business in a country may ensue not only from actions by that country's government, but also from actions by governments in other countries. For example, in June 2017, Saudi Arabia led a coalition of the United Arab Emirates, Bahrain, Egypt, the Maldives, Mauritania, Senegal, Djibouti, the Comoros, Jordan and others to sever diplomatic relations with Qatar, alleging it had supported terrorism, hence violating an agreement with the countries of the Gulf Cooperation Council. The countries demanded Qatar downgrade diplomatic relations with Iran, stop military coordination with Turkey, and close Al-Jazeera. Saudi Arabia and partners also banned Qatari registered airplanes and ships from entering their airspace and sea routes. The European Union and the Brexit negotiations is another example.

Political risk may affect several aspects of a business, including personnel, capital assets, contracts, operations, partners and reputation. Asset risks may include the risk of seizure or nationalization, sudden changes on ownership, eg increasing the local ownership equity requirements or an insistence on (designated) locally-owned shareholders or appointment of local directors.

Where the legal system is less mature, anti-foreign legislation or administrative procedures may be enforced that retrospectively vary contractual terms. These contractual risks may also be due to regime change, civil war or a new government being elected. Of particular importance to multinationals is transfer risk, where exchange controls, profit repatriation, and restrictions on royalty payments can severely impact the viability of an overseas operation.

Risks to personnel may include risk to person (intimidation, kidnapping of foreign nationals, minority groups with no legal protections eg LGBT+ staff, certain nationalities or even female staff). Finally, risk to operations may include changes in taxation regime (eg when the country is under fiscal stress and imposes ad hoc windfall taxes), rise of anti-foreign sentiment in organized groups, shifts in labour relations, restrictions on technology or key personal movements, sabotage and terrorism.

Social externalities

Here the focus is on the attitudes, assumptions, perceptions and beliefs of the people that matter to you. Ultimately, you are trying to know things about these groups (their profile), the kinds of issues important to them (their identity/attitudes) and their likely behaviour towards your organization, the sector and your products and services.

Profiling is fairly well established, covering demographics, socio-economic class, ethnicity, education and so on. Their attitudes and beliefs include the causes they support, their faith/religion, cultural referents and attitudes on a range of issues such as money, saving, the environment, sustainability, migration, politics, work, career, leisure, lifestyle, family and so on. Specifically, you'll want to know how these groups feel towards your organization and whether what you do is of value to them, to society and, possibly, to the planet.

Earlier in this chapter we explored examples of how the different drivers can affect identity. Technology has radically altered how people live in modern economies and changed expectations, such as 24/7 access to services seamlessly and unrestricted by place. The way in which groups express their unhappiness about corporate behaviour is now very public, rapid and geared towards the need for round-the-clock media feeds. The technologies for understanding the attitudes, motivations and predicted actions is also improving, from focus groups to gaming and simulations using virtual reality and gamification of choices.

Understanding the motivations of groups that emerge and seemingly disappear again could provide insight into the quieter voices that in time may re-emerge to shape public discourse. The recent flash climate protest group that stopped parts of central London, Extinction Rebellion, was organized and purposeful. This group harnessed the frustration of those who care deeply about climate change to disrupt normal life. Their modus operandi was one that flummoxed the police, and one I suspect will be adapted by other groups.

Environmental/sustainability externalities

This is an area that is usually regulated, and an environmental audit of projects is fairly routine. However, organizations can be held to account for decisions taken many years earlier and it is sensible to ensure that potential environmental impacts take a longer-term view.

Environmental factors entail everything that changes the environment. Examples of environmental factors include soil, water, climate, natural vegetation and land forms. Planned activity that changes the environment may also be affected by the impact of climate change, as droughts, floods, land movements and storms affect the resilience of nations, regions, and local economies. Also, just as you have to anticipate the agenda for new laws and regulations for business operations, what is likely, over time, is higher minimum standards for materials, water management, waste management, recycling and so on.

In many future scenarios, for example, potable water is going to be a contested resource in many parts of the world and, as this is essential to life, a source of tension between those who have it, those who can control it and those who need it. The decarbonization agenda is another that will entail continued monitoring and measurement. Such standards will also evolve to incorporate more sophisticated models of environmental interdependencies.

Economic externalities

This refers to the macro-economic factors affecting the business environment in which your organization operates. Many medium to large businesses will probably monitor many of the indicators to support strategy, planning and investment/divestment decisions. Macroeconomic analysis comprises economic trend analysis (eg growth rates and assumptions), sector growth, seasonal factors, foreign exchange movements, key inputs costs like energy and raw materials, trade, factors affecting labour costs and availability, credit or capital raising conditions, consumer sentiment, disposable income, interest rates, monetary policy, fiscal policy, long-term macroeconomic projections, analysis of alternative trends, and counterfactual simulations of the economy. Macroeconomic models are an essential aspect of these analyses.

While many economic trends are directed at the near term, operations are scanning for broader shifts in the macro-economic environment. Examples include billion-dollar initiatives to change the business ecosystem, such as Made in China 2025 (investing in home-grown high-tech) or the Belt-and-Road infrastructure project linking Asia to Europe and Africa, in part to address protectionism in some key markets. Others include monitoring the flow of international capital and where emergent centres of capital may be signalling capital-hungry growth regions.

ECONOMIC EXTERNALITIES AND HCM

In the area of human capital development, unaccredited tech education start-ups meeting particular skills gaps are enjoying success in graduate placements. This is challenging the orthodoxy that a tertiary level education from a good institution is required for employment. This shift towards learning skills in blocs on a need-to-know basis brings to the fore the tensions between a traditional education which serves to inculcate the skills for learning, and a more platform/app architecture approach where there is a smorgasbord of micro-learning opportunities via YouTube, online Massive Open Online Courses, peer networks and community forums that reflect an on-demand culture both for the learner as well as for seizing the opportunities presented by potential employers.

Second, there will come a time as technologies stabilize where standards will be applied and demanded by employers to reference trustworthy records of learning. Standards like ISO/IEC 17024:2012 *Conformity assessment – General requirements for bodies operating certification of persons* ensure that certifying bodies conform to a quality of process. The certifying process may in time be supported by distributed ledger technologies like Blockchain. When a person completes some recognized micro-learning and fulfils all the requirements, a block, or record, can be added to that person's learning ledger. The verification of successful completion to warrant a record on the ledger is done by 'miners' (someone with recognized authority to confirm that the micro-learning has taken place satisfactorily). The Blockchain locks the blocks in a chain so that any tampering will show up, making the record more trustworthy.

In the global marketplace for talent, the OECD has measured the demand for skills across 40 countries. In highly-developed economies like Finland, highly-skilled jobs account for 90 per cent of employment in all jobs in hard-to-fill occupations. In Mexico and Chile, highly-skilled jobs account for only 20 per cent of the jobs. In general, emerging economies seem to have shortages concentrated in occupations requiring lower skill sets.

Skills shortages and mismatches result in suboptimal use of human capital. As new technologies emerge to address some of these, new standards on those technologies will emerge to support industry practices. What the OECD database is also flagging up is that while the shortages and mismatches are global, the structure of the economies matter. Automation and investments in AI machines will reflect these structural distinctions and so the impact will be uneven.

These are just some examples of how scanning for macro-economic drivers can open up strategic options and signal risks and opportunities. The key issue is to see if there are economic factors favouring and hampering the organization's overall strategic direction and whether adjustments to existing plans or contingencies need to be put in place. Areas that organizations will immediately look at is the impact on pricing, revenues and costs. However, there are implication for your workforce as well. In a tighter labour market, there are questions about retention of valued workers and ensuring that the various teams within and between organizations work well and are supported by appropriate policies and hygiene factors. The standards discussed in this book focus on a variety of people management concerns, and in each you'll find guidance on where attention should be paid and available levers to organizations.

Technological externalities

This is a major driver and one explored quite extensively earlier in this chapter. Technology can have a profound impact on the way you conceptualize, make, distribute and market your products and services. Areas that may be scanned include ICT infrastructure (eg 5G will spawn whole new ecosystems), legislation around technology, standards around technology, consumer access (eg what services are being touted, however clunky, at trade events), competitor technology and development, emerging technologies, adoption of automation, research and innovation (eg scouring research papers or looking at special calls by research funding agencies), intellectual property regulation, industrial strategies of countries/regions, technology incentives, and so on.

As we've highlighted, technologies like ICT have a transformative effect over time as more and more is digitized. Automation, for example, when applied to replace jobs currently done by humans, will remove those jobs. When autonomous vehicles reach a reliable, critical mass, drivers will no longer be needed. Where technology augments or enhances human actors, there is the opportunity to develop designs for jobs and new ways of working between machine and human (that are likely to be subject to standards).

We have witnessed the power of 'platforms' to disintermediate incumbent businesses. Every business relying on intermediation is vulnerable, from professional services (see will writing and conveyancing shops removing bread and butter businesses from lawyers) to professional bodies who seek to set standards. Where these are not part of a regulated system, many of the services once delivered by individuals can be automated, removing the intermediary position of many professionals. This is especially the case where their professional judgement may be augmented heavily by data analytics. The greater the access to data, the more potential for the data to gain predictive power and insights into the business model.

TECHNOLOGICAL EXTERNALITIES AND HCM

Communications technologies are also disintermediating. The modern workplace is now full of tools like SharePoint, Yammer and so on to encourage workers to share information for collaboration. With modern project teams blurring the traditional lines between employees and contingent specialists, a lot of sensitive information is no longer kept within the traditional boundaries of the organization. With such open access to information, required to benefit from working in a networked way, many operational decisions will be made not at the apex of the hierarchy but collectively in a defused manner.

In effect, the traditional hierarchical leadership model will be disintermediated from many decisions now still under their purview, given that the inputs they require (from business insights and sensor data) will be available to all involved. Management standards currently assuming the use of 'top management' for sponsorship and accountability are likely to respond to these alternate forms of organizational governance.

Learning technologies are likely to evolve to meet industry needs, with simulators and virtual techniques already tested in aviation and surgical training.

Roth (nd) predicts that by 2022, one in five workers will have AI as their co-worker. An example is the deployment of chatbots to service customer enquiries, both internal and external. Chatbots reduce response times to queries, and free up employee time to focus on more interesting aspects of their jobs and develop skills beyond repetitive tasks. This is the kind of AI/ human job design interface that can enhance skills, improve job design to increase diversity and challenge and consequently build the human capital talent pipeline.

While this will be uneven, with some jobs being lost, new ones will emerge where operators are more skilled in interfacing with their AI counterparts to generate new forms of value. The metrics of performance is also likely to evolve. Currently we see productivity in terms of quantity of outputs, while in the knowledge economy it is the quality and potential impact of an idea that matters. With operational and transactional tasks being automated and offshored to shared service centres, the expectation is that the people are freed to think about the issues at a more fundamental, conceptual level and to address these laterally and creatively.

This type of work is more difficult to quantify, and new metrics on the value and impact of these ideas and the effectiveness of execution will matter.

Legal and regulatory externalities – implications for standards in HCM

The significance of this externality is that most businesses operate in a rules-based environment. Compliance with laws and regulations applicable to the organization, its workforce and its partners is required and forms an important part of the calculus of risk and cost. It ensures that all affected parties are subject to the same rules and level playing field. Where the rule of law is weak or lacks integrity, businesses assume greater risks of sudden shifts in policy and an inability to enforce judgements, and cannot reliably protect their investments or personnel.

Areas for legal and regulatory due diligence include consumer rights, discrimination, intellectual property, health and safety, employment, fraud, capital transfers, import/export laws, immigration, bribery, data protection and so on. In the European Union, one of the major pieces of legislation impacting businesses globally is the GDPR. This lays down the clear principle that any data collected about any individual is owned by that person. Any legal person who holds that data can only do so with their express consent and only for the purposes for which it was collected. The upper limit for infringement of the GDPR is €20 million or 4 per cent of the worldwide annual revenue of the prior financial year, whichever is higher.

Data security standards under the ISO 27000 family have incorporated these principles with national adjustments. In fiscal year 2018, the US Securities and Exchange Commission (SEC) annual report (SEC, nd) stated that it assessed $3.945 billion in disgorgement and penalties across 821 enforcement actions, slightly up from fiscal year 2017 with 754 actions totalling $3.7 billion. The Serious Fraud Office in the UK publishes the names of all its cases. So breaches can be financially costly. More than that, it can irreparably damage the trustworthiness of your brand to key stakeholders.

Compliance with laws and regulations should be viewed as the minimum for organizations. The present environment with activist shareholders and numerous grassroots organizations and movements holding large corporations to account, standards expected are higher. A recent example is the collapse of Rana Plaza, killing 1,135 workers housing five garment factories supplying Western retailers. The low cost of labour, averaging some $68 per worker per month was a draw for companies like Benetton, Mango, Primark and Kik but the consumer backlash was immediate, and meant shifting production elsewhere. It is clear that reputational risk cannot be 'outsourced'.

The challenges and opportunities of standards

This chapter has explored many of the drivers shaping the way we live, work and socialize. I have pointed out where standards exist and where these are likely to evolve in response to some of the drivers of change. In this section, I briefly summarize where I see standards adding value, and where standards and standard development itself has to evolve.

As indicated in Chapter 2, one the key considerations for all standards is the UN Agenda for Sustainable Development 2030. Adopted by all UN member states in 2015, the agenda provides a shared blueprint of development imperatives for humanity and the planet we depend on. What it signals is the urgency in using whatever levers we may have – including ISO standards

– to achieve the 17 sustainable development goals (SDGs), but also that the SDGs are all interconnected, interdependent systems and require focused, long-term partnerships to move the agenda forward.

The strength of standards is that the development of standards brings together global expertise and, usually, the inputs from key stakeholders in that particular outcome of the standard. This development pathway involving industry practitioners, academic experts, policy developers, industry bodies and industry technical experts has delivered a generation of standards that have made products safer and cheaper, and allowed for various technologies to develop products and services that apply interoperating standards across industry sectors. The process is open and transparent with opportunities for interested parties to participate during public commenting periods. User feedback is then incorporated into future editions of the standards, improving them over time.

However, the development of standards remain very much within an industrial paradigm, and given the discussions earlier in this chapter, it is clear that the process of standards development is not keeping pace with the intersectionalities of technology, ways of working and the evolution of organizations. There are many areas where the current typologies of knowledge, sectoral and professional divisions are fraying and require more multi-disciplinary, multi-sectoral, multi-function constituents. While ISO has provision for joint working groups of experts from two committees, the challenge is that for good standards in a networked world, we will require greater diversity in inputs.

This book focuses on human capital standards, principally on its management and development. In the development of these standards, it became clear to me that the role of people in the success of standards is key. As a psychologist, I am, of course, biased but I think you'd agree that factors that enable a person to thrive personally and professionally are important if you hope to engage them (as your workforce) to the importance of whatever outcome you desire organizationally using standards, in particular management standards. Their needs, motivations and welfare should be integral to all standards involving people.

I would agree that there are thousands of technical standards that determine the specifications of widgets that I would exclude, but, increasingly, human factors is a recurring theme in a broad spectrum of standards – AI, robotics, algorithms, resource management, governance, data management, innovation, risk analysis, healthcare, health and safety, military and defence standards, and so on. To leverage standards in support of the SDGs, and recognizing the imperative for organizations and governments to deliver on these, standards development processes need to reimagine how they should work in a world where expertise from different domains meet at the intersections.

The following are areas where those involved in existing standards may find rich opportunities for development and innovation.

Machine–human interfaces

There will be numerous standards covering this, from ergonomics to voice/face recognition technologies. There will also be many outcomes envisioned by these standards. Some will focus on health and safety, some on ease of use by the human user, some on surveillance/security/identity verification, someone establishing communications channels, some on sifting through vast quantities of data to manage cognitive overload, some on how to make predetermined decisions on and for humans (eg social/credit rating), and so on.

What these standards need to include in their development (and I don't pretend to argue that this is not already happening at an informal level) is clarity on the ethical frame of reference. One of foremost science fiction writers of the twentieth century, Isaac Asimov published the Three Laws of Robotics (Asimov, 1942). These are:

- First Law: A robot may not injure a human being or, through inaction, allow a human being to come to harm.

- Second Law: A robot must obey orders given it by human beings, except where such orders would conflict with the First Law.

- Third Law: A robot must protect its own existence as long as such protection does not conflict with the First or Second Law.

What is so elegant is that in establishing the Three Laws, Asimov has established his vision of how AI will interact with a human. It establishes that the robot is there in a subordinate position to the human. This addresses very human fears of being displaced or overruled. It sets down a cast-iron rule that under no circumstances can a robot harm a person or through omission allow harm to a person, even if ordered by a person to do so – for example, if a person orders a robot to harm another person, or where a person is taking their life and a robot is witness to that. The robot in the former would disobey the human command and, in the latter, intervene, to stop the person from self-harm.

The rule also protects the robot from harm in recognition that it is a valuable, useful asset and must have some self-preservation protocols built in. In essence, these robots would have a moral protocol incorporated that makes them decent.

The necessity of starting with clear principles is that it becomes clear where human agency is located. In the principles designing algorithms, the building blocks of 'smart' machines, where is the informed consent of the individual? When Google presents the first page of choices on the search pages, are you aware that advertisers are bumped to the top? It is now clear to the user that this happens, but it wasn't always the case. Likewise, the setting up of principles governing a machine–human interface standard should set out clearly where human agency sits.

So while a standard on AI may have nothing to do with a human being, where it affects a human being, it must establish what the underpinning principles are. Does it take a utilitarian approach where the algorithm acts to some predetermined greater good in a paternal manner where consent is implied, or does it allow the person to see that the choices are actually predicated on those assumptions and to make that consent informed? To that end, the expertise of an ethicist to facilitate that discussion would be helpful in highlighting the consequences of choices made by the technical experts in that committee.

Another consideration raised in Asimov's Three Laws is the vision of robots and humans working alongside each other, and where robots are looking after humans – eg vulnerable adults or children. Current standards of machine–human interface focus on usability, safety and interoperability. Future standards with smart machines will have to consider the nature of the relationship between machine and human. If you have a robot as a co-worker, where each works to their strengths will require work processes designed for both to work together as colleagues or as master–servant (ie Asimov). Those in the care of a robot for instance run the risk of anthropomorphization. and the many complications such a relationship can bring. What are the protocols to protect both the machine and the person?

There is a lot invested in AI, and in neuroscience, both of which will make tremendous progress in the intervening years. Machine learning AIs will generate much benefit socially and economically and in the short term augment the decision choices we have to make.

Improvements and innovation

As highlighted previously in this chapter, organizations increasingly require knowledge and expertise from many disciplines and stakeholders obtained through complex partnerships. This kind of interorganizational working is not new. Developing the modern airliner brings together many parties, and the Boeing Dreamliner placed the development of new components on their global partner suppliers. There will be more co-opetition and co-creation with many partners.

What is trickier is managing relationships for innovation using the Wirearchy approach, where power is flowing between partners, negotiated on the basis of knowledge, trust, credibility and a focus on results, enabled by interconnected diverse people and technology. Managing partnerships where every person has earned their place to be an equal contributor will challenge traditional approaches of accountability. This way of working raises question about intellectual property, collusion, loss of commercially valuable knowledge, and falling foul of anti-trust legislation.

This is an area where ISO already have a track record in setting out the hygiene factors upon which innovation can occur. Juxtaposing standards and innovation may appear paradoxical, but there are many stories and instances shared by those involved in innovation and how standards are enabling (ISO, nd). In the evolution of innovation systems in a looser, less controlled ecosystem, the challenge is to use standards to establish platforms and protocols where the focus is not control but trust. There remain many challenges to this system of innovation and it will require some experimentation and experiential inputs.

Another promise of innovating in innovation standards is to take this opportunity to re-think the improvement cycles inherent in many standards. The PDCA cycle has proven very robust in incremental improvements of standards over time incorporating invaluable user feedback. Mindful of how innovation is becoming more devolved and distributed, how can ISO improve on the feedback loop so that a greater diversity of stakeholders can potentially re-invent the standard instead of taking incremental steps?

Evidence, measurement and audits

One of the key requirements of standards is that organizations act on that which is required or suggested to achieve desired outcomes. For the organization, that means establishing a system of collecting the evidence that the actions have in fact been carried out. The evidence collected serves the metrics agreed at the outset so the before and after measures provide an indication of the success of the interventions. Should the organization choose to have the results audited independently and certified, an external competent party then examines the veracity of the evidence, the integrity of the process and the metrics to ascertain how well the interventions have worked towards the desired outcome.

Given the foregoing discussions on advances in digitization and algorithms, I anticipate that this process of evidence collection can be automated. This is true of manufacturing processes where quality parameters can be collected as part of the process. For human capital, as sensors and wearable technologies advance, a lot of identification verification, physiological data, social data and performance data can be collected by the organization. These are already envisioned by standards in data management. Where the data is logged in a secure system like Blockchain, external assessors can automatically access that data in order to verify and certify the process, the outcomes and the interventions.

For that to happen, the evidence has to be in a machine-readable form that can work across platforms. There is already some standardization in this area. Financial reports, in order to be machine readable, have to be XBRL-tagged. That allows analysts' systems to read the figures into their software without having to enter the data. Ratios can then be computed and a preliminary report generated. All this can be done by the software. While this standardization is limited to a particular industry, I am hopeful given the energies devoted to standards and standards certification that a standard on the data presented as evidence for standards certification is established to enable machine readability.

Apart from ethical considerations around the automated collection, storage, analysis and manipulation of workforce data using sensors (which I discussed in an earlier section), there is the question of how algorithms themselves are analysed for bias. Do these have to incorporate agreed ethical protocols and sub-routines to self-check (a sort of bias antivirus) or is the procedure to look at the performance of the algorithm over time? So, say a piece of AI-enabled machine is used to sift machine-readable video CVs of people applying for vacancies in a firm, and the organization is seeking certification against an ISO standard for D&I. How do we ascertain that automated processes used by that organization to manage its people adhere to the principles and recommendations of that standard?

Summary

Developing standards in HCMD is a relatively recent development. The first HRM standards were only published by ISO in 2016. This book provides a snapshot of standards in HRM and HCMD to date. This chapter looks ahead, exploring the drivers shaping the spaces and places where current standards affecting human capital operate already and how future standards may evolve.

The subject of human capital is difficult in at least two ways. First, standards and standardization in areas involving human beings require quite mature conversations about human rights and ethics. Reading the standards discussed in this book, you can see how important it is to be clear about the philosophical starting point. Are people inputs and cost, are they an asset to be deployed, or are they human beings with rights independent of their contribution to the organization? The journey for BS 76000 was challenging, and the first principle was not universally acclaimed by all stakeholders.

Second, setting aside the tricky exercise of deciding which drivers to discuss and how the interactions may be described, the directions of the interacting drivers are uncertain. The breadth of the drivers discussed showcases how and where human capital is located in a variety of economic spaces and where they interact with a wide range of standards as user, implementer, actor or possibly even victim.

The vignettes and examples sketched out briefly in this chapter are the possible interactions between drivers, small 'what ifs' for illustration and provocation. We would be hostages to fortune if this chapter made the discussion out to be sure-fire predictions, but that would be dishonest. The future will be a function of these and other drivers, but also the actions of many individuals who will influence the choices made and foreground some drivers over others. And none of the drivers discussed here in this chapter are likely to play out consistently in every country, in every region and in every sector along the same timescale.

The ambition of this chapter was to explain the complex interactions as a mosaic of the landscape, and that this landscape holds the potential for many futures of work. The chapter also encourages organizations to constantly scan the horizon for incoming opportunities and threats using the PESTLE framework. It is, admittedly, a discipline to look above one's parapet to get a fresh perspective and to take the longer view. As more standards in HRM and HCMD are published, we hope to capture those and the emerging patterns, intersections, priorities and impact of these standards affecting human capital.

References and further resources

Asimov, I (1942) Runaround, *Astounding Science Fiction*, **29** (1), 94–103

BLS (2018) Contingent and Alternative Employment Arrangements Summary, *BLS* www.bls.gov/news.release/conemp.nr0.htm (archived at https://perma.cc/BU6A-3K7Z)

Brynjolfsson, E and McAfee, A (2016) *The Second Machine Age: Work, progress and prosperity in a time of brilliant technologies*, W W Norton & Co Ltd, New York

BSI (2015) BS 76000:2015 *Human Resource. Valuing People. Management System. Requirements and Guidance*, https://shop.bsigroup.com/ProductDetail/?pid=000000000030298954 (archived at https://perma.cc/SP2U-NSEG)

Castells, M (2010a) *The Rise of the Network Society*, 2nd edn, John Wiley & Sons Ltd, Chichester, UK

Castells, M (2010b) *The Power of Identity*, 2nd edn, John Wiley & Sons Ltd, Chichester, UK

Church, A H and Burke, W W (2017) Four trends shaping the future of organizations and organizational development, *OD Practitioner*, **49** (3), pp 14–22

Economist. Platforms: something to stand on, *The Economist* www.economist.com/special-report/2014/01/16/something-to-stand-on (archived at https://perma.cc/7N4F-SL63)

Husband, J (2013) What is Wirearchy?, *Wirearchy* wirearchy.com/what-is-wirearchy/

International Organization for Standardization (ISO) (2018) ISO 30401 *Knowledge management systems – Requirements* www.iso.org/standard/68683.html (archived at https://perma.cc/3YHP-8YXT)

International Organization for Standardization (ISO) (2018) ISO/IEC 27000 *Information technology – Security techniques – Information management systems – Overview and vocabulary* www.iso.org/standard/73906.html (archived at https://perma.cc/7WSV-4WWZ)

IOM. Global Migration Trends, *IOM* www.iom.int/global-migration-trends (archived at https://perma.cc/U6TS-MUD6)

ISO (2012) ISO/IEC 17024:2012 *Conformity assessment – General requirements for bodies operating certification of persons*, www.iso.org/standard/52993.html (archived at https://perma.cc/FZ37-5KDV)

ISO. Standardization and innovation: CERN conference proceedings, *ISO* www.iso.org/iso/standardization_and_innovation.pdf (archived at https://perma.cc/FKS8-PUVC)

Kässi, O and Lehdonvirta, V (2018) Online Labour Index: Measuring the Online Gig Economy for Policy and Research, *Technological Forecasting and Social Change* (forthcoming)

Lampland, M and Star, S L (eds) (2009) *Standards and Their Stories: How quantifying, classifying and formalizing practices shape everyday life*, Cornell University Press, Ithaca, London

Lin, P, Abney, K and Bekey, G A (2012) *Robot Ethics: The ethical and social implications of robotics*, The MIT Press, Cambridge, Mass

Lipsey, R G, Carlaw, K I and Bekar, C T (2005) *Economic Transformations: General purpose technologies and long term economic growth*, Oxford University Press, Oxford

Manuti, A and de Palma, P D (eds) (2014) *Why Human Capital is Important for Organizations: People come first*, Palgrave Macmillan, London, New York

Mozur, P. One Month, 500,000 Face Scans: How China Is Using A.I. to Profile a Minority, *New York Times* www.nytimes.com/2019/04/14/technology/china-surveillance-artificial-intelligence-racial-profiling.html (archived at https://perma.cc/5QVE-V5MD)

OECD. OECD Employment Outlook 2019: The future of work, *OECD* www.oecd.org/employment/outlook/ (archived at https://perma.cc/8WAC-Q82N)

OECD. Skills for Jobs Database, *OECD* www.oecdskillsforjobsdatabase.org/#UK/ (archived at https://perma.cc/E34K-E9QP)

OII. Online Labour Index, *University of Oxford* http://ilabour.oii.ox.ac.uk/online-labour-index/ (archived at https://perma.cc/7P3X-A3UA)

ONS. Trends in self-employment in the UK: Analysing the characteristics, income and wealth of the self-employed, *ONS* www.ons.gov.uk/employmentandlabourmarket/peopleinwork/employmentandemployeetypes/articles/trendsinselfemploymentintheuk/2018-02-07 (archived at https://perma.cc/KBR4-KC6M)

Ployhart, R E *et al* (2014) Human capital is dead; long live human capital resources!, *Journal of Management*, 40 (2), pp 371–98

Roth, C. By 2022, One in Five Workers Engaged in Mostly Nonroutine Tasks Will Rely on AI to Do Their Jobs, *Gartner Blog Network* blogs.gartner.com/Craig-Roth/2017/12/05/489/

SEC. Agency Financial Report, Fiscal Year 2018, *SEC.GOV* www.sec.gov/files/sec-2018-agency-financial-report.pdf (archived at https://perma.cc/T8A3-3WGE)

Stevenson, D and Farmer, P [accessed 15 March 2019] Thriving at work: a review of mental health and employers, *GOV.UK* www.gov.uk/government/publications/thriving-at-work-a-review-of-mental-health-and-employers (archived at https://perma.cc/YM73-9ZJT)

UKCES. The future of work: Jobs and skills in 2030, *GOV.UK* www.gov.uk/government/publications/jobs-and-skills-in-2030 (archived at https://perma.cc/67XX-BLMJ)

UNFPA. World Population Trends, *UNFPA* www.unfpa.org/world-population-trends (archived at https://perma.cc/K9U2-VGQV)

World Wide Web Foundation. Leaders Edition: From Promise to Progress, *Open Data Barometer* https://opendatabarometer.org/leadersedition/report (archived at https://perma.cc/XZ6X-6RCN)

APPENDIX 1

Glossary of terms

TABLE A.1   Glossary of terms

TERM	SOURCE	CHAPTER
accreditation: The process of formal approval and certification, by an awarding body, to recognize the achievement of a standard or level of qualification.		Introduction
accreditation: Often used interchangeably with 'recognition' but implies a more formal approach. Used in many different fields, accreditation is a process whereby formal approval and certification is given, usually by an awarding body, to demonstrate some authority or credibility in that area or sphere.		10
artificial intelligence (AI): The development and application of computing technologies to perform in areas hitherto requiring human intelligence. Examples of these involve decision-making, facial recognition and interpretation, learning from prior experience and adapting to new stimuli.		9 and 11
assessment: A systematic method and procedure for ascertaining work-related knowledge, skills, abilities or other characteristics of people or a group of people, or the performance of people or a group of people.	ISO 30405	4
assessment and evaluation: In the context of learning and development, these terms refer to formal or informal valuation of the quality, effectiveness and impact of learning, development and competence management systems and processes. Many approaches to assessment and evaluation involve a series of levels to assess the return on investment of learning, training or development interventions, measured through changes in behaviour, competency profiles and levels of productivity, effectiveness and efficiency.		5

TABLE A.1   *continued*

TERM	SOURCE	CHAPTER
audit: A systematic, independent and documented process for obtaining audit evidence and evaluating it objectively to determine the extent to which the audit criteria have been fulfilled.	ISO 30400:6.13	2
audit: This term is often used by awarding bodies themselves and the standards specialists developing the standards, as well as those working as assessors and organizational stakeholders who are helping to prepare for a formal review. The term, which is often synonymous with that used within the field of finance and accountancy, is sometimes also considered when describing the assessment process. It implies a careful review of information and evidence by an authorized person to check and officially verify against facts.		10
benchmarking: Comparing attributes, processes or performance between organizations.	ISO 30400:3.17	2
business case: How organizations value individual differences as commodities to be attracted and exchanged for value. The business case for recruiting individuals from minority ethnic backgrounds, for example, has been promoted as a means of enabling the mirroring of the demographic make-up of potential consumers, capturing the knowledge of different cultures and contributing to organizational renewal and innovation.		6
business continuity planning: The process of mutual planning by organizations and other stakeholders.	ISO 30400:3.6	2
business model: An organization's approach to operating in its environment.	ISO 30400:3.4	2
business model: The value proposition of an organization to its stakeholders and its operation to ensure its sustainable success. This requires identifying the business context, eg competitors and substitutes, sources of revenue, target markets, products and services, business intelligence such as market research for shifts in tastes and trends, evaluation and redesign.		11

TABLE A.1 *continued*

TERM	SOURCE	CHAPTER
capacity management: The process used to manage the human capital necessary to execute organizational commitments and delivery excellence.		3
capacity plan: A view of resource requirements over a defined period that reflects planned numbers of resources by roles and skills. The capacity plan can include consideration of skills development, retraining, redeployment, recruitment, redesign, and use of organizational partners, third-party subcontractors, contingent workforce and volunteer workforce.		3
career stage: A distinct phase of a person's career. Can include entry, establishment, advancement, maintenance, transition and maturity.		3
communications plan: This informs and engages organization leaders, workforce and other stakeholders in the objectives, methods, deliverables and outcomes of workforce planning.		3
competence: The ability to apply knowledge and skills to achieve intended results, particularly those that are essential for an organization's success.		3
competence framework: A structure that defines the competence of people within an organization to achieve intended results.		3
competence model: The process of analysing and describing knowledge, skills and ability of people.		3
competency management system: An organizational-level system that takes a comprehensive approach to profiling behaviours and qualities needed for organizational performance to a given standard. This involves analysing where skills gaps may be occurring, and planning and managing processes to generate sustainable competency across the organization.		5
compliance: Doing what is necessary to meet a specified requirement.	ISO Online Browsing Platform (ISO-OBP)	2

TABLE A.1   *continued*

TERM	SOURCE	CHAPTER
conformity: The fulfilment of a requirement.	ISO-OBP	2
corporate governance: The procedures, systems and principles in place to enable effective management of organizations by directors and their stakeholders. Corporate governance standards will differ between jurisdictions. Corporate governance is commonly understood to be concerned with: 'Holding the balance between economic and social goals and between individual and communal goals... the aim is to align as nearly as possible the interests of individuals, corporations and society'.	Cadbury, 1992	1
critical position: A job role that has a direct and significant impact on organizational outcomes. Critical positions are identified by organizations as part of their organizational strategy, and will vary by industry, sector and organizational type. They are not always high-level positions.	ISO/TS 30410	4
criticality assessment: A method applied within the organization to determine level of job role criticality.		3
current workforce demand: Based on current business requirements to deliver business outcomes.		3
current workforce supply: Baseline data on the size of the workforce.		3
dismissal: The termination of employment for substantial reasons. These reasons may be economic, technical or organizational. Reasons for dismissal include employee misconduct, lack of capability, poor performance or role redundancy. Dismissal usually involves serving notice of the end of the employment relationship or making payment in lieu of notice. In certain circumstances (such as serious or gross misconduct by an employee), the dismissal may be made without notice. Many countries have legal or regulatory provision in place to protect individuals who believe that they have been subject to unfair or unwarranted dismissal.		8

TABLE A.1   *continued*

TERM	SOURCE	CHAPTER
diversity: Characteristics of differences and similarities between people. Two supplementary notes are included in this definition: • 'Diversity includes factors that influence the identities and perspectives that people bring when interacting at work.' • 'Diversity can foster learning from others who are not the same, about dignity, respect and inclusiveness for everyone, and about creating workplace environments and practices that foster learning from others to gain advantages of diverse perspectives.'	ISO 30400.9:1	6
divisional workforce plan: This provides an overview of nominated divisions in relation to the broader organizational plan.		3
ecosystem: In the business and management context, refers to the complex system or network of organizations, including suppliers, distributors, customers, competitors, government agencies, and so on, involved in product or service delivery. Ecosystems involve both competition and cooperation as each entity affects and is affected by the others. Ecosystems involve constantly evolving relationships and, as in a biological ecosystem, flexibility and adaptability are needed in order to survive.		11
employ: To engage the services of a person or put a person to work.		4
environmental scan: Gathering and reporting on information on external and internal workforce demand and supply influences.		3
equal opportunities: A type of management initiative or legislation that requires all candidates and employees to be treated equally. It is a means of eliminating discrimination against members of particular social groups and is often motivated by a desire for social justice.		6

TABLE A.1   *continued*

TERM	SOURCE	CHAPTER
ethical climate: This describes 'correct behaviour, and how ethical decisions should be handled in organizations'.	Victor and Cullen, 1987	1
ethical culture: This describes the 'systems, procedures, and practices for guiding and supporting ethical behaviour' in organizations.	Kish-Gephart *et al*, 2010	1
external quality award: An award which is given in recognition of an organization achieving certain agreed levels of activity in its field of operation. The award is given by the organization which 'owns' it, eg the Best Companies Award.		10
external quality model: A way of operating that is based on a specific way of doing things, built on both good practices and ongoing research to ensure the currency of the model. Sometimes 'external quality framework' is used interchangeably. An example of an external quality model would be the European Foundation Quality Model.		10
external quality standard: An external set of rules or principles to which an organization must adhere to receive accreditation. It provides an accepted way of doing things relevant to the organization operating in its sector/industry. An example of an external quality standard would be one sitting within the ISO 9000 family of standards.		10
focus areas: Those areas identified as important to the organization. May include age, indigenous representation, diversity, areas of undersupply, areas of oversupply, retirement impact, and retirement projections.		3
future of work: An umbrella term encompassing approaches to the nature of work, the shape of workplaces and workforces in the future.		11
future-focused business scenarios: Identification of plausible alternative future business scenarios. Used to determine workforce shift scenarios.		3

TABLE A.1   *continued*

TERM	SOURCE	CHAPTER
futures: The study of alternate futures (the possible, the probable and the preferred) and the study of the drivers (eg legacies, technologies, worldviews and mythologies) shaping these futures.		11
governance: The way a whole organization is led, directed, controlled and held accountable.	ISO 30400:3.1	2 and 3
hazard: Source with a potential to cause injury and ill health. Hazards can also include sources with the potential to cause harm or hazardous situations, or circumstances with the potential for exposure leading to injury and ill health.	ISO 45001	7
human capital: The terms 'human capital' and 'human capital resources' are contested expressions. Human capital resources refers to individual, unit or corporate level capabilities relating to knowledge, skills, abilities, and other relevant characteristics. At a strategic level, human capital resources are the basis for the achievement of sustainable competitive advantage. The debate about the use of the term revolves around whether the individual contribution that people can make to their workplace is overlooked or undervalued if economic logics associated with terms such as 'capital' and 'investment' dominate decision-making in organizations. However, the term human capital as used in the book connotes the view that people contribute far more than their labour to the organization. People are important sources of value through their individuality, their skills, ideas and networks. Regardless of terminological differences, human capital management is all about people in the workplace and the combined contribution of skills, attributes, knowledge, talent, and expertise that people make in work organizations.	Ployhart *et al*, 2014	Intro
human capital: The value of the collective knowledge, skills and abilities of an organization's people.	ISO 30400:4.1	2 and 3

TABLE A.1   *continued*

TERM	SOURCE	CHAPTER
human capital: This term describes the value of the workforce: 'the knowledge, skills, abilities and other capabilities which describe individual capacities'.	Ployhart *et al*, 2014	1, 3 and 11
human capital management: Managing from a 'human capital' approach involves valuing people in terms of their actual (or potential) contribution flowing from their unique skills. When applied to diversity and inclusion, this approach entertains the notion that a diversity of human capital can lead to the creation and maintenance of social capital within the organization.	CIPD, 2019	6
human capital reporting: Reporting focused on core elements including human capital costs, structure, skills and capabilities, sustainability, culture and productivity.		3
human governance: The way the people within the organization are led, directed, controlled, managed and held accountable, taking into account human and social factors at the highest and every level of decision-making.	ISO 30400:7.1	2 and 3
human resource management: Refers to all practices concerned with people in work organizations, taking into account their management as well as their development. This includes systems and practices associated with recruitment and selection, deployment, development and general management of the organization's employees.		Intro and 3
human resource management and information systems: Technology that supports human resource management.		3
identity: A 'sense of self' constructed from, among other things, a person's memories, ambitions, desires, values, hopes and beliefs.		11

TABLE A.1   *continued*

TERM	SOURCE	CHAPTER
inclusion: The 'practice of including all stakeholders in organizational contexts', noting that 'stakeholders from different groups are to be accepted and welcomed (eg offered opportunities on the basis of abilities, talents and skills)'. A range of factors that can lead to exclusion (such as language, dialect or bodily appearance), and embedding an inclusive culture requires a transparent approach that goes beyond legal compliance.	ISO 30400:9.5 and BS 76005	6
individual learning: The process whereby an individual experiences growth and fulfilment (knowledge, skills and behaviours) which result in behaviour change. Individual learning is personal and unless there are opportunities for this learning to be shared, the knowledge, skills and behavioural attributes of individuals is lost from the organization should they leave or decide to withhold what they have learned.		5
Industry 4.0: Term often used by practitioners to refer to what they term the Fourth Industrial Revolution. This follows previous revolutions such as mechanization (Industry 1.0), mass production (Industry 2.0) and automation (Industry 3.0). Industry 4.0 is the label given to the gradual combination of traditional manufacturing and industrial practices with increasing technological functionality. Industry 4.0 provides the potential for large-scale machine-to-machine communication to leverage increased automation, improved communication and monitoring, self-diagnosis and analysis as the basis for productive and service efficiency.		9
injury and ill health: An adverse effect on the physical, mental or cognitive condition of a person. These adverse effects include occupational disease, illness and death. The term 'injury and ill health' also implies the presence of injury or ill health, either on their own or in combination.	ISO 45001	7

TABLE A.1   *continued*

TERM	SOURCE	CHAPTER
insight reports: Executive summary relating to workforce planning and key elements of core delivery including snapshot reporting on focus areas, workforce shift scenarios and areas for attention, areas to monitor and areas well-placed. These are delivered via automated workforce planning system.		3
integrated location plan: This enables broader scope workforce planning if organization has more than one site/location.		3
the Internet of Things (IoT): A system of interrelated computing devices, mechanical and digital machines, objects, animals or people that are provided with unique identifiers with the ability to transfer data over a network without requiring human-to-human or human-to-computer interaction.	IoT Agenda, 2019	9
intersectionality: Can refer to the intersection of oppressions (eg racism and sexism) and/or the intersection of social groupings (eg as defined by ethnicity and gender). It is a useful means of identifying the complex and subtle ways in which disadvantage is sometimes manifest in relation to these intersecting characteristics, and has become an important consideration in the discussion of diversity.		6
job families: The segmentation of jobs into similar occupation groups based on related competencies.		3
key demographic indicators: These identify organizational demographics by core delivery, core enabling, administrative support and enabling job families.		3
learning technology: Although this term is often used as a synonym for e-learning, here it refers to the broad range of information and communication technologies that can be used to identify learning needs, deliver and assess learning, and provide the basis for organization-wide learning and competency management systems.		5

TABLE A.1   *continued*

TERM	SOURCE	CHAPTER
machine Learning (ML): An application of AI that provides systems with the ability to automatically learn and improve from experience without being explicitly programmed. ML means that computer programs can access and use data autonomously.	Expert Systems, 2019	9
managing diversity: This term refers to a range of management interventions designed to encourage diversity of individuals, rather than only applying to those in protected groups. This approach has been criticized for concentrating on all the ways in which individuals differ, without referring to issues of equality and fairness, and some argue that it risks diversity becoming 'meaningless'.	Tatli, 2011	6
materiality: A measure of the significance of an element to organizational results.	ISO 30400:3.15	2
meta-standards: Management system standards that focus on organization-wide systems and managerial practices that can be audited. Well-known examples of meta-standards are the Quality Management Systems standard, ISO 9001 and the ISO 14001 environmental management systems standard.		Intro
national/international standards: Explicitly formulated consensual rules or guidelines published by accredited national or international standardization bodies such as BSI and ISO. They provide an accepted way of doing things relevant to specific products, services or management processes. Initially, standards served technical design and manufacturing purposes, but over time, accredited standards for organization-wide management systems have been agreed and implemented.	Anderson, 2017 and Mulvie, 2019	Intro
occupational health and safety (OH&S) opportunity: A circumstance or set of circumstances that can lead to improvement in OH&S performance.	ISO 45001	7

TABLE A.1   *continued*

TERM	SOURCE	CHAPTER
OH&S risk: A combination of the likelihood of occurrence of a work-related hazardous events or exposures, and the severity of the injury and ill health that can be caused by the events or exposures.	ISO 45001	7
operational workforce planning: This typically covers a defined period, generally the ensuing 12 months, and is aligned to the organization's planning cycle. The focus is on gathering, analysing and reporting on workforce risk and risk mitigation.		3
organization design: A systematic approach to reviewing and intentionally developing an organization's ways of working, systems and processes (eg workflow, procedures, structures, systems and layout).		11
organization structure: The hierarchical arrangement of authority, responsibility and accountability in an organization.	ISO 30400:3.3	2
organizational culture: 'The values, norms and traditions that affect how individuals of a particular group perceive, think, interact, behave and make judgments about their world.'	Chamberlain, 2005	1
organizational culture: Values, beliefs and practices that influence the conduct and behaviour of people and organizations.	ISO 30400:3.2	2
organizational learning (OL): This term is distinct from the term 'organization-wide learning'. OL refers to all processes and activities involved in creating, retaining and transferring knowledge both within and beyond organization boundaries. OL is experiential; it requires processes, practices, methods and activities to value 'lessons learned' from within and outside the organization as a feature of systematic performance improvement and adaptability.		5

TABLE A.1   *continued*

TERM	SOURCE	CHAPTER
organizational values: Aspirational or articulated standards, behaviour, principles or concepts that an organization considers important.	ISO 30400:4.7	2
organization-wide learning: The process, rarely achieved in organizations, where all members of the organization are able to access different learning processes, practices, methods and activities (both formally and informally), as individuals and as members of work groups, to systematically and intentionally improve their performance at individual, work group and organizational levels.		5
outsourcing: An arrangement where an organization hands over activities, functions or processes that could be performed 'in house' to external process or service providers, resulting in the loss or transfer of jobs from the original organization.		8
people risk: Possible negative outcomes that arise as a consequence of the behaviour and activities of people.	ISO 30400:4.10	2
planning: The process of thinking about an organization's activity required to achieve a desired outcome.		3
principle: A fundamental basis for decision-making or behaviour.	ISO-OBP	2
principles: Fundamental truths or propositions that serve as the foundation for a system of belief or behaviour, or to a chain of reasoning of a person, a plan, an organization or a nation on which policies, processes, laws, decisions and institutions are built.		11
protected groups: Social groupings against whom it is unlawful to discriminate (eg in the UK this covers age, gender reassignment, marriage and civil partnership status, pregnancy and maternity, disability, race, religion and belief, sex, and sexual orientation).		6

TABLE A.1   *continued*

TERM	SOURCE	CHAPTER
recruitment: The process of sourcing, attracting, assessing, and employing talent for an existing or new position within the organization.	ISO 30405	4
redundancy: A form of dismissal that occurs when an employee's job no longer exists. This may be due to an employer deciding to reduce their workforce or to close the business. It may also occur when the work undertaken in the specific role is no longer needed, or when a decision has been made to outsource work to a third-party service or process provider.		8
requirement: A need or expectation that is stated, generally implied or obligatory.	ISO-OBP	2
resignation: Leaving a job as the result of the employee's decision, communicated either verbally or in writing. Threatening to leave or looking for work elsewhere is not the same as formally resigning. The intention to resign is usually accompanied by giving notice to the employer of the intention to leave. However, in some circumstances, it is possible to resign without notice. In some countries, if an employee feels forced to resign because of the actions of their employer, this may be regarded as 'constructive dismissal'.		8
retention: The observation, analysis and description of the extent an organization retains its workforce. Retention may be measured as a proportion of workforce with a specified length of service, typically one year or more, expressed as a percentage of overall workforce numbers. Retention rate is the ratio of the total workforce that is retained over a defined period.	ISO 30400	8
retirement: Leaving a job at the point that the person considers the end of their active working life. In different countries a person may choose to retire at different ages and different tax laws and pension rules mean that a 'standard retirement age' is impossible to specify in a general publication. In some countries, retirement ages are different for males and females.		8

TABLE A.1   *continued*

TERM	SOURCE	CHAPTER
risk: The effect of uncertainty – an effect is a deviation from the expected, whether positive or negative. Uncertainty is the state, even partial, of deficiency of information relating to, understanding or knowledge of, an event, its consequence, or likelihood. Risk is often characterized by reference to potential 'events' and 'consequences', or a combination of these. Risk is often expressed in terms of a combination of the consequences of an event, and the associated 'likelihood' of occurrence.	ISO Guide 73:2009 3.6.1.1	3 and 7
risk mitigation strategies: Strategies designed to reduce workforce risk.		3
robotic process automation (RPA): The use of software with AI and ML capabilities to handle high-volume, repeatable tasks that previously required human input. These tasks can include queries, calculations and maintenance of records and transactions. RPA allows computer software configuration and robotic processes to emulate and integrate human actions within digital business process systems.		9
social groupings: Defined as 'groups of people recognized by law, self-identification or self-organization, who share a set of similar characteristics that are defined through demographic attributes for societal exclusion'. The term may include protected groups (noted above) as well as those who might share characteristics but who are not protected by legislation (such as those sharing similar economic backgrounds).	BS 76005	6
social responsibility: The responsibility of an organization for the consequences of its decisions and activities on society and the environment, through transparent and ethical behaviour.	ISO 30400:3.9	2
source: To identify a pool of potential applicants.		4

TABLE A.1   *continued*

TERM	SOURCE	CHAPTER
stakeholder/interested party: A person or organization that can affect, be affected by, or perceive itself to be affected by a decision or activity.	ISO 30400:5.1	2
standardization: The process of development, publication and application of guidelines, specifications and rules by a consensus of relevant stakeholders in order to ensure compatibility, interoperability, safety and consistency.		Intro and 11
strategic plan: The formulation, development, implementation and evaluation of factors that are relevant to an organization's long-term or overall interests, and the means of achieving its objectives.	ISO 30400:3.8	2 and 3
strategic workforce planning: This usually covers a defined period aligned to organizational strategy – generally 3–5 years or more. The scope of planning can include identifying the workforce, assessments and benchmarking, human resource policy, framework and associated processes related to current and future organizational strategic objectives, structure and design.		3
strategy: An organization's high-level plan or approach designed to bring about one or more goals under conditions of uncertainty to achieve its objectives,	ISO 30400:3.5	2, 3 and 11
succession planning: A process for identifying and developing current or external employees with the potential to fill key positions in the organization.		2
sustainable employability: The long-term capability to acquire or create and maintain work. Sustainable employability can be the responsibility of people, organizations or governments.	ISO 30400:8.1	4
talent pool: A group of people who possess the knowledge, skills, abilities and other characteristics necessary to carry out a specific job.		5

TABLE A.1   *continued*

TERM	SOURCE	CHAPTER
team learning: A social and relational process that occurs when collaborative processes between individuals involve coordination of knowledge and behaviours as a feature of their work processes. Where systemic team learning occurs, it can enhance the performance of the team and can contribute to the improvement of organizational performance.		5
top management: The person or group of people who direct and control an organization at the highest level. In a non-hierarchical structure, top management implies ultimate decision-makers, who might be business owners.		6
turnover: A measure often used to observe, analyse and describe the proportion of the workforce (employees, contractors, and contingent/temporary labour) that leave their employment over a defined period, usually a year, and is calculated as a percentage of total workforce numbers. At its broadest, turnover assesses the rate at which workers are leaving the organization for both voluntary and involuntary reasons.		8
underrepresentation: The 'disproportionate absence or recognition of people from social groupings', with a note that the 'under-representation of social groupings can be an indication of exclusion and could lead to subsequent disadvantage'. This is a useful way of ensuring that diversity can refer both to individuals and to groups of individuals who might share similarities.	BS 76005	6
value: The merit and worth of people due to their unique knowledge, skills and abilities (noting that inherent value refers to the principle that people are valued for who they are; not just because they deliver monetary value or money equivalents to their organization).	BS 76000:3.26	2

TABLE A.1   *continued*

TERM	SOURCE	CHAPTER
values: Principles, ethics or rules applied to make moral judgements, and consequently people's standards of behaviours and attitudes.	BS 76000:3.27	2
work life stage: Phases of a person's work life, which can include new entry, early, mid, transition and end career. People can move in and out of these work life stages at different ages and life stages.		3
worker: A person performing work or work-related activities that are under the control of the organization. Note that persons perform work or work-related activities under various arrangements, paid or unpaid, such as regularly or temporarily, intermittently or seasonally, casually or on a part-time basis. In addition the term 'workers' includes top management, managerial and non-managerial persons. It is also the case that the work or work-related activities performed under the control of the organization may be performed by workers employed by the organization, workers of external providers, contractors, individuals, agency workers, and by other persons to the extent the organization shares control over their work or work-related activities according to the context of the organization.	ISO 45001	7
workforce: People who provide a service or labour to contribute to business or organizational outcomes. This may include the contingent, contract, volunteer, and outsourced workforce.		3
workforce design: The design of the workforce resulting from workforce planning reports on the efficiency of the current workforce design. It includes design, supply, mobility and utilization.		3
workforce mix and scenario modelling: This details investment break-up and the ability to scenario plan workforce needs based on changing demand and business needs.		3

TABLE A.1   *continued*

TERM	SOURCE	CHAPTER
workforce mobility: The intra- and inter-movement of people within an organization.		3
workforce planning: The systematic identification, analysis and planning of organizational needs, in terms of people. It is a process used to generate business intelligence to inform an organization of the current and future impact of the external and internal environment on the business, enabling it to be resilient to structural and cultural changes, and thereby to better position itself for the future.		3
workforce planning process: An active and continuous process in the organizational planning cycle. Workforce planning is the responsibility of the organization's senior management, and should be aligned and consistent with organizational strategies and governance.		3
workforce segmentation: This is used to classify the different types of job families, functions, roles, competencies and/or locations within an organization. It is used to focus workforce planning on the most critical business positions, employee capabilities and locations identified in the strategic and business plan as core to organization performance. There are two basic workforce segmentation approaches: role-based, where jobs are segmented by value or type of work performed and employee-based segmentation by demographic, other observable or inferred characteristics.		3
workforce supply/recruitment plan: This aligns the recruitment plan to affordability and future needs. It includes the stable operating model and the scenario reflecting changing business needs.		3

TABLE A.1   *continued*

TERM	SOURCE	CHAPTER
workplace: An area or place in which work activities are carried out. It could be a place under the control of the organization where a person needs to be or to go for work purposes. It is important to note an organization's OH&S responsibilities depend on the degree of control over the workplace.	ISO 45001	3 and 7

The table shows a list of terms and definitions as used in the book

APPENDIX 2

Standards

TABLE A.2 Human capital management and people-related British standards

Standard number	Standard title	Chapters
BS 76000	Human Resource. Valuing People. Management System. Requirements and Guidance https://shop.bsigroup.com/ProductDetail/ ?pid=000000000030298954 (archived at https://perma.cc/G7TH-D7QB)	Intro, 2, 5, 6, 8, 10 and 11
BS 76005	Valuing People Through Diversity and Inclusion: Code of Practice for Organizations https://shop.bsigroup.com/ProductDetail/ ?pid=000000000030338898 (archived at https://perma.cc/2V29-GGPT)	Intro, 2, 6, 8 and 10
BS PD 76006	Guide to learning and development https://shop.bsigroup.com/ProductDetail/ ?pid=000000000030350673 (archived at https://perma.cc/2V29-GGPT)	Intro, 2, 5 and 10
PAS 3000	Smart Working. Code of Practice https://shop.bsigroup.com/ProductDetail/ ?pid=000000000030324355 (archived at https://perma.cc/M533-E329)	2
PAS 3001	Travelling for work. Responsibilities of an organization for health, safety and security. Code of practice https://shop.bsigroup.com/ProductDetail? pid=000000000030331555 (archived at https://perma.cc/KAP3-JR8A)	2
PAS 3002	Code of Practice on Improving Health and Wellbeing Within an Organization https://shop.bsigroup.com/ProductDetail? pid=000000000030384539 (archived at https://perma.cc/XHU4-ZU6C)	2

TABLE A.2   *continued*

Standard number	Standard title	Chapters
BS 45002-0	Occupational health and safety management systems. General guidelines for the application of ISO 45001 https://shop.bsigroup.com/ProductDetail/ ?pid=000000000030334815 (archived at https://perma.cc/7YZH-HKGS)	7
BS 45002-1	Occupational health and safety management systems. General guidelines for the application of ISO 45001. Guidance on managing occupational health https://shop.bsigroup.com/ProductDetail/ ?pid=000000000030362021 (archived at https://perma.cc/Q4DC-ZDBB)	7
BS 45002-2	Occupational health and safety management systems. General guidelines for the application of ISO 45001. Risks and opportunities https://shop.bsigroup.com/ProductDetail/ ?pid=000000000030362019 (archived at https://perma.cc/XG6W-BYVT)	7
BS 45002-3	Occupational health and safety management systems. General guidelines for the application of ISO 45001. Guidance on incident investigation https://shop.bsigroup.com/ProductDetail/ ?pid=000000000030362017 (archived at https://perma.cc/RZK5-ZRL4)	7
BS ISO 45003	Occupational health and safety management – Psychological Health and Safety in the Workplace – Guidelines https://standardsdevelopment.bsigroup.com/ projects/2018-02515 (archived at https://perma.cc/JCQ2-QP9W)	7

The table shows a list of relevant British standards

TABLE A.3   ISO human resource management standards

Standard number	Standard title	Chapters
BS ISO 30400	Human resource management. Vocabulary https://shop.bsigroup.com/ProductDetail/ ?pid=000000000030324720 (archived at https://perma.cc/3ZAP-4HSD)	2, 3, 6 and 8
ISO 30405	Human resource management – Guidelines on recruitment www.iso.org/standard/64149.html (archived at https://perma.cc/5ZWG-55UJ)	Intro and 4
ISO 30406	Human resource management – Sustainable employability management for organizations www.iso.org/standard/72327.html (archived at https://perma.cc/FYK8-BUBV)	2
ISO 30407	Human resource management: Cost per Hire www.iso.org/standard/62975.html (archived at https://perma.cc/CA79-H6QQ)	4
BS ISO 30408	Human Resource Management – Guidelines on human governance https://shop.bsigroup.com/ProductDetail/ ?pid=000000000030284701 (archived at https://perma.cc/JL9M-9HN8)	2, 8 and 9
ISO 30409	Human Resource Management – Workforce Planning www.iso.org/standard/64150.html (archived at https://perma.cc/Z3Z2-H5GW)	Intro, 2, 3 and 8
ISO 30401	Knowledge management systems – Requirements: www.iso.org/standard/68683.html (archived at https://perma.cc/9JG3-VFD8)	11
ISO 30410	Human resource management: Impact of hire www.iso.org/standard/68219.html (archived at https://perma.cc/JB3R-3E33)	4
ISO 30411	Human resource management: Quality of hire www.iso.org/standard/68220.html (archived at https://perma.cc/4RZE-XPT2)	4
ISO 30414	Human resource management – Guidelines for internal and external human capital reporting www.iso.org/standard/69338.html (archived at https://perma.cc/9S36-NTTB)	Intro, 1, 2, 3 and 9

TABLE A.3   *continued*

Standard number	Standard title	Chapters
ISO/AWI TS 23378	Human Resource Management: Turnover and Retention: www.iso.org/standard/75372.html (archived at https://perma.cc/K5PB-WR6P)	8
ISO/IEC 17024	Conformity assessment – General requirements for bodies operating certification of persons https://www.iso.org/standard/52993.html (archived at https://perma.cc/LTR3-KV3W)	11
ISO/IEC 27000	Information technology – Security techniques – Information security management systems – Overview and vocabulary: www.iso.org/standard/73906.html (archived at https://perma.cc/E9C4-CALP)	11
ISO/AWI 30419	Guidelines for ensuring a positive candidate experience during the recruitment process www.iso.org/standard/68696.html (archived at https://perma.cc/GDF6-5Q7P)	4
BS OHSAS 18001/18002	Occupational Health and Safety Management – BS OHSAS 18001:2007 Occupational health and safety management. Requirements: https://shop.bsigroup.com/ProductDetail?pid=000000000030148086 (archived at https://perma.cc/LZ28-CEDP)	7

The table shows a list of relevant ISO standards

TABLE A.4   Other ISO standards

Standard number	Standard title	Chapters
ISO/DIS 10015	Quality management – Guidelines for competence management and people development www.iso.org/standard/69459.html (archived at https://perma.cc/7VQF-TACV)	Intro and 2
ISO/DIS 10018	Quality management systems – Guidelines on people engagement www.iso.org/standard/69979.html (archived at https://perma.cc/597J-USQH)	2
ISO 10667	Assessment service delivery – procedures and methods to assess people in work and organizational settings (Parts 1 and 2) www.iso.org/standard/56441.html (archived at https://perma.cc/4LUB-ZTKG)	4 and 9
ISO 14000	Environmental management www.iso.org/iso-14001-environmental-management.html (archived at https://perma.cc/84W5-2V2K)	5, 7 and 10
ISO/IEC 17024	Conformity assessment – General requirements for bodies operating certification of persons www.iso.org/standard/52993.html (archived at https://perma.cc/NWL4-23EK)	11
ISO 26000	Guidance on social responsibility www.iso.org/standard/42546.html (archived at https://perma.cc/MU5H-AQSW)	2 and 6
ISO 27500	The human-centred organization – Rationale and general principles www.iso.org/standard/64239.html (archived at https://perma.cc/3C8W-V8MQ)	2
ISO 27501	The human-centred organization – Guidance for managers www.iso.org/standard/64241.html (archived at https://perma.cc/S3MQ-P3CK)	6 and 8
ISO 29993	Learning services outside formal education – Service requirements www.iso.org/standard/70357.html (archived at https://perma.cc/KF29-5MRK)	5

TABLE A.4   *continued*

Standard number	Standard title	Chapters
ISO 37001	Anti-bribery management systems – Requirements with guidance for use www.iso.org/standard/65034.html (archived at https://perma.cc/FF83-ZH9T)	2
ISO 37500	Guidance on outsourcing www.iso.org/standard/56269.html (archived at https://perma.cc/RYS6-AL3D)	8
BS ISO 45001	Occupational health and safety management systems. Requirements with guidance for use https://shop.bsigroup.com/ProductDetail? pid=000000000030299985 (archived at https://perma.cc/KKC8-B3XU)	Intro, 7 and 8
BS ISO 9001	Quality management systems. Requirements https://shop.bsigroup.com/ProductDetail? pid=000000000030273524 (archived at https://https://perma.cc/3YZY-NQVM)	Intro, 2, 5, 7 and 10
ISO/AWI 37000	Guidance for the governance of organizations https://www.iso.org/standard/65036.html (archived at https://https://perma.cc/C8DK-ESAM)	2
ISO/IEC/JTC 36	Information technology for learning, education and training https://www.iso.org/committee/45392.html (archived at https://perma.cc/L94T-M2KN)	5
ISO/NP 37002	Whistleblowing management systems – Guidelines https://www.iso.org/standard/65035.html (archived at https://perma.cc/9LTU-WAKJ)	2
ISO/TS 22330	Security and resilience – Business continuity management systems – Guidelines for people aspects of business continuity https://www.iso.org/standard/50067.html (archived at https://perma.cc/NRQ2-EP7X)	2

The table shows a list of other ISO standards

INDEX